D0329010

Cooking
with the
Young
Chefs
of France

OTHER BOOKS BY ELISABETH LAMBERT ORTIZ

The Complete Book of Mexican Cooking
The Complete Book of Caribbean Cooking
The Complete Book of Japanese Cooking

ROUBAIX
LILLE

Sedan

LE HAVRE
ROUEN
REIMS
Epernay
NANCY
St. Germain en Laye
STRASBOURG
PARIS
Ribeauville
Fontainebleau
Remirmont
RENNES
LE MANS
Bescançon
ANGERS
DIJON
NANTES
Beaume
Poitiers
Digoin
Roanne
Bourg en Bresse
La Rochelle
LIMOGES
LYON
CLERMONT-FERRAND
ST. ETIENNE
GRENOBLE
BORDEAUX
Albi
Nîmes
Avignon
NICE
Auch
TOULOUSE
Montpellier
Arles
Castlnaudary
MARSEILLE
TOULON
Tarbes
Carcassonne

France

Cooking
with the
Young
Chefs
of France

Contemporary Interpretations
of Traditional Cuisine

ELISABETH LAMBERT ORTIZ

Illustrations by Lizbeth Patrone

M. EVANS AND COMPANY, INC.

New York

Library of Congress Cataloging in Publication Data

Ortiz, Elisabeth Lambert.
    Cooking with the young chefs of France.

    Includes index.
    1. Cookery, French.   I. Title.
TX719.77   641.5944   81-15309

ISBN 0-87131-360-X   AACR2

M. Evans and Company, Inc.
216 East 49 Street
New York, New York 10017

Design by RONALD F. SHEY

Manufactured in the United States of America

9 8 7 6 5 4 3 2 1

*To the chefs and cooks of France whose generosity
made this book possible, and to my literary agent,
Oliver G. (Ollie) Swan, who has encouraged me through
years of culinary journeyings.*

CONTENTS

Acknowledgments   xi

Preface   xiii

Unusual Ingredients and

Basic Recipes and Techniques   1

Hors-d'Oeuvre and Salads   35

Soups   85

Fish and Shellfish   111

Poultry   175

Meats   209

Vegetables   259

Desserts and Breads   287

Index   317

ACKNOWLEDGMENTS

I could not have written this book without the help of the many chefs who let me visit their kitchens, who talked with me, cooked for me, and gave me recipes suitable for American kitchens. I also owe a debt of gratitude to friends in France who were equally generous with their help.

My special thanks are due to M. Joseph Olivereau, International President of the Relais and Châteaux Organisation, and his assistant Mme Elizabeth Robertson, who gave me unstinting help in planning trips, and to Jean-Pierre Fava of the Hôtellerie du Bas-Bréau at Barbizon, for good advice and help. My special thanks also to Pierre Duvauchelle, President of France-Mapotel and manager of the Hôtel de l'Aigle Noir at Fontainebleau, and to Mme Martine Bonnamy of the Chaîne Hotelière Frantel. And finally I would like to thank Ruth Buchan for her excellent editorial advice.

ELISABETH LAMBERT ORTIZ

PREFACE

The history of French cuisine is one of continuous change, with every hundred years or so a major change of great depth and importance. Familiar food patterns and attitudes disappear and new tastes, new techniques and new points of view are presented to us. The evolution of the French kitchen began with Taillevent back in the fourteenth century, continued through La Varenne in the seventeenth, Antonin Carême in the eighteenth, to Escoffier who died only in 1935. Each man had something special to offer with added inspiration and technical improvements, simplifying and clarifying menus as well as individual recipes, taking the cuisine to new heights. Today we have a whole group of young chefs, men and women, bursting with fresh ideas and creative skills, giving us dishes we find perfect for today's life-style; and the French cuisine stimulates our interest and our appetites in a way no other cuisine can.

Recently I had the great good fortune to be asked by *Gourmet* magazine to write some of the chapters in *Gourmet's France*, a book not just of food but of many aspects of French culture. It was on a holiday trip after I had finished my work on the *Gourmet* book that the idea for this book

was born. It was suggested to me by a prestigious chef whose suggestions I took seriously.

I've had a happy time traveling all over France, meeting chefs who are generosity itself, eating in restaurants both large and small, grand and simple, famous and unknown; eating with friends at home; visiting markets and food shops, always an important source of knowledge, to find out what has been happening to food and attitudes to food in France in recent years. The answer is very simple really. It can be summed up into eating more fish and poultry, and less meat; having more vegetables that are cooked *croquant,* that is crisp, and not limp and overdone; having more, and more imaginative, salads; and having meals that are unstructured, more flexible. If you want to begin with a salad, fine. If you want a double portion of salad as a main course, fine. It is a lovely attitude to food. It says: eat what you like, how you like it, and enjoy it. Perhaps the best thing of all is that sauces have not ceased to be rich, in fact I think they are richer, but you get less of them. Not a plate swimming in gravy, but a meat, poultry or fish napped with a tablespoon or two of an exquisite sauce. And you are given a small, flat spoon to make sure that none of the sauce is missed. Since that last bit of sauce is tasted without the intervention even of flavors of the main course it enhances, it comes to the palate unadulterated by any other taste, absolutely pure. This is utter luxury. There has also been an influence from Japan and Vietnam, especially in presentation, so that food looks prettier. Natural flavors are stressed and food comes tasting as it should taste, of itself, its own true flavor enhanced by the cooking process, not masked by it.

Technology has played a most important role in helping to create today's food. There are so many dishes that would not be possible or practical without the blender and that newest and most welcome kitchen helper, the food processor. There have also been, over recent years, innovations and improvements in cook stoves, cookware, and other kitchen equipment as well as fine catalogues that tell us what and where to buy. In addition more fresh foods are

available from all over the country as well as from all over the world, and processed foods reach us from just about everywhere. There are very few things we cannot cook if we want to.

This is a very personal book. I have not made any attempt to cover the whole of the current scene. There surely must be a number of very fine chefs I have not had the privilege of meeting, but, if I had tried to embrace the total genius of the French kitchen, this would not be a small modest book, but a series of huge ones. This is the only apology I can make for what I have missed. The loss is wholly mine. I have chosen the recipes I have most enjoyed. I have tested them all and found them entirely workable in a small kitchen with ingredients easy enough to buy, though sometimes a little searching was necessary. And sometimes extra kitchen time was needed too. I do hope that readers will want to cook these dishes and will enjoy them as much as I have. It is such fun and so very rewarding to have one's culinary horizons expanded.

ELISABETH LAMBERT ORTIZ
1981

Cooking
with the
Young
Chefs
of France

UNUSUAL INGREDIENTS AND BASIC RECIPES AND TECHNIQUES

STOCKS

Nowadays there are available excellent canned beef and chicken stocks, and in a crisis there are bouillon cubes, packed by several good companies, that can be useful in enriching an otherwise thin-tasting stock, a long-indulged-in shortcut recently legitimized by Michel Guérard. For those who prefer to make their own stock, it should be remembered that the stockpot must not become a dumping place for all or any leftovers, though it can be used to make stock that is less formal than a restaurant chef would accept. Here are recipes for the main stocks with suggestions for shortcuts. Most cooks will have their own, as few of us nowadays have kitchens large enough, or freezers big enough, or time sufficient to make stocks as perfect as we would wish. There is, however, room for reasonable compromise.

CHICKEN STOCK

MAKES ABOUT 3 QUARTS.

1 fowl, 4 pounds, with chopped giblets, excluding liver
2 medium-size onions, each stuck with a clove
2 leeks, well washed, split
2 medium-size carrots, scraped and sliced

1 celery rib, chopped
1 garlic clove
4 parsley sprigs
6 whole peppercorns
1 bay leaf
1 teaspoon salt
4½ quarts water

In a large saucepan or kettle combine all the ingredients and bring to a boil over moderately high heat, skimming the froth as it rises. Reduce the heat and simmer, partially covered, for 2½ hours.

Lift out the fowl, let it cool, and bone it. Return the bones to the kettle and set the meat aside for another use. Simmer, skimming from time to time, for another 30 minutes. Strain the stock through a fine sieve. Let it cool, then refrigerate and remove the solidified fat.

The stock can be frozen.

If a fowl is not available, use an equivalent weight of wings and backs, which can be bought in supermarkets and in stores that sell chicken parts. If you have chicken bones or veal bones, or meat bones other than lamb, from previous cooking, add them to the stockpot. If you have kept water in which vegetables have been cooked, use this instead of plain water. Use the stock for soups or sauces or whenever it is called for in recipes.

BROWN (BEEF) STOCK

MAKES ABOUT 2 QUARTS.

2 pounds beef shanks, chopped into about 2-inch pieces

2 pounds veal knuckles and bones, chopped into about 2-inch pieces

2 medium-size carrots, scraped and sliced

2 medium-size onions, coarsely chopped

1 garlic clove, chopped

¼ pound mushroom stems or whole mushrooms, chopped

1 celery rib, chopped

4 parsley sprigs

1 bay leaf

6 whole peppercorns

1 teaspoon salt

2 medium-size tomatoes, coarsely chopped

3 quarts water

½ cup dry white wine

Put the beef shanks and the veal knuckles and bones into a roasting pan without any liquid, and put the pan into a pre-heated hot oven (450°F.). Let the bones brown, turning them over once or twice, for 15 minutes. Add the carrots, onions, garlic and mushroom stems, or mushrooms, and cook for 5 minutes longer. Transfer to a large kettle or stockpot with all the remaining ingredients except the wine. Pour the wine into the roasting pan and deglaze the pan over moderately high heat, scraping up any brown bits. Add the deglazing to the kettle. Bring liquid to a boil and skim the froth as it rises. Simmer, partially covered, for about 3 hours.

Strain through a fine sieve, cool, and refrigerate. Remove the solidified fat.

Use in stews, soups and sauces, or whenever it is called for in recipes.

The stock can be frozen.

TO CLARIFY STOCK

Make sure all the fat has been removed from the stock. Beat 2 egg whites for about 6 cups of stock. Pour the cold stock into a saucepan, add the egg whites, and place saucepan over low heat. Using a wire whisk, beat the mixture until it comes to a simmer. Simmer for 5 minutes, uncovered. Let the mixture stand for at least 10 minutes. Strain it through a colander lined with a double layer of dampened cheesecloth, pouring carefully so as to disturb the coagulated mixture as little as possible.

GLACE DE VIANDE

(Meat Glaze)

MAKES 2 CUPS.

This is extremely useful to have in the refrigerator as it makes a superb enrichment for sauces and meat soups, improving both taste and color. In a crisis a tablespoon or two of the meat glaze can be turned into brown stock with the addition of a cup of boiling water, but for most purposes only a teaspoon of glaze is needed. In addition to being economical, it has the added merits of being easy to make and of keeping indefinitely in the refrigerator. It is a good idea to make 2 cups and freeze three quarters of the amount in small containers, keeping the remainder for current use in the refrigerator.

Make 2 quarts of Brown Stock (see Index) and carefully remove all fat. Pour the stock into a medium-size saucepan and simmer, uncovered, over moderate heat until it is reduced to 2 cups and has a syrupy consistency. Let it cool and pour into containers.

WHITE VEAL STOCK

MAKES ABOUT 6 CUPS.

This is the most elegant of all the stocks. It looks beautiful and is lovely to use; it is worth the trouble it takes. Get the butcher to chop up or saw the veal shanks and bones into convenient pieces.

2 pounds meaty veal shank, chopped into 2-inch pieces
2 pounds veal bones, chopped into 2-inch pieces
1 pound chicken wings and backs, or 1 pound chicken giblets (without livers), or the carcass of a chicken, chopped
1 pig's foot, split
2 medium-size carrots, scraped and sliced
2 medium-size onions, chopped
1 celery rib, chopped
1 leek, well washed and split
2 whole garlic cloves
2 cloves
1 bay leaf
3 parsley sprigs
¼ teaspoon dried thyme
1 teaspoon salt
3 quarts water

Put the veal shank and bones into a large saucepan or kettle. Pour on enough boiling water to cover, bring back to a boil over high heat, and boil for 1 minute. Drain and rinse. Rinse out the saucepan and return the meat and bones to it. Add all the rest of the ingredients and bring to a boil. Reduce the heat to a simmer and skim off any froth that rises. Partially cover the saucepan and simmer over low heat for 3 hours, skimming the surface from time to time as necessary.

Let the stock cool, then strain through a sieve lined with a double layer of cheesecloth. Refrigerate the stock; when cold, remove the solidified fat. The stock will set to a light golden-colored jelly. It is a good idea to freeze some of it by cupfuls in plastic bags. Use in sauces or interchangeably with chicken stock.

ASPIC

Stocks made with calf's feet, pig's feet or veal knuckles usually contain enough natural gelatin for the stock to set into aspic. Fish stock usually has enough gelatin from the fish bones to set. Sometimes, however, the jelly is not sufficiently firm. In this case it may be reinforced by the addition of a little unflavored powdered gelatin. One envelope (7 grams) will set 2 cups of liquid into a firm aspic. One envelope of gelatin will set 3 cups of liquid into jellied soup. Use in the amount needed. One envelope is about 1 tablespoon.

To use powdered gelatin, sprinkle 1 envelope onto ¼ cup cold water and let stand until softened. Stir into the rest of the liquid and simmer over moderate heat until gelatin has completely dissolved. Remove from the heat and chill in the refrigerator to set.

COURT BOUILLON

MAKES ABOUT 8 CUPS.

Fish may be cooked in a court bouillon which can then form the basis of a fish stock or *fumet,* or the fish may be cooked in the stock itself. The *fumet,* if frozen, will keep for several weeks.

2 tablespoons butter	Several parsley stalks
1 cup finely chopped onions	1 sprig of thyme
	1 bay leaf
1 cup scraped and diced carrots	6 cups water
	Salt, white pepper
½ cup chopped celery	2 cups dry white wine
1 garlic clove, minced	

In a saucepan heat the butter and add the onions, carrots and celery; cook, stirring, over moderate heat until the vegetables are softened. Add all other ingredients except the wine, with salt and pepper to taste, and simmer for 15 minutes. Add the wine, bring back to a boil, and simmer for 15 minutes longer. Let the broth cool.

Use to poach fish or shellfish. After poaching fish the broth may be used as a light fish stock and as the basis for fish soup or sauce, or as the basis of a *fumet*.

FISH STOCK OR FUMET

MAKES ABOUT 3 CUPS.

When buying fish always ask for the head and bones.

2 tablespoons butter
1 pound fish heads and bones of any nonoily white fish, coarsely chopped
1 cup chopped onions
1 shallot, chopped (optional)
½ cup diced mushrooms
12 parsley stalks

1 bay leaf
½ teaspoon dried thyme
2 tablespoons lemon juice
½ cup dry white wine
3½ cups water, or use strained court bouillon (preceding recipe)

In a saucepan combine all the ingredients except the wine and water. Stir to mix, cover, and cook over low heat for 5 minutes. Add the wine and water, bring to a boil and simmer, uncovered, skimming the froth as it rises to the surface, for about 20 minutes. Strain through a fine sieve, pressing down to extract all the juices. Cool and chill. The stock may be frozen.

Use leftover court bouillon in place of the water if available.

7

MAYONNAISE

MAKES ABOUT 2 CUPS.

2 large egg yolks
1 teaspoon Dijon
   mustard
   Salt, freshly ground
   white pepper
1½ cups olive oil or
   vegetable oil (corn or
   peanut), or a mixture
   of both

4 teaspoons wine vinegar
   or lemon juice, or a
   mixture of both

Put the egg yolks into a bowl and beat them lightly with a fork or a whisk. Beat in the mustard and salt and pepper to taste. Beat in the oil drop by drop until the yolks thicken. When half of the oil has been beaten in, add the vinegar, beating vigorously. Beat in remaining oil, pouring it in a thin, steady stream. Taste the mayonnaise and add more vinegar or lemon juice, or more salt and pepper. If the mayonnaise is too thick, thin it with a tablespoon or so of cream or water.

SAUCE VINAIGRETTE

(Oil and Vinegar Dressing)

MAKES ABOUT 1 CUP.

This is the basic French salad dressing. It may be varied by using different oils and vinegars or by using lemon juice instead of vinegar.

¼ cup wine vinegar
   Salt, freshly ground
   pepper

¾ to 1 cup olive or salad
   oil

Combine the vinegar with about ½ teaspoon or more of salt and pepper to taste in a bowl. Whisk in the oil in a steady stream until the mixture is well blended.

Variations: Add Dijon mustard to vinegar and salt and pepper, mixing thoroughly before adding the oil. Use ½ teaspoon to 1 tablespoon mustard according to taste.

For walnut oil dressing, use ¾ cup salad oil and ¼ cup walnut oil.

Use herb vinegar (tarragon, basil), or raspberry or sherry vinegar instead of wine vinegar.

Add ½ to 1 teaspoon Dijon mustard and 1 crushed garlic clove to the vinegar with the salt and pepper, mixing well.

BEURRE BLANC OR BEURRE NANTAIS

(White Butter Sauce)

MAKES ABOUT 1 CUP.

¼ cup finely chopped shallots	½ pound (2 sticks) chilled butter, cut into bits
¼ cup dry white wine	Salt, white pepper
¼ cup white-wine vinegar	

In a small heavy saucepan combine the shallots, wine and vinegar and simmer, uncovered, over moderate heat until the liquid has reduced to about 1 tablespoon. Over low heat whisk in the bits of butter, one at a time, adding a new piece as soon as the previous one has almost melted into the sauce. Continue until all the butter is used up, beating constantly. Do not let the sauce get hot as the butter will turn oily and the sauce will thin instead of being thick and creamy. Season with salt and pepper and serve as soon as possible.

Some cooks make the sauce with ½ cup dry white wine instead of a mixture of wine and vinegar.

JUS LIÉ

(Simple Brown Sauce)

MAKES ABOUT 2 CUPS.

Simmer 2 cups of brown (beef) stock (see Index) over moderate heat, uncovered, for 10 minutes. In a small bowl combine 1 tablespoon arrowroot with about 4 tablespoons cold water, stirring to mix well. Stir into the stock and simmer until the sauce is lightly thickened, about 2 minutes.

SAUCE BÉCHAMEL

(White Sauce)

MAKES 2 CUPS.

2 tablespoons butter	2 cups milk
3 tablespoons flour	Salt, white pepper

In a heavy saucepan melt the butter over low heat and stir in the flour with a wooden spoon. Cook, stirring, without letting the mixture color, for 2 minutes. Gradually pour in the milk, stirring constantly to mix, and bring to a boil. Simmer, stirring, for 5 minutes. Season with salt and pepper.

Variations: For a very thick sauce reduce the liquid to 1 cup. For a thinner sauce increase the liquid to 2½ cups.

For Sauce Velouté substitute veal or chicken stock for the milk.

BEURRE MANIÉ

Work equal quantities of flour and butter together with a fork in a cup or small bowl until completely amalgamated. Stir small pieces of the mixture into boiling liquid, stews for example, and stir constantly until the liquid has thickened to the degree required.

TO CLARIFY BUTTER

Clarified butter is used whenever high heat is needed, such as in sautéing. It does not burn in the way ordinary butter does. Using clarified butter eliminates the need for adding oil, which is the other method used to cook over high heat without burning the butter.

Cut the butter into large chunks and put it into a small heavy saucepan over low heat. Let the butter heat but do not let it brown. Skim off the white froth that rises to the top. Let the butter sit for a minute or two, then carefully pour off the clear yellow liquid. The white residue in the bottom of the pan need not be discarded. Stir it into soups, stews or sauces.

BEURRE D'ESCARGOTS

(Snail Butter)

MAKES ABOUT ½ CUP.

Thoroughly mix together 2 large garlic cloves, crushed, ¼ pound butter, 1 teaspoon finely chopped shallot, salt and pepper to taste and 3 tablespoons finely chopped parsley. For use in other recipes, if liked, ⅛ teaspoon ground dried mixed herbs may be added, but not when the butter is used for snails.

A NOTE ON BUTTER

Butter is sold as lightly salted, or unsalted, often called "sweet butter." I have not specified which type to use in these recipes because I use unsalted (sweet) butter always, for its more delicate flavor. As the degree of saltiness varies greatly from one butter to another, using salted butter can make judging the saltiness of a dish difficult, especially for guests on low-salt diets.

TO NAP WITH A SAUCE

This term is used specifically with sauces that have *du corps,* body or consistency. This type of sauce will adhere because it is thick but will not obliterate the outline of the food. It is spooned or brushed on right before serving.

TO PEEL AND SEED TOMATOES

Choose tomatoes that are ripe and red and, if possible, thin skinned, as these are usually more flavorful. Drop them one at a time into boiling water for about 10 seconds. Lift out and peel from the stem end. Cut out the stem. If the tomato does not peel easily, drop it back into the water for a few seconds longer. Cut the tomato crosswise into halves and gently squeeze out the seeds. Use as directed.

There are times, especially in winter, when really red-ripe tomatoes cannot be found. Choose a good brand of canned tomatoes—Italian plum tomatoes are usually very flavorful—and use them as a substitute in appropriate dishes.

COULIS DE TOMATES FRAÎCHES

(Fresh Tomato Purée)

MAKES ABOUT 1½ CUPS.

Peel and seed 4 medium-size tomatoes (about 1 pound) and chop them coarsely. Purée the tomatoes in a food processor fitted with the steel blade or in a blender. (For a finer sauce force the tomatoes through a sieve into a bowl.) Season with salt and freshly ground pepper and stir in 1 tablespoon tomato paste or thick tomato purée to intensify the flavor. (If the tomatoes are really sweet and red-ripe, omit this addition.) Use as directed.

VINAIGRETTE DE TOMATES FRAÎCHES

(Tomato Vinaigrette)

MAKES ABOUT 1¾ CUPS.

Peel and seed 4 medium-size tomatoes (about 1 pound) and chop them coarsely. Purée the tomatoes in a food processor fitted with the steel blade, or in a blender, and force the purée through a fine sieve into a bowl. Season with salt and freshly ground pepper. Beat in 3 tablespoons olive or vegetable oil and 1 tablespoon white-wine vinegar or lemon juice. If liked, and to suit the dish, stir in 1 tablespoon of minced herbs in any combination (basil, tarragon, chives, parsley, chervil or mint). Use as directed.

CHIFFONADE D'OSEILLE

(Sorrel Chiffonade)

MAKES ABOUT ½ CUP.

My friend and fellow food writer Norman Kolpas says that sorrel is the only vegetable that purées itself, a most apt description. It has a refreshing acidity.

| ½ pound sorrel, about 4 cups | 2 tablespoons butter |

Thoroughly wash the sorrel leaves in cold water and shake to remove excess water. Cut away and discard the stems and center veins of the leaves. Stack the leaves and roll them up. Slice them very finely. Heat the butter in a small heavy saucepan, add the sorrel, and cook over low heat, stirring once or twice, until the vegetable has melted into a purée, about 10 minutes. Let it cool. Transfer to a covered container and refrigerate until ready to use. It will keep for about a week.

MIREPOIX

MAKES ABOUT 2½ CUPS.

2 tablespoons butter
2 cups scraped and diced
   carrots
½ cup peeled and diced
   turnips

½ cup finely chopped well-
   washed leeks or onions
¼ cup diced celery

Heat the butter in a saucepan and add the vegetables. Sauté over moderate heat until the vegetables are soft but not browned. Use as directed in recipes.

DUXELLES

MAKES ABOUT 1 CUP.

½ pound mushrooms
4 tablespoons butter
¼ cup finely chopped
   shallots or scallions

Salt, freshly ground
   pepper

Wipe the mushrooms and chop finely, using both the caps and stems. Heat the butter in a small heavy saucepan and sauté the mushrooms with the shallots until all the moisture has evaporated, stirring from time to time. The *duxelles* should be quite dry. Season to taste with salt and pepper. Refrigerate in a covered container until ready to use as a flavoring for stuffings and for sauces.

CROUSTADES

(Bread Cases)

These can be either large or small according to the planned use. Essentially they are hollowed-out bread from which the crusts have been removed. A whole loaf may be used, or a thick slice, 2 to 4 inches of bread. The walls of the case should be about ¾ inch thick. The case is brushed all over, inside and out, with butter or oil and baked in a preheated hot oven (400°F.) until golden brown, about 10 minutes.

CROÛTES À L'AIL

(Garlic-Flavored Toasted Bread)

Rub slices of French bread, or any firm homemade type of bread, with a cut garlic clove. Sprinkle the bread with olive oil or vegetable oil, and bake in a preheated moderate oven (375°F.) for 10 to 15 minutes, or until golden brown. If liked, the crusts may be trimmed from the bread.

CROÛTONS

(Little Crusts)

Cut bread, preferably French or firm homemade type, into ¼-inch slices; remove the crusts and cut the slices into ¼-inch cubes. Sauté in clarified butter or in oil until they are golden all over. Alternately they may be sprinkled with melted butter or oil and baked in a preheated moderate oven (375°F.) until browned, about 10 minutes.

CROÛTES

(Crusts)

These are larger pieces of bread; they may be the same as Melba toast, that is, thin slices of bread dried in a slow oven. They may also be cut into triangles or other shapes and browned in clarified butter or oil; or buttered or sprinkled with oil and browned in the oven.

PÂTE BRISÉE

(Short Paste, Piecrust)

MAKES ENOUGH PASTRY FOR AN 8- TO 9-INCH PIE SHELL OR FOR SIX 4-INCH TARTLET TINS.

1¼ cups all-purpose flour
¼ teaspoon salt
5 tablespoons chilled
   butter, cut into bits
3 tablespoons chilled
   vegetable shortening,
   cut into bits

2 to 3 tablespoons cold
   water

Sift the flour with the salt into a large bowl. Rub the fats into the flour with the fingertips until the mixture resembles coarse meal. Sprinkle with 2 tablespoons of the water, mix quickly, and form the dough into a ball. Add more water if necessary to hold the dough together. It should be soft but not sticky. On a floured pastry board knead the dough with the heel of the hand for about 30 seconds to distribute the fat evenly. Form the dough into a ball, dust it with flour, put it into a plastic bag or wrap in plastic wrap, and refrigerate for at least 1 hour before using. Pastry dough can be made ahead of time as it will keep, refrigerated, for about 3 days. It can be frozen successfully.

The pastry can be made in a food processor using the steel blade. Pour in the flour and salt, add the cut-up butter and shortening, and process until the mixture resembles coarse meal, about 30 seconds. With the machine running add 2 tablespoons of water through the feed tube to make a fairly soft ball of dough. Add remaining tablespoon of water if necessary. The dough should not be damp or sticky. Wrap up the dough and refrigerate for 1 hour before using.

For a 10- to 11-inch pie shell increase the flour to 2 cups and use ½ teaspoon salt, 8 tablespoons butter, 4 tablespoons vegetable shortening or lard and 4 to 5 tablespoons water.

TO BAKE BLIND

To bake a pastry shell blind, roll the dough on a floured surface to ⅛-inch thickness, drape it over the rolling pin, and fit it into the pie pan. Press the dough firmly into the pan. Cut off excess pastry with the rolling pin. Prick the bottom of the pastry with a fork and chill for 1 hour.

Line the pan with foil and fill about half full with dried beans or rice. Bake a pie shell in a preheated hot oven (425°F.) for 15 minutes, tartlet shells for 8 minutes. Remove the beans or rice and keep them to use again. Remove the foil and bake the pie shell for 8 minutes longer, tartlet shells for about 5 minutes, or until the pastry is golden. Remove from the oven and let the shell cool. It is now ready to be filled and the baking finished.

If the filling is not to be baked, increase the baking time after the foil has been removed to about 18 minutes, or until the pastry is golden brown.

Shallow flan pans with removable rings can be used instead of pie pans.

PÂTE BRISÉE SUCRÉE

(Sweet Short Pastry)

This is the pastry that is used for dessert tarts and fruit pies. Omit the salt from Pâte Brisée ingredients (see preceding recipe). Use all butter instead of a mixture of butter and vegetable shortening. Add 3 tablespoons sugar to the flour when sifting. Mix the dough with 1 egg, lightly beaten, instead of cold water. Add water only if necessary. If you like, ¼ teaspoon vanilla extract may be added to the egg when beating it.

For the 10- to 11-inch tart increase the sugar to 4 tablespoons and use 1 large egg or 2 small eggs. Increase the flour to 2 cups.

PÂTE FEUILLETÉE

(Puff Pastry)

MAKES ABOUT 1 POUND.

2 cups all-purpose flour
1 teaspoon salt
½ pound (2 sticks) butter,
    divided

1 cup ice water

Sift the flour and salt together into a large bowl. Cut 4 tablespoons butter into bits and work it into the flour with the fingertips until the mixture resembles coarse meal. Add about ½ cup ice water and work the dough quickly to form a ball. Sprinkle with flour, put into a plastic bag, and refrigerate for about 1 hour.

Using the fingers, work the rest of the butter into a square. Put it between 2 sheets of wax paper and roll it out with a rolling pin to make a 4-inch square. Peel off the wax paper, sprinkle the butter with flour, and wrap up in fresh paper. Refrigerate until butter is firm. On a lightly floured board roll the dough out to a 7-inch square and put the butter diagonally in the center. Fold the dough over the butter, as if making an envelope, to enclose it. Turn it over.

Dust the board and the dough lightly with flour and roll out the dough into a rectangle 6 by 10 inches. Fold the top over all but the bottom third of the rectangle. Fold the bottom third over the top, as if folding a letter into thirds. Turn the dough so that one of the open ends faces you. With the rolling pin roll the dough away from you from the center almost to the edge. Turn it around and roll the other half away from you to make a rectangle about 10 inches long, taking care to stop rolling about ½ inch before the edge so as not to let the butter ooze out. Fold the dough once more into thirds as for a letter, flouring the surface and the board as necessary. This completes 2 turns. Wrap the dough in wax paper and chill in the refrigerator for 30 minutes. Take out the dough, remove the wax paper, flour both board and dough, and roll out as before with an open

18

Preparing Puff Pastry

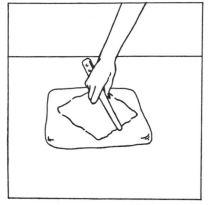

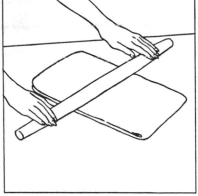

1. Place a square of softened butter diagonally on the square of dough.

2. Fold the dough over the butter as if making an envelope. Turn it over and roll out dough into rectangle.

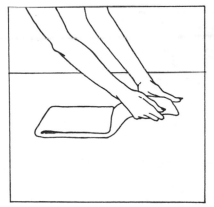

3. Fold the dough into thirds as if folding a letter.

4. With the open end facing you, roll out the dough into a rectangle.

end facing you. Fold it up again into thirds. Roll out again and fold up. Chill the dough, wrapped in wax paper, for at least 30 minutes. It is now ready to be used.

The dough can be kept, refrigerated, for about 1 week. It can be kept frozen, wrapped in foil. Thaw before using.

Cleaning a Leek

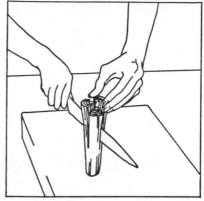

1. Slit the trimmed leek down in half through the green to the white part.

2. Cut across in the same way so leek top is divided into four parts.

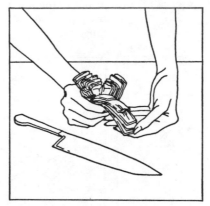

3. Leek can now be thoroughly washed in cold water to get rid of any sand or dirt.

TO WASH LEEKS

Leeks need careful washing as there is always dirt between the outer layers of the leaves. Trim the roots and remove any tough or wilted outside leaves. Slit the leeks from the green tops down in 2 places to within 2 inches of the white part. Soak in cold water and rinse thoroughly. Cut off the green parts that have been slit and use them in making soups or stock. The leeks are now ready to be cooked.

TO CLEAN MUSSELS

Mussels need a great deal of cleaning. Scrub them in several changes of water and scrape off the beards, or cut off the beards with a small sharp knife. Soak the mussels in cold water to cover for several hours, changing the water once or twice, to get rid of sand. Some cooks add a tablespoon of cornmeal to the water to speed up the process. Rinse the mussels thoroughly and drain. They are now ready to cook.

MOULES À LA MARINIÈRE

(Steamed Mussels)

SERVES 6.

This is the most usual method of cooking mussels, and it is a good basis for mussels cooked in other ways. Estimate 2 pounds mussels in the shell per person.

12 pounds mussels in the shell
2 cups dry white wine
½ cup minced shallots, green onions or onion
Salt, freshly ground pepper
4 tablespoons butter

Bouquet garni: 4 parsley sprigs, 1 bay leaf, 1 thyme sprig, 1 garlic clove, tied in a square of cheesecloth

Thoroughly scrub and clean the mussels and put them in a heavy saucepan or kettle with all other ingredients. Cover, bring to a simmer over moderate heat, and cook, shaking the pot from time to time, for 5 to 6 minutes, or until the shells have opened. Discard any unopened mussels.

To serve the mussels, ladle them out into large rimmed soup plates and strain the cooking liquid over them. Serve with soup spoons as well as finger bowls, and crusty bread and butter.

21

Cutting Up a Rabbit

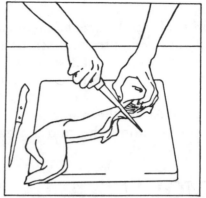

1. Cut the rabbit into two parts, severing the backbone where the rib cage ends.

2. Make the incision between the second and third ribs; then cut off rib cage and forelegs.

TO CUT UP AND BONE A RABBIT

I'm grateful to my friend Richard Olney who showed me the best way to cut up and bone a rabbit, a surprisingly easy operation. However, I always ask the butcher to remove and split the head for me if I am using it to enrich the stock, and I tend to look the other way when I put it in, or take it out of, the pot.

Cut the rabbit in two under the rib cage; two of the ribs will remain with the lower part. There is very little meat on the rib cage or forelegs. Cut up these parts and use with the head to make a stock or to enrich the gravy. They can, of course, be used in a rabbit stew in which case cut off the forelegs and cut the rib cage in two.

To bone the hind legs and meaty saddle, the part with the kidneys, use a small, sharp-pointed paring knife; loosen the flesh and work it away from the backbone. Pull the bone

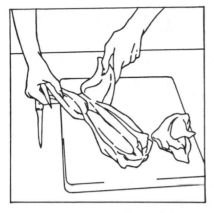

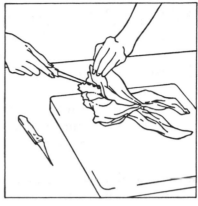

3. Lay the rabbit on its back and open out legs. Set rib cage aside.

4. Using a small, sharp-pointed paring knife or boning knife, start to cut the backbone away from the flesh. Use the tip of the knife to free the vertebrae, taking care not to pierce the flesh.

5. If cutting the rabbit into serving pieces, cut across the back just above the legs.

6. Cut the saddle into halves and separate legs, cutting them apart.

gently away. Try not to pierce the flesh. It is easier to work by breaking off sections of the backbone as they are freed from the flesh. The rabbit is now ready to be stuffed. To serve, separate the hind legs and cut the saddle in two, crosswise.

TO PREPARE SWEETBREADS

Soak sweetbreads in cold water to cover for 2 to 3 hours, changing the water once or twice. Drain and transfer to a saucepan with cold water to cover. Bring to a simmer over moderate heat, cover, and simmer for 10 minutes. Lift out the sweetbreads into a bowl of cold water. When they are cool enough to handle, peel away the membrane and remove the tube and any fat. Place the sweetbreads on a flat surface, such as a plate or board. Top with another plate or board and weight with a 2- to 3-pound weight for several hours. The sweetbreads are now ready to be cooked. If not to be used immediately, wrap in wax paper and refrigerate.

LARDONS

(Lardoons)

These are small strips, 1 to 1½ inches long and about ¼ inch thick, cut from fresh belly of pork (fresh bacon), or blanched salted belly of pork or slab bacon. To blanch the salted and/or smoked meat, simmer the whole piece in water to cover by several inches for 10 minutes, then drain, pat dry, and cut into strips. Heat about 1 tablespoon vegetable oil in a heavy skillet and sauté the *lardons* until they are browned and have released most of their fat. Lift out with a slotted spoon and drain on paper towels if using in a salad, or use as recipe indicates.

A NOTE ON BACON, FRESH AND UNSMOKED

The bacon used in French cooking is not usually smoked. If unsmoked bacon is not available, blanch smoked bacon by simmering it in water to cover for about 10 minutes. Drain and pat dry before using.

Belly of pork (fresh bacon) with the rind on and the bone in, is available in Chinese markets. Otherwise ask a pork butcher to supply the pork belly with the rind. The rind can be cut off and used when *couennes,* bacon or pork rinds, are called for. If fresh belly of pork is not available, you may use salt pork. Simmer it in water to cover for about 10 minutes. Drain and pat dry before using.

TO PREPARE AND COOK CHESTNUTS

Most cooks have a favorite method for removing the hard outer shell and the bitter inner skin of chestnuts to prepare them for cooking. I do them the Japanese way: Cut the peel from the flat end of each nut with a small sharp knife. Put the nuts into a heavy skillet (cast iron is perfect for this), and cook them, turning them constantly, over moderate heat until the shells are browned and begin to crack. Chopsticks are best for turning the chestnuts but any kitchen implement that does the job is fine. As soon as they are cool enough to handle, remove the peel with a knife. It should come away quite easily. If the nuts get too cold and difficult to peel, warm them up in the skillet.

Another method is to peel a thin strip off one side of the nut, or make a horizontal slash in the flat side. Put the chestnuts in a large saucepan with cold water to cover, bring to a boil over moderate heat, and boil for about 3 minutes. Remove from the heat and take out the chestnuts a few at a time, peeling them as soon as they are cool enough to handle. If any get too cold to peel, warm them up again in the saucepan.

There are approximately 35 to 40 raw chestnuts to the pound. They will yield 2½ cups peeled. Whole, unsweetened chestnuts are available canned, and can be used in place of cooked fresh chestnuts. Sweetened chestnut purée is also available canned and is useful for desserts.

To cook chestnuts, simmer them in chicken or beef stock or water until tender, about 30 minutes.

CRÈME FRAÎCHE

MAKES 1 CUP.

French *crème fraîche* is a matured cream that has thickened naturally through the action of lactic acid organisms, but it remains sweet, not sour. Our heavy cream can be used instead very successfully. However, it is easy enough to turn heavy cream into a close approximation of *crème fraîche.* Combine buttermilk with heavy cream in the proportion of 1 tablespoon buttermilk to 1 cup cream. Stir thoroughly to mix, cover, and let the mixture stand at room temperature until it has thickened, 8 or more hours usually, though the time varies with the weather. Store in the refrigerator. It will keep for about 1 month.

TECHNIQUES

Boning a Chicken

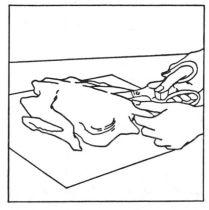

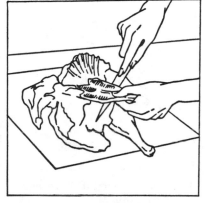

1. To partially bone chicken, lay breast down and cut out the backbone with poultry shears or scissors.

2. Cut away and pull out the breastbone.

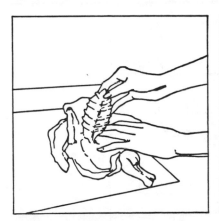

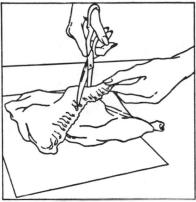

3. Using a sharp-pointed paring knife, cut and pull out the rib cage.

4. Cut off the wing tips.

Boning a Fish through the Back

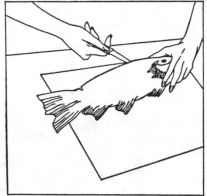

1. Boning cleaned fish through back by cutting open along backbone.

2. Pulling out the backbone.

Chopping

Chopping onions with a chef's knife.

EQUIPMENT

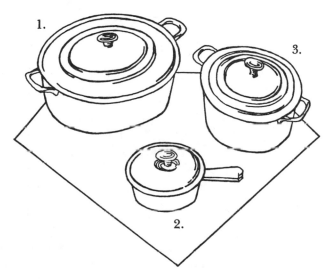

1. Large round enameled cast-iron casserole. **2.** Small enameled cast-iron saucepan. **3.** Small round enameled cast-iron casserole.

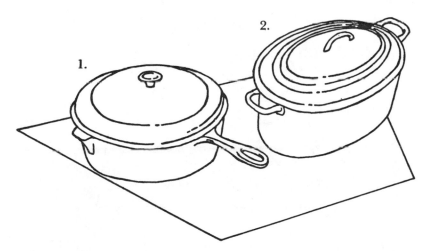

1. Enameled cast-iron sauté pan. **2.** Oval enameled cast-iron casserole.

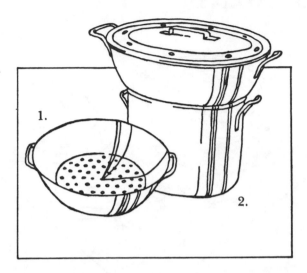

1. Perforated inner basket of *couscoussière,* a special steamer traditionally used for couscous. 2. Aluminum *couscoussière* with lid.

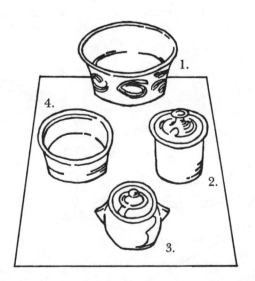

1. Earthenware terrine. 2, 3. Earthenware *rilletes* pots. 4. Porcelain soufflé dish.

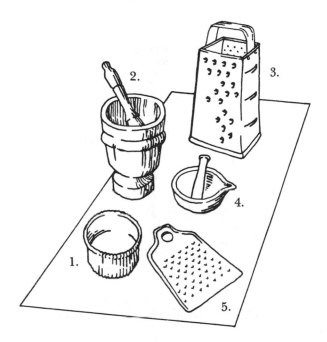

1. Small fluted porcelain ramekin. 2. Wooden mortar and pestle for dry herbs and spices. 3. Four-sided grater and shredder. 4. Small marble mortar and pestle for garlic, basil and so on. 5. Small porcelain grater for nutmeg or ginger.

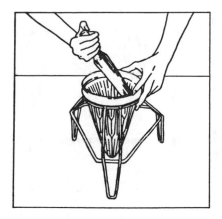

Perforated tinned-steel *chinois* (conical sieve) with stand and wooden pestle.

1. Sauce whisk. 2. Large wooden-handled balloon whisk for egg whites and cream. 3. Smaller stainless steel-handled balloon whisk for egg whites and cream.

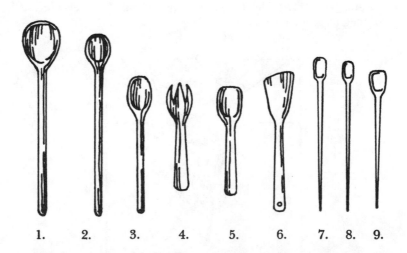

1. Large beechwood mixing spoon. 2. Thin-handled wooden spoon. 3. Small beechwood mixing spoon. 4,5. Beechwood fork and spoon for serving salads and other foods. 6. Olivewood spatula. 7,8,9. Small variously sized thin-handled wooden mixing spoons for stirring sauces.

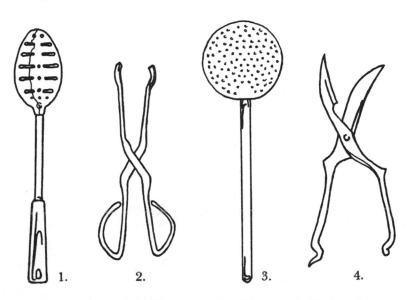

1. Slotted spoon. 2. Lifting tongs. 3. Skimmer. 4. Poultry shears.

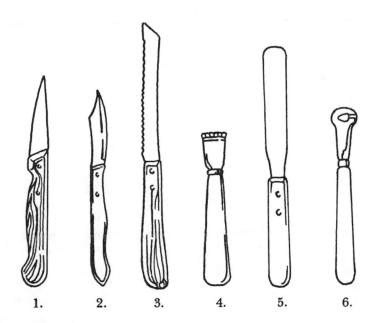

1. Paring knife. 2. Small paring knife. 3. French tomato knife.
4. French citrus peeler. 5. Stainless steel spatula. 6. Lemon zester.

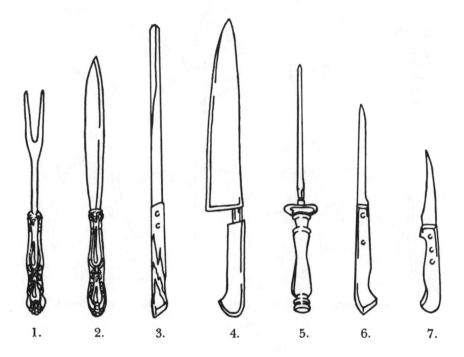

1. Carving fork. 2. Carving knife. 3. Round-tipped slicing knife.
4. Chef's knife. 5. Round sharpening steel. 6. Boning knife.
7. Small paring knife.

HORS-D'OEUVRE
AND SALADS

Perhaps the best thing that has happened to food recently is that menus have become unstructured, which is a way of saying that we can eat as we like. The hors-d'oeuvre which were once relegated to the beginning of rather formal meals can now be served generously enough to be the main course of the meal itself, or they can still be first courses with a main course to follow.

Salads are now universally accepted as first courses, but can also still be served after the main course if preferred. They can also become the main course of a light meal, lunch or dinner.

SALADE DE FOIE GRAS AUX NAVETS ET ÉPINARDS

(Foie Gras Salad with Turnips and Spinach)

SERVES 4.

This salad makes an unusually good first course. The *foie gras* is in luxurious contrast with the simplicity of the turnip and spinach. It is not always possible to find *foie gras* and I have more than once substituted a really good *pâté de foie* in its place. The French accompany the salad with good chewy *pain de campagne,* country bread, the type sometimes found in Italian bakeries. Any good, firm bread will do, or enthusiasts can make their own (see Index).

1 pound trimmed spinach leaves, about 4 cups tightly packed

¾ pound white turnips, 4 or 5 small turnips

½ cup Sauce Vinaigrette (see Index), made with walnut oil

6 ounces foie gras, cut into ¾-inch squares about ½ inch thick

Finely shred the spinach and put into a salad bowl. Peel the turnips, slice thinly, then cut into julienne strips. Drop into briskly boiling salted water and boil for 1 minute. Drain and cool. Add to the spinach and toss with the vinaigrette. Arrange on 4 plates and top with the squares of *foie gras.*

Serve with toasted slices of country-style bread and crocks of unsalted butter.

SALADE ROYALE

(Royal Salad)

SERVES 2.

This makes an elegant beginning to a lunch or dinner. It is typical of the inventiveness of Gérard Truchetet. M. Truchetet, of the Relais et Châteaux Château d'Isenbourg, Rouffach, is a widely traveled chef who appreciates other cuisines while remaining faithful to his own.

4 leaves of Boston or other soft-leaf lettuce
1 medium-size avocado, pitted and peeled
1 cup cooked green beans, cut if large, left whole if small
1 large cooked artichoke heart, chopped
4 medium-size mushroom caps, wiped and finely chopped

1 ounce foie gras, cut into small cubes
4 tablespoons Sauce Vinaigrette (see Index), preferably made with Sherry vinegar
Freshly ground pepper

Arrange the lettuce leaves on 2 salad plates. Arrange the vegetables according to your own taste and sprinkle them with the *foie gras.* Pour the vinaigrette dressing over the salad and finish with a few grinds from the pepper mill.

Variation: Instead of *foie gras,* use cubes of a good *pâté de foie,* or substitute 4 medium-size shrimps, halved, or a little crab meat or lobster, or whatever seems appropriate.

SALADE DE TOMATES, HARICOTS VERTS ET CHAMPIGNONS

(Tomato, Green Bean and Mushroom Salad)

SERVES 6.

This makes a refreshing beginning to a meal, and has the advantage of being low-calorie, too.

4 cups cooked green beans, cut into ½-inch slices, about 1 pound
2½ cups sliced fresh mushrooms, about ½ pound
1 cup Sauce Vinaigrette (see Index), made with 1 tablespoon Dijon mustard

6 medium-size tomatoes, thinly sliced
Chopped parsley, or basil, or chervil

In a bowl combine the green beans and mushrooms. Toss with ¾ cup of the vinaigrette. Arrange on 6 salad plates. Surround with the tomatoes. Pour the rest of the vinaigrette over the tomatoes and sprinkle with the herbs.

SALADE DE COURGETTES, HARICOTS VERTS, AVOCAT ET FOIE DE VOLAILLE

(Zucchini, Green Bean, Avocado and Chicken-Liver Salad)

SERVES 6.

This is a robust salad, excellent as a first course followed by a soufflé or a light fish dish.

4 cups cooked green
  beans, cut into ½-inch
  slices, about 1 pound
2 cups thinly sliced cooked
  zucchini, about ½
  pound
1 medium-size avocado,
  peeled and cubed

1 medium-size endive,
  thinly sliced
1 cup Sauce Vinaigrette
  (see Index)
3 large chicken livers
2 tablespoons butter

In a salad bowl combine the green beans, zucchini, avocado cubes and endive. Toss with the vinaigrette.

In a skillet heat the butter and sauté the chicken livers over moderately high heat until they are lightly browned all over but still pink inside, about 6 minutes. Lift out, cool, and cut into ¼-inch slices. Arrange on top of the salad.

SALADE CHAUBUISSON

(Shrimp, Artichoke Heart and Avocado Salad)

SERVES 4.

This very pretty salad comes from Jacques Sourisseau of the Relais et Châteaux Le Manoir at Fontenay-Trésigny. The textures and flavors are beautifully balanced, complementing each other.

1 large avocado, peeled,
  pitted and sliced
4 cooked large artichoke
  hearts
1 cup cooked tiny shrimps
2 medium-size tomatoes,
  sliced

¼ pound raw mushrooms,
  sliced, about 1¼ cups
Chopped Boston lettuce
Sauce Vinaigrette (see
  Index)

On 4 salad plates arrange sliced avocado on one side. In the center of each plate put an artichoke heart filled with shrimps. Around the edge of each plate put tomato slices, sliced mushrooms and chopped lettuce. Moisten with the Sauce Vinaigrette.

SALADE DES GASTRONOMES

(Gourmet Salad)

SERVES 6.

This attractive salad, the creation of Paul Pauvert, chef of the Nantes Frantel restaurant Le Tillac, has similar ingredients to those of Salade Chaubuisson, but the crunchy quality of walnuts and the difference in technique—tossing the ingredients together—give a very different result.

6 large or 12 medium-size cooked artichoke hearts, chopped
3 medium-size avocados, pitted, peeled and cubed
2 cups chopped raw mushrooms
2 cups walnut meats
½ cup snipped chives
¼ cup chopped chervil (if not available use parsley)

1 recipe Sauce Vinaigrette (see Index), made with Sherry vinegar if possible, 1 tablespoon Dijon mustard and heavy cream instead of oil
1 head of Boston lettuce

Combine all the ingredients in a bowl and toss lightly. Serve decorated with lettuce leaves.

AVOCAT AU VINAIGRETTE ET CERFEUIL

(Avocado with Vinaigrette and Chervil)

SERVES 1.

The chopped chervil turns this simple presentation of avocado into something special, emphasizing and contrasting with the bland flavor of the avocado. The two shades of green make the salad look very pretty and appetizing.

1 medium-size avocado
2 tablespoons Sauce
   Vinaigrette (see Index),
   approximately

1 tablespoon finely
   chopped fresh chervil

Peel the avocado carefully. Cut it into halves and remove and discard the pit. Cut each half into ⅛-inch crosswise slices and arrange the slices on each side of a plate so that they follow the curve of the plate. Moisten with vinaigrette and sprinkle with chervil.

    A large avocado will serve 2.

SALADE DE CHOUCROUTE CRUE ET CERVELAS

(Sauerkraut and Cervelat Sausage Salad)

SERVES 6.

Cervelat or cervelas sausage is a semidry sausage similar to salami. It is sometimes called "summer sausage." It is used very imaginatively in this salad created by chef Claude Praz, who is from Lorraine.

1 head of Boston lettuce
1 pound sauerkraut,
   rinsed, drained and
   chopped
1 large onion, Bermuda-
   type, finely chopped
3 medium-size tomatoes,
   quartered

½ pound Swiss cheese,
   cut into strips
1½ pounds cervelas
   sausage, thinly sliced
1 cup Sauce Vinaigrette
   (see Index), made
   with 1 tablespoon
   Dijon mustard

Arrange the salad in 6 individual salad bowls. Line each bowl with lettuce leaves and arrange the sauerkraut on top. Place the onion on top of the sauerkraut and put 2 quarters of tomato at the sides of the bowl. Top the onion with cheese and sausage. Pour some dressing over each salad bowl.

41

TOMATES FARCIES AUX NOIX ET MARRONS

(Tomatoes Stuffed with Walnuts and Chestnuts)

SERVES 6.

This simple dish makes a marvelous first course. I find that canned whole chestnuts, well drained, are fine for the purée, though freshly cooked ones have a firmer drier texture. About 1 pound raw chestnuts are needed for the stuffing. (For preparation, see Index.) It is worth searching for really red, garden-ripe tomatoes for this.

6 large ripe but firm
   tomatoes
  Salt, freshly ground
   pepper
4 tablespoons butter
1 cup walnut meats,
  coarsely chopped

3 cups cooked chestnuts
  Oil
  Chopped parsley or
   chervil or snipped
  chives

Cut a slice off the stem end of each tomato and carefully hollow them out, leaving a wall about ½ inch thick. Sprinkle the insides with salt and pepper, turn upside down, and leave to drain for 30 minutes.

In a skillet heat 2 tablespoons butter and sauté the walnuts until they are lightly browned. Purée the chestnuts in a food processor fitted with the steel blade, or in a blender, and mix with the walnuts. Season with salt and pepper. Spoon the mixture into the tomatoes. Top each tomato with 1 teaspoon butter. Oil a baking dish and arrange the tomatoes in it. Bake the tomatoes in a preheated moderate oven (400°F.) for 10 minutes. Sprinkle with the parsley, chervil or chives. Serve hot.

SALADE DE PETITS LÉGUMES AU SAUMON FUMÉ

(Salad of Spring Vegetables with Smoked Salmon)

SERVES 4.

I am in the debt of M. Leyssalles of the Mapotel Cro-Magnon for this charming salad which I find makes an original first course or, if served more generously, a good main course for lunch.

2 medium-size tomatoes, peeled and sliced
1 cup ½-inch slices of cooked green beans
1 cup sliced mushrooms
4 cooked asparagus spears, cut into ½-inch slices
2 medium-size carrots, cooked, halved lengthwise, and cut into 1-inch slices

4 lettuce leaves
¾ cup Sauce Vinaigrette (see Index)
¼ cup heavy cream
4 slices of smoked salmon, each about 2 ounces

Arrange the salad on 4 plates. Around the edge of each plate arrange slices of tomato, a small heap of green beans, a small heap of mushrooms, 1 asparagus spear topped with the asparagus tip, and the carrot slices in a lettuce leaf. Moisten the vegetables with the vinaigrette mixed with the cream. Cut each of the smoked salmon slices into crosswise pieces and arrange some in the center of each plate. Serve any extra dressing separately.

FILET DE POISSON À LA TAHITIENNE

(Fish, Tahitian style)

SERVES 8 AS A FIRST COURSE, 4 AS MAIN COURSE OF A LIGHT LUNCHEON.

This is an original recipe from the chef of the Mapotel Pont Royal in Paris. It makes an unusual change from *seviche* though the method of "cooking" the fish with lime juice is the same.

2 pounds any firm-fleshed nonoily white fish, cut into small cubes
¾ cup fresh lime or lemon juice
1 small coconut
2 medium-size green bell peppers, seeded and cut into small cubes
2 medium-size tomatoes, peeled and coarsely chopped
2 firm bananas, peeled and sliced
1 medium-size onion, finely chopped
Salt, freshly ground pepper

In a bowl combine the fish with the lime juice and refrigerate it for 2 hours, turning fish two or three times.

Meanwhile, with a screwdriver or icepick, pierce 2 of the 3 eyes of the coconut and drain out the water. Strain the water to remove any coconut fibers and set it aside. Bake the coconut in a preheated hot oven (400°F.) for 15 minutes. Put the coconut on a hard surface and hit it with a hammer to break the hard shell. Lever out the coconut and peel off the brown skin with a small sharp knife. Cut coconut into small pieces and grate in a blender or food processor. Set aside half of the grated coconut. In a bowl mix the reserved coconut water with the rest of the grated coconut and let it stand for 30 minutes. Line a sieve with dampened cheesecloth and add the grated coconut mixture. Let it drip through, then gather up the cheesecloth and squeeze out all the liquid. Discard the coconut and set the coconut milk aside. There will be about ¾ cup milk.

In a large salad bowl combine the fish and the lime juice in which it has been marinating with the green peppers, tomatoes, bananas, onion, the reserved grated coconut and the coconut milk. Season with salt and pepper and mix lightly. Refrigerate for 2 to 3 hours. Before serving drain off the excess liquid.

POISSON FUMÉ EN SALADE

(Smoked Fish Salad)

SERVES 4.

Jacques Le Divellec of the Relais Gourmand Le Yachtman in La Rochelle smokes his own bass for this. The salad is tasty with any smoked fish and makes an unusual first course.

1 pound of any smoked white fish fillets, thinly sliced
1 lemon, cut into quarters
1 medium-size cucumber, peeled, coarsely grated and drained

1 tablespoon shredded fresh ginger root
2 tablespoons chopped parsley
Freshly ground pepper (optional)

Arrange the slices of fish on 4 salad plates in a fan shape. Put a quartered lemon at the top, and a heap each of cucumber and ginger at the bottom. Sprinkle with the parsley.

Serve with toasted coarse-textured bread and butter. To eat, squeeze on the lemon juice and eat the fish with a little ginger and cucumber. Sprinkle with freshly ground pepper if liked. Drink a fresh, slightly acid dry white wine.

Variation: Use thinly sliced smoked salmon instead of a white fish.

45

LES HUÎTRES DE BELONS AU CHAMPAGNE

(Oysters Poached in Still Champagne)

SERVES 2.

A delectable recipe from the charming restaurant Daniel et Denise, in Lyon, perfect for a special dinner for two. Any type of oyster can be used; Belons simply indicates an oyster from a specific part of Brittany.

12 oysters in the shell, opened	Salt, freshly ground pepper
1 cup Côteaux Champenois, or other dry white wine	¼ cup heavy cream
1 tablespoon very finely chopped shallot	2 tablespoons butter, cut into bits

The fishmonger will usually open oysters. If not, thoroughly scrub the shells. Hold the shell, deep side down, in the left hand which should be protected by a cloth or glove. Using an oyster knife, work the point into the hinge and cut the ligament which holds the shells together.

Remove the oysters from their shells, and transfer them with their liquor to a small saucepan. Reserve the lower shells. Add the wine, shallot, and salt and pepper to taste to the oysters; over moderate heat bring to just under a boil. Immediately remove the oysters from the liquid and replace in the reserved shells on 2 plates. Keep them warm, covered, over hot water.

Reduce the liquid in the saucepan over high heat to ¾ cup. Stir in the cream and reduce over high heat to ½ cup. The sauce should be quite thick. Lower the heat. Whisk in the butter, bit by bit, adding each new piece as the previous piece is incorporated into the sauce. Spoon the sauce over the oysters.

Serve with Melba toast. Drink Champagne or a dry white wine, preferably from the Champagne region.

HUÎTRES FRÉMIES AVEC LA LAITUE DE MER

(Oysters Cooked with Seaweed)

SERVES 4.

This could be translated as oysters that have sighed themselves into being cooked, so delicate is the cooking process. The *laitue de mer* is the fine green seaweed *Ulva lactuca,* called sea lettuce. Japanese *wakame,* available dried and packaged from Japanese stores, is perfect for this. It is an exquisite dish created by Jacques Le Divellec of the Relais Gourmand Le Yachtman in La Rochelle on the Atlantic Coast of France, where the seafood is magnificent.

2 cups liquor from steamed mussels (see Index); or use 1 cup clam juice and 1 cup dry white wine	8 fronds of wakame (lobe-leaf seaweed), each 8 inches long
24 large oysters	12 tablespoons (1½ sticks) butter, cut into bits
	Freshly ground pepper

Steam mussels; strain the liquor Set the mussels aside and reserve for another use. Measure the liquor, or mix together the clam juice and dry white wine. Pour the resulting liquid into a saucepan. Open the oysters and pour off the liquor. Strain it and add it to the mussel liquid or clam-juice mixture. Reduce it over high heat until it is syrupy. While the liquid is reducing, put the *wakame* to soak in water to cover for 10 minutes. Drain, squeeze lightly, cut away any hard ribs, and chop coarsely. Set aside.

Whisk the butter into the reduced shellfish liquid, adding each new piece as the previous one is incorporated into the sauce. Stir in the reserved seaweed and season with pepper.

Put the oysters into 4 small dishes and cover with the sauce. Place under a preheated broiler about 2 inches from the source of heat for about 2 minutes, just until the sauce is glazed and the edges of the oysters curl.

LES HUÎTRES EN PAQUETS

(Oysters in Packets)

SERVES 2 OR 4.

I feel privileged to have been given this delectable recipe by its creator, Georges Paineau of the Relais Gourmand Le Bretagne at Questembert. I had to wait until there was an "r" in the month and until I could get the large tender-leafed spinach I wanted before making this at home. One day they came together and the dish was as fabulous as I had remembered. The quantities for this can be successfully doubled or trebled, so the dish can be served as the main course of an elegant lunch or supper.

8 large tender spinach leaves	2 tablespoons water
	Salt, white pepper
24 oysters, with their liquor	12 tablespoons butter (1½ sticks), chilled and cut
¼ cup lemon juice	into bits

Wash the spinach leaves and trim the stems. If the spinach leaves seem coarse, blanch them in boiling salted water for 15 seconds. If the leaves are not big enough to enfold the oysters, use more than 1 leaf. Put 3 oysters on each leaf and fold them up into neat packages. Place them in an oven-proof dish or in a skillet and strain the oyster liquor over them. Cover and poach in a preheated moderate oven (350°F.), or on top of the stove, for 3 minutes.

In a small saucepan reduce the lemon juice with 2 tablespoons water and salt and white pepper to taste to half its volume over high heat. Reduce the heat and beat in the butter, adding each new piece as the previous piece is incorporated into the sauce.

Lift out the packets of oysters and, according to appetite, the cost of oysters and the type of main dish to follow, distribute them on heated plates—4 packets on 2 plates, or 2 packets on 4. Pour the butter sauce around each packet in a thin ribbon.

Drink a dry white wine such as Chablis or Pouilly-Fuissé.

PÂTÉ DE SAUMON

(Salmon Pâté)

SERVES 8.

This pâté is a wonderful way to begin a special meal. It is the creation of a very gifted young chef, Jacques Rochard of the Relais et Châteaux Cazaudehore et La Forestière at Saint-Germain-en-Laye. At times when fresh salmon was very expensive I've made it with two thirds sole and one third salmon, keeping the salmon for the decorative part of the pâté.

2 pounds fresh salmon, skinned and boned	1 tablespoon finely chopped chervil
1½ cups cooked rice	Salt, freshly ground white pepper
3 hard-cooked eggs, chopped	⅔ cup heavy cream
¼ cup finely chopped parsley	1 tablespoon Cognac or other brandy
2 tablespoons finely snipped chives	3 whole raw eggs Butter

Cut one third of the salmon into ½-inch cubes and put them into a bowl with the cooked rice, hard-cooked eggs, chopped herbs, and salt and pepper to taste. Toss lightly to mix. Set aside.

Coarsely chop the rest of the salmon. In a food processor fitted with the steel blade, or in a blender in batches, purée the chopped salmon with the cream, Cognac and raw eggs. Season with salt and pepper. The mousse should be light and fluffy. Fold the mousse gently into the salmon, rice and egg mixture, then transfer it to a buttered 2-quart terrine. Set the terrine in a baking pan with enough hot water to reach two thirds up the sides of the terrine. Cover the terrine and bake in a preheated moderate oven (350°F.) for 1 hour, or until the mousse is set. Remove the terrine from the baking pan and let it cool. Chill in the refrigerator.

Serve the pâté sliced, garnished with lettuce leaves and with Mayonnaise (see Index) served separately, if liked.

TERRINE DE SAUMON AVEC SAUCE AU CRESSON

(Salmon Terrine with Watercress Sauce)

SERVES 4.

This recipe, which comes from Jean-Paul Bossée, the young chef at the Relais et Châteaux Hostellerie La Cheneaudière at Colroy-la-Roche, can be made very successfully in a food processor. The ingredients must be very cold before starting. I am indebted to my friend Richard Sax for the good kitchen trick of chilling the container of the food processor and the steel blade as well as the ingredients. The fish for the mousse should include one with red-colored flesh, ideally salmon, or sea trout or red mullet; the other fish may be halibut, haddock or cod. Serve as a first course or as a main course for a light lunch or dinner.

½ pound salmon, sea trout or red mullet	4 tablespoons butter, cut into bits
¼ pound halibut, haddock, or cod	1¾ cups heavy cream
1 teaspoon salt	4 fillets of sole, 1¼ to 1½ pounds altogether
Freshly ground white pepper	2 cups Fish Stock, (see Index)
1 large egg	Watercress Sauce
2 large egg whites	(recipe follows)

Pat the salmon and halibut dry with paper towels and chop coarsely. Season with salt and pepper to taste and put into a food processor fitted with the steel blade. Run the machine for about 30 seconds. With the machine running, pour the whole egg and egg whites through the feed tube, then add the butter, bit by bit, until mixture is well blended. Add the cream little by little, as one adds oil to a mayonnaise. The mixture will be light and fluffy. If not using a food processor or blender, pound the mixture in a bowl set over ice.

Place the fillets of sole between 2 pieces of wax paper and flatten them lightly with the blade of a knife. Spread each fillet with a thin layer of the fish mousse. Roll them up; if necessary fasten them with toothpicks. Simmer the fillets in the fish stock for 6 minutes. Lift out and allow to cool.

In an ovenproof baking dish, about 6½ by 5 inches, spread a layer of one third of the remaining mousse. Arrange the rolled-up fillets on top and cover with the rest of the mousse; smooth it down lightly. Cover the dish with foil, or a lid, and set in a baking pan with water to come about halfway up. Bake in a preheated moderately hot oven (400°F.) for about 45 minutes, or until the mousse is firm. Cool completely before unmolding. Chill and serve with watercress sauce.

WATERCRESS SAUCE

1 bunch of watercress
⅓ cup heavy cream,
    whipped
½ cup Mayonnaise (see
    Index)

Salt, freshly ground
    pepper

Remove any yellow or wilted leaves from the watercress and cut off any coarse stems. Chop coarsely, then reduce to a purée in a blender or food processor. In a bowl fold the cream into the mayonnaise. Add puréed watercress and mix lightly but thoroughly. Taste for seasoning; add salt and freshly ground pepper if necessary.

Pour a little of the sauce onto 4 serving plates. Arrange the sliced mousse, each portion containing a sole fillet, on top of the sauce so that the mousse is surrounded with sauce. Serve the rest of the sauce separately.

ÉCREVISSES À LA NAGE AU CHAMPAGNE

(Crayfish Poached in Still Champagne)

SERVES 6.

Crayfish, or crawfish, are hard to find in the eastern part of the U.S.A., but they are available in the West and Midwest. Jumbo shrimps make an admirable substitute. The pure flavor of crayfish or shrimps comes through beautifully in this recipe from chef Jacques Courgnaud of the Hôtel des Berceaux in Épernay. It makes a refreshing first course in summer weather.

30 crayfish or jumbo shrimps
1 cup thinly sliced carrots
12 small white onions, peeled
Bouquet garni: 1 bay leaf, 4 parsley sprigs, 2 thyme sprigs, 1 garlic clove, peeled, all tied in a square of cheesecloth

Salt, freshly ground pepper
2½ cups still Champagne or any dry white wine
1 cup water

Rinse the crayfish or shrimps in cold water. Hold the body of the crayfish in the left hand and with the right hand twist the middle section of the tail and pull it straight out, removing and discarding the intestines. There is no need to do anything to the shrimps except to devein them if liked. Set aside.

Combine all remaining ingredients in a heavy saucepan or skillet and bring to a boil over moderate heat. Reduce the heat, cover, and simmer gently until the carrots are tender, about 15 minutes. Drop the crayfish into the boiling liquid and simmer for 6 minutes. If using shrimps, simmer for only 3 minutes. Remove from the heat and allow the shellfish to cool in the stock.

Remove and discard the *bouquet garni*. Pour the bouillon into 6 small bowls and arrange the crayfish or shrimps in the center of the bowls.

Serve with thinly sliced buttered bread. Have finger bowls at each place and a large bowl for the shells. If liked, the shrimps may be slightly chilled; otherwise serve at room temperature.

MOUSSE DE BROCHET

(Pike Mousse)

SERVES 6.

The secret of this mousse is to have the ingredients very cold, otherwise the mousse will be dense instead of airy. I like it very much as a first course, but it can also, in more generous portions, make a very pleasant luncheon main course. If the fishmonger does the hard work of filleting and boning the pike, then it is also an easy dish to make. If pike is not available, ask the fish store to suggest an alternative. This is a favorite dish that Daniel Robin serves in his restaurant near Chénas in the Beaujolais.

2 pounds boneless fillets of pike, cut into 1-inch pieces	¼ pound (1 stick) butter, cut into bits
1 teaspoon salt	2 cups heavy cream
¼ teaspoon white pepper	Beurre Fondu (Melted Butter Sauce) (recipe follows)
6 eggs	

Chill the fish, season with salt and pepper, then purée it in a food processor fitted with the steel blade, or in an electric blender in batches. Add the eggs, one by one, through the feed tube of the food processor with the machine running

(recipe continues)

53

and blend thoroughly. Add the butter, bit by bit. Scrape the mousse into a bowl and chill in the refrigerator for at least 1 hour.

Set the bowl of mousse in a larger bowl filled with cracked ice and beat in the cream, 2 tablespoons at a time, until the mousse is very light and fluffy. Put the mousse into a well-buttered 4-cup mold, or divide among 6 smaller molds, and set in a baking pan with hot water to come about two thirds the way up the sides of the molds. Cover with foil. Bake in a preheated hot oven (400°F.) for 25 minutes, or until a knife inserted in the mousse comes out clean. Run a thin knife round the inside of the mold and invert the mousse onto a warmed serving dish. Pour the sauce over the mousse.

Drink a dry white wine like Pouilly-Fuissé.

BEURRE FONDU
(MELTED BUTTER SAUCE)

½ pound (2 sticks) butter   1 teaspoon lemon juice
   Salt, white pepper

Put the butter, cut into bits, into a heavy saucepan and melt over very low heat. Season with salt and white pepper and add the lemon juice.

FEUILLETÉ D'OSEILLE AU PARFUM D'ANCHOIS

(Puff Pastry Stuffed with Sorrel and Anchovy Purée)

SERVES 4.

Jacques Le Divellec, of the Relais Gourmand Le Yachtman at La Rochelle, is one of his country's young and gifted chefs. He is also immensely generous. I spent considerable time with him and he was endlessly helpful talking to me about the subtleties of the changes taking place in French cooking at home and in restaurants. This is a lovely recipe.

1 recipe Pâte Feuilletée
   (see Index)
1 recipe Chiffonade
   d'Oseille (see Index)

2 cans (1¾ ounces each)
   flat fillets of anchovies
Salt, freshly ground
   pepper

Make *pâte feuilletée* (puff pastry) and give the dough 2 more turns.

Reserve 4 anchovy fillets for a garnish. Drain remaining anchovies and mash them to a paste. Mix with the sorrel chiffonade. Season with salt if necessary, and pepper.

Roll out the pastry into a rectangle ¼ inch thick and 6 by 10 inches. Cut the dough into 4 equal pieces. Chill the dough for 20 minutes. Arrange it on a baking sheet and bake in a preheated hot oven (400°F.) for 20 minutes, or until the pastry is puffed and golden brown. Split the pastries horizontally and spread with the sorrel-anchovy filling. Replace the top halves and garnish with the reserved fillets.

Serve on plates garnished with a lettuce leaf or with watercress sprigs.

Variations: Cut the pastry into 2-inch squares. Omit the garnish and use all the anchovies for the purée. Serve at room temperature to accompany drinks.

Add ½ cup grated Parmesan or Gruyère cheese to the sorrel-anchovy purée.

There seems to be no end to Jacques Le Divellec's originality. This is is his own variation on his own recipe and it is as delicious as the original: In place of the anchovies use 1 cup shredded crab meat. Mix the crab meat with the sorrel chiffonade, season with salt and pepper, and use as directed.

FEUILLETÉ D'ESCARGOTS À LA CRÈME D'AIL

(Puff Pastry with Snails in Garlic Sauce)

SERVES 6.

Daniel Léron, of Daniel et Denise in Lyon, created this dish for snail and garlic lovers.

1 recipe Pâte Feuilletée (see Index)
2 recipes Snail Butter (see Index)

3 dozen snails
1 cup heavy cream

Make *pâte feuilletée* (puff pastry) and give the dough 2 more turns. Roll the dough out about ¼ inch thick and cut into six 3-inch squares. Arrange the pastry squares on a baking sheet and bake in a preheated hot oven (400°F.) for 20 minutes, or until the pastry is puffed and golden brown. Make 2 recipes of Snail Butter. In a saucepan heat 36 snails in 1 cup heavy cream; stir in the snail butter. Pour a layer of the sauce onto 6 plates. Put a pastry square on each and divide the snails among them. Cover the snails with the remaining sauce.

If liked, use 3 recipes of snail butter instead of 2.

LAPIN EN COMPOTE

(Jellied Rabbit)

SERVES 10 TO 12 AS A FIRST COURSE, 6 AS MAIN COURSE.

French chefs make good imaginative use of rabbit, especially in recipes for jellied rabbit, which makes an attractive first course or can be served in summer with salads as the main course of a hot-weather lunch or dinner. Jacques Rochard, the chef at the Relais et Châteaux Cazaudehore et

La Forestière at Saint-Germain-en-Laye, gave me this very good dish. He recommends a Pouilly-sur-Loire as the accompanying wine. Excellent packaged ready-to-cook frozen rabbit is available in many supermarkets, and specialty butchers often carry it. Rabbit is lean and small-boned so there is little waste.

2 to 2½ pounds rabbit,
    cut into serving pieces
    Salt, freshly ground
    pepper
½ pound fresh pork
    belly, cut into ¼-inch
    cubes
10 garlic cloves, chopped
6 medium-size onions,
    coarsely chopped
6 medium-size carrots,
    scraped and thinly
    sliced

8 thyme sprigs
3 bay leaves
1½ cups dry white wine
½ cup finely chopped
    parsley
¼ cup snipped chives
1 tablespoon finely
    chopped chervil

Season the rabbit pieces with salt and pepper, and put them in a large heavy casserole or terrine with the pork belly, garlic, onions, carrots, thyme and bay leaves. Pour in the white wine, cover, and refrigerate for 24 hours.

The next day cover the casserole or terrine with aluminum foil and the lid and stand in a baking tin with water to come halfway up. Bake in a preheated moderate oven (350°F.) for 2 hours. Allow to cool, then remove the rabbit pieces. Strain the liquid. Discard the onions, thyme and bay leaves. Reserve the carrots and cubes of pork. Rinse out and dry the terrine. If using a casserole, choose a suitable bowl or a soufflé dish for the rabbit.

Bone the rabbit and cut the meat into bite-size pieces. Transfer them to the terrine or bowl. Add the pork cubes and some or all of the carrot slices, according to taste. Sprinkle with the herbs. Taste the reserved cooking liquid and season with salt and pepper if necessary. Pour it over

(recipe continues)

the rabbit mixture and refrigerate for several hours, until the liquid has set into a jelly. It is a good idea to test the liquid ahead of time by putting a small amount on a saucer in the freezer. If it does not jell, add a little unflavored gelatin to the liquid.

Variation: Paul Pauvert of the Nantes Frantel's restaurant Le Tillac has a version I like very much. Cut up a 2-pound rabbit with an equal weight of belly of pork and combine in a casserole or terrine with 1 chopped onion, 1 bay leaf, 1 thyme sprig, 1 unpeeled garlic clove, salt, freshly ground pepper, and enough dry white wine barely to cover, about 1½ cups. Cover with foil, then with a lid, and put into a baking tin with water to come about halfway up. Bake in a preheated, slow oven (250°F.) for 4 hours. Allow to cool.

Lift out and bone the rabbit, and cut into bite-size pieces. Remove and discard the thyme, bay leaf and garlic clove. Return the rabbit to the terrine, mixing thoroughly. Taste for seasoning and add salt and pepper if necessary. Chill in the refrigerator until the jelly has set.

Serve with a salad of white and red cabbage, finely chopped, seasoned with salt and pepper, and tossed with hot cider vinegar.

RILLETTES DE LAPIN CLEMENTINE

(Potted Minced Rabbit)

MAKES 8 TO 9 CUPS.

During a visit I made to Alsace, I stayed at the Relais et Châteaux Clos Saint Vincent at Ribeauvillé and had Bertrand Chapotin's Rillettes de Lapin for the beginning course of a delightful meal. With the *rillettes* we drank a 1976 Trimbach Gewürztraminer, a lovely spicy white wine perfect with the rabbit. M. Chapotin was good enough to let me have the recipe and M. Trimbach presented me with a bottle of his wine to take home. It made testing the recipe a very rewarding experience. I've since had the *rillettes* with a California Gewürztraminer which was very good indeed. The cooking time may seem very long these energy-conscious days, but really very little heat is needed to keep the meats at a bare simmer, and little attention need be paid to the pot except toward the end of the cooking time.

3 pounds rabbit	1 cup dry white wine
2 medium-size carrots, scraped and sliced	4 cups water, approximately
2 medium-size onions, chopped	1½ pounds fat bacon, diced
2 garlic cloves, chopped	1½ pounds fresh pork belly, diced
1 thyme sprig, or ¼ teaspoon dried thyme	Lard
1 bay leaf Salt, freshly ground pepper	

Cut all the meat off the rabbit. Chop it coarsely and set it aside. There will be about 2 pounds of meat. In a saucepan combine the rabbit bones, carrots, onions, garlic, thyme, bay leaf, salt and pepper to taste, white wine and water to cover, about 4 cups. Bring to a boil, reduce the heat and simmer, covered, for 3 hours. Cool and strain.

In a heavy saucepan or casserole combine the reserved rabbit meat, diced fat bacon and fresh pork, and pour in enough of the strained stock to barely cover the meats. Cover and simmer over very low heat for 6 hours. Towards the end of the cooking time stir frequently with a wooden spoon; this helps shred the meats. Check for seasoning and add salt and pepper if necessary. The stock should have evaporated completely during the cooking. If there is too much liquid towards the end, cook partially covered.

Cool the *rillettes* and pack them into 2- or 3-cup earthenware pots. When the *rillettes* are completely cool, cover with a layer of melted lard, then cover with aluminum foil. The *rillettes* will keep refrigerated for 2 weeks.

To serve, remove the layer of lard and allow the meats to come to room temperature. Serve with toast.

TARTE À L'OIGNON

(Onion Tart)

SERVES 8 AS A FIRST COURSE, 4 AS MAIN COURSE FOR LUNCH.

I'm very fond of onion tart, and this one from the Relais et Châteaux Hostellerie Claire-Fontaine at Saint-Nabord in the Vosges is a favorite of mine. It makes a good accompaniment to drinks.

3 tablespoons vegetable oil
1 pound onions, quartered
   and thinly sliced
   Salt, freshly ground
   pepper

1 partially cooked 8-inch
   pastry shell (see Index)
2 large eggs
1 cup heavy cream

Heat the oil in a heavy skillet, add the onions, and cook over very low heat, stirring gently from time to time, until they are golden brown; it will take about 45 minutes. Season the onions with salt and pepper, cool them, then spread in the prepared pastry shell. Lightly beat the eggs with the cream. Season with salt and pepper and pour the mixture over the onions. Bake in a preheated moderately hot oven (375°F.) for 30 minutes or until the tart is set and golden. Serve warm.

Variations: The Claire-Fontaine's Quiche Lorraine is simple and good and I like to serve slivers of this quiche as well as the onion tart to accompany drinks. It is convenient to make both at the same time. Have ready a partially baked 8-inch pie shell. In a skillet sauté 8 slices of bacon cut into pieces 1 inch by ½ inch until they are crisp and lightly browned. Drain on paper towels. In a bowl beat together 3 large eggs and 1½ cups heavy cream, ½ teaspoon salt, ¼ teaspoon white pepper and a little grated nutmeg. Scatter the bacon pieces over the bottom of the pie shell and pour the custard mixture over it. Bake in a preheated moderately hot oven (375°F.) for 30 minutes, or until the quiche is puffed and golden.

TARTE À L'OIGNON

(Onion Tart)

SERVES 8 AS A FIRST COURSE, 4 AS MAIN COURSE FOR LUNCH.

Another favorite onion tart of mine is a family one. The recipe was very generously given to me by the Vicomtesse du Breil de Pontbriand, of the Manoir de Vaumadeuc at Pléven, which she has turned into an elegant small hotel. This tart is quite different from any others I've had.

1 partially cooked 8-inch pastry shell (see Index)	1 tablespoon sugar
4 slices of bacon, chopped	2 hard rolls, cut up
Vegetable oil	1½ cups milk
1½ pounds onions, peeled and chopped	3 large eggs
	Salt
	Pepper

Have the pie shell ready. In a heavy skillet sauté the chopped bacon in a little vegetable oil until it is crisp and has released all its fat. Lift out the bacon bits with a slotted spoon and drain on paper towels. In the fat remaining in the skillet, sauté the onions until they are soft and golden brown. Add a little more vegetable oil if necessary. Sprinkle with sugar. While the onions are cooking, soak the hard rolls, cut up, in the milk until they are soft. Add more milk if necessary. Simmer the bread mixture over low heat, stirring constantly, to form a thick *panade*. When the mixture is smooth, mix it with the onions. Set aside. Beat the eggs with salt and pepper and fold into the onion-bread mixture. Pour into the prepared pastry shell, sprinkle with the bacon bits, and bake in a preheated moderate oven (350°F.) for 35 to 40 minutes, or until the tart is puffed and golden brown.

Variation: The Vicomtesse has a variation on her own recipe which I find deliciously unusual. Omit the eggs from the tart rec-

(recipe continues)

ipe. Soak ¾ cup golden raisins in red wine to cover overnight. Drain and fold into the onion mixture with ¼ pound uncooked beef marrow cut into cubes. Bake as above.

FLAMICHE AUX POIREAUX

(Leek Quiche)

SERVES 8 AS A FIRST COURSE, 4 AS MAIN COURSE.

6 medium-size leeks (about 1 pound)
4 tablespoons butter
½ cup Chicken Stock (see Index)
3 eggs
1½ cups heavy cream
⅛ teaspoon grated nutmeg
Salt, freshly ground pepper
1 pie shell, 8 to 9 inches, baked blind (see Index)

Wash the leeks (see Index) and chop coarsely. In a heavy skillet heat the butter, add the leeks, and sauté for about 5 minutes without letting them brown. Pour in the chicken stock and simmer until the leeks are soft. Let the moisture evaporate over low heat, about 10 minutes. Set aside.

In a bowl beat the eggs lightly, then beat in the cream. Add the nutmeg and salt and pepper to taste. Beat to mix. Put the leeks into the pastry shell, pour on the cream and egg mixture, and bake in a preheated moderate oven (375°F.) for 25 to 30 minutes, or until the custard is set and the top golden brown.

TARTELETTES AUX CHAMPIGNONS

(Mushroom Tartlets)

MAKES 12, SERVES 4.

These tartlets, a favorite with Rémy André and his wife, who run the Au Bon Pasteur restaurant in Carcassonne, make a delicious first course. They are also good as an accompaniment to drinks.

> 1 recipe Pâte Brisée (see
>   Index)
>   Butter
>   Flour
> 1 egg, lightly beaten

FILLING

4 tablespoons butter	Salt, freshly ground
2½ cups chopped	pepper
mushrooms	⅛ teaspoon grated
⅓ cup flour	nutmeg
½ cup milk	1 tablespoon chopped
¼ cup grated Gruyère	parsley
cheese	6 tablespoons heavy
1 tablespoon finely	cream
chopped shallot	

Butter 12 muffin tins, 1 inch by 2½ inches. Flour them lightly, shake out the excess, and line them with the pastry rolled out ⅛ inch thick. Prick the bottoms with a fork, brush the edges with beaten egg, and bake in a preheated moderate oven (325°F.) for 8 minutes. Allow pastry to cool in the muffin tins.

Make the filling: Heat the butter in a skillet, add the mushrooms, and sauté over moderate heat for about 5 minutes. Lift out the mushrooms and set aside. Leave the butter in the skillet and add a little more if necessary. Stir in the flour and cook, stirring, over low heat for 1 or 2 minutes. Gradually add the milk, stirring constantly, then return the cooked mushrooms to the pan together with the cheese, shallot, salt and pepper to taste, nutmeg and parsley. Cook for a few minutes longer. Remove from the heat and stir in the cream.

Spoon the mushroom mixture into the pastry-lined muffin tins. Bake in a preheated hot oven (450°F.) for 5 minutes. Serve hot or at room temperature.

RAMEQUINS AU FROMAGE

(Cheese Puffs)

MAKES ABOUT 40 SMALL PUFFS, 30 MEDIUM-SIZE PUFFS.

Jacques Sourisseau of the Relais et Châteaux Le Manoir at Fontenay-Trésigny loves to cook and his recipes show it. This is an updated version of an older recipe. A delicious variation of the *gougère*, it is richer and softer than Jean-Pierre Billoux's cheese puffs (see following recipe). I find them both delicious, not only for a party but for casual drinks with friends when kitchen time is short.

1 cup milk	½ cup grated Gruyère cheese
¼ pound (1 stick) butter	
½ teaspoon salt	½ cup ⅛-inch cubes of Gruyère cheese
⅛ teaspoon pepper	
1½ cups all-purpose flour	½ cup grated Parmesan cheese
6 eggs	

In a saucepan bring to a boil the milk, butter, salt and pepper, stirring until the butter is melted. Remove from the heat and add the flour all at once, stirring with a wooden spoon or spatula until the batter is well mixed and leaves the sides of the pan. Return it to the heat and cook for 2 minutes, stirring. Off the heat beat in the eggs, one by one, not adding another egg until the first one has been thoroughly incorporated into the paste. Stir in all the cheese. The mixture should be quite smooth.

Butter 1 or more baking sheets. Drop batter by teaspoon for small puffs, or by tablespoon for medium-size puffs, onto the sheet, 1 or 2 inches apart. (The puffs may be piped onto the cookie sheet using a pastry bag.) Bake in a preheated hot oven (425°F.) for 15 to 20 minutes. Cool in the turned-off oven with the door slightly ajar.

Serve either hot or cold as cocktail appetizers.

GOUGÈRES

(Cheese Puffs)

MAKES ABOUT 30 PUFFS.

While I was talking with Jean-Pierre Billoux, the gifted young chef of the Relais Gourmand Restaurant Bonnevay-Billoux in Digoin, I ate several small *gougères* with my apéritif as a prelude to lunch. They were so good I asked Jean-Pierre for his recipe. Here it is.

1 cup water	1¼ cups all-purpose flour
4 tablespoons butter	4 eggs
¼ teaspoon salt	1 cup tiny cubes of
⅛ teaspoon pepper	Gruyère cheese
Pinch of grated	Egg wash
nutmeg	

In a saucepan bring to a boil the water, butter, salt, pepper and nutmeg. When the butter has melted, remove the pan from the heat and stir in the flour, all at once. Beat the mixture with a wooden spoon until it is well mixed and leaves the sides of the pan. Return batter to the heat and cook for 2 minutes, stirring. Off the heat beat in the eggs one by one, then add the cheese. The mixture should be smooth.

Butter 1 or more baking sheets and drop the mixture by teaspoons onto the sheets, about 1 inch apart. Brush with egg wash (1 egg beaten with 1 tablespoon water). Bake in a preheated hot oven (425°F.) for 15 to 20 minutes. Cool in the turned-off oven with the door slightly ajar. Serve either hot or cold as cocktail appetizers.

Larger puffs can be made using a tablespoon, or batter can be piped onto the cookie sheet using a pastry bag.

GÂTEAU DE FOIES DE VOLAILLE ET JAMBON

(Chicken Liver Pâté and Ham Loaf)

SERVES 8 TO 10.

This makes a luscious beginning to a special lunch or dinner. With a green salad, it becomes a good summer lunch or, in these happy days of unstructured meals, it makes an adequate main course for dinner if followed by a favorite dessert.

6 tablespoons butter
1 pound chicken livers, cleaned and halved
1 garlic clove, minced
⅛ teaspoon ground thyme
   Salt, freshly ground pepper
2 tablespoons Cognac
¼ cup dry Madeira wine
3 tablespoons heavy cream

1 envelope unflavored gelatin (7 grams)
¼ cup cold water
1 cup Chicken Stock (see Index)
1 cup dry white wine
1 pound thinly sliced boiled ham

In a heavy skillet heat 3 tablespoons of the butter. Pat the chicken livers dry with paper towels and add to the skillet. Sauté the livers over moderate heat for 5 minutes, turning them once or twice. They should be cooked but still pink inside. Lift out the livers and transfer to a blender or food processor fitted with the steel blade. Add the garlic, thyme, salt and pepper to taste, the Cognac and Madeira to the skillet, and simmer for 1 or 2 minutes. Pour the mixture over the chicken livers. Add remaining 3 tablespoons butter, cut into bits, and the cream, and blend until smooth. Transfer to a bowl and chill slightly.

Sprinkle the gelatin over ¼ cup cold water in a small bowl. Combine the chicken stock and wine in a small saucepan, add the softened gelatin, and stir over low heat until the gelatin is dissolved. Chill until syrupy.

Rinse a mold 8½ by 4¾ inches in cold water, and pour in a thin layer of the syrupy aspic. Refrigerate the mold until the aspic is set. Make a layer of ham slices on the aspic, then spread with a layer of pâté. Pour in another layer of aspic and chill until set. Repeat until all the ingredients are used, ending with a layer of aspic. Chill thoroughly for several hours or overnight.

Unmold by inverting on a flat serving dish and rapping the bottom sharply; or hold a cloth dampened in hot water on the bottom of the mold to release the gelatin. Cut the loaf into slices.

Serve garnished with lettuce leaves and parsley sprigs.

GÂTEAU DE FOIES BLONDS

(Chicken Liver Mousse)

SERVES 6.

It is impossible to translate this airy dish into "chicken liver cake" without giving a wrong impression of its delicate quality. Jean-Pierre Vullin, the young and gifted chef of the Michelin two-star Auberge Bressane restaurant at Bourg-en-Bresse, gave me his own recipe which is served in the restaurant as an appetizer. I find it makes a splendid beginning for a special dinner. I also like it served in more generous portions as the main course of a Sunday brunch, or weekday lunch. If I can't get light-colored chicken livers, I settle for regular ones. So long as they are large and fresh I have not found it makes a difference except in appearance. The light-colored livers just look prettier.

(recipe continues)

6 large chicken livers,
    light colored if possible
1 garlic clove, cut
    Salt, freshly ground
    pepper
⅛ teaspoon grated nutmeg

4 whole eggs
2 extra egg yolks
2 cups heavy cream
1 tablespoon chopped
    parsley
    Butter

Purée the chicken livers in a food processor fitted with the steel blade, or in a blender. Rub a bowl with the cut garlic clove. Push the livers through a sieve into the bowl and season with salt and pepper to taste and nutmeg. Beat in the whole eggs, one by one, then beat in the extra egg yolks and the cream. Fold in the parsley. Butter a 1-quart mold and pour in the mixture. Set the mold in a baking pan with water to come halfway up the mold. Bake in a preheated moderate oven (375°F) for about 45 minutes, or until set. Lift mold out of the baking pan and let it stand for 2 or 3 minutes. Run a knife round the inside of the mold, invert a plate on top of the mold, and unmold the mousse. If preferred it can be served direct from the mold.

Serve with Coulis de Tomates Fraîches (see Index). Pour some of the tomato purée around each serving of mousse.

LE SALMIS DE PALOMBES

(Squab Salmis)

SERVES 4 AS A FIRST COURSE, 2 AS MAIN COURSE.

This makes a luxurious first course, especially if it is followed by a main course of fish. It is the creation of chef

Peyrefitte of La Rotonde, the restaurant of the Mapotel Poste et Golf at Luchon.

2 squabs, each about 8 ounces	Bouquet garni: 1 thyme sprig, 1 small celery
8 tablespoons butter	rib, 1 bay leaf, 1 garlic
¼ cup finely chopped shallots or spring onions	clove, 2 parsley sprigs, tied with a piece of
3 tablespoons Armagnac or Cognac or other brandy	cotton, or tied up in a square of cheesecloth
1 cup dry white wine	2 tablespoons lemon juice
Salt, freshly ground pepper	Garlic-flavored Croûtes (see Index)

Remove and reserve the livers of the squabs. Roast the birds in a preheated hot oven (425°F) for 20 minutes. Remove from the oven and let them rest for 10 minutes. Remove the legs and breasts and set aside. Chop the carcasses and put them into a casserole with the butter and the shallots. Warm the Armagnac and flame the carcasses with it. Pour in the wine, season with salt and pepper, add the *bouquet garni*, cover, and simmer for 20 minutes. Coarsely chop the reserved squab livers and add to the casserole. Simmer for 1 minute longer. Remove and discard the *bouquet garni*. Strain the casserole contents through a sieve, pushing down hard to extract all the juices. Rinse and dry the casserole and return the sauce to it. Add the lemon juice, taste for seasoning, and add salt and pepper if necessary. Add the squab legs and breasts and any juices that have accumulated and simmer over very low heat for about 5 minutes, or until the squabs are heated through. Place a breast and a leg on each of 4 *croûtes* and nap with the sauce.

TAPENADE

(Olive and Anchovy Spread)

MAKES ABOUT 1½ CUPS.

This tapenade comes from M. Mayard of the Relais et Châteaux hotel La Mayanelle at Gordes. It is a good accompaniment to *crudités,* as a stuffing for hard-cooked eggs, or as a spread for toast to accompany drinks.

½ pound oil-cured black olives, pitted and coarsely chopped

1 can (1¾ ounces) flat fillets of anchovies, with their oil, 10 to 12 fillets

4 large garlic cloves, peeled and chopped

Freshly ground pepper

2 tablespoons olive oil

In a food processor or in a blender combine the olives, anchovy fillets and their oil, garlic, pepper to taste and the olive oil; blend until smooth. The mixture should be thick and quite heavy. Transfer to a small bowl and chill before serving.

Variation: Add ¼ cup capers, rinsed and drained, to the mixture when puréeing.

CHAMPIGNONS À L'ANCHOÏADE

(Mushrooms with Anchovy Sauce)

SERVES 4.

I was enchanted by deep-fried mushrooms with anchovy sauce served as an hors d'oeuvre at the Frantel in Mulhouse, the creation of a brilliant young chef, Roger Boni. This recipe, however, is not all Boni. It is a mixture of Boni and M. Mayard of La Mayanelle, a Relais et Châteaux at Gordes in Vaucluse. M. Mayard is an exceptional chef in an exceptional setting; it was he who gave me this *anchoïade* recipe.

1 pound mushrooms, preferably with small uniform caps	⅛ teaspoon grated nutmeg
2 medium-size eggs, lightly beaten	2 tablespoons heavy cream
Salt, freshly ground pepper	1½ cups dry bread crumbs
	Oil for deep-frying
	Anchoïade (recipe follows)

Wipe the mushroom caps and trim the stems. Set aside. In a bowl combine the eggs, salt and pepper to taste, nutmeg and heavy cream, mixing thoroughly. Dip the mushrooms into the egg mixture, then dip into the bread crumbs. Fry in batches in hot oil (375°F.) in a deep-fryer for 2 minutes, turning once. Drain on paper towels and keep warm. Serve with Anchoïade.

L'ANCHOÏADE

(Anchovy Sauce)

MAKES ABOUT ½ CUP.

2 cans (1¾ ounces each) flat fillets of anchovies	1 teaspoon red-wine vinegar or lemon juice
1 tablespoon olive oil, approximately	Freshly ground pepper

Put the anchovies and the oil from the cans into a small heavy saucepan. Mash them over low heat to a purée. Beat in the olive oil. Off the heat beat in the vinegar or lemon juice. Season with pepper.

Use as a dipping sauce for the mushrooms. This is also good as a dipping sauce for celery.

TORTILLA MONTAGNARDE

(Omelet Mountaineer Style)

SERVES 4.

This omelet can make the first course of a hearty meal, or a light main course of a meal by itself. It comes from the kitchen of the Mapotel Poste et Golf's restaurant La Rotonde in Luchon.

4 tablespoons butter	Salt, freshly ground pepper
1 medium-size onion, finely chopped	Pinch of ground thyme
2 medium-size tomatoes, peeled and chopped	2-ounce slice of ham, cut into 4 pieces
1 4-ounce chorizo sausage, peeled and sliced	⅓ cup heavy cream
	½ cup coarsely grated Gruyère cheese
8 eggs, lightly beaten	Paprika

In a small skillet heat 2 tablespoons of the butter and sauté the onion in it until soft but not brown. Add the tomatoes and cook until the mixture is well blended. In another skillet sauté the chorizo in its own fat for a few minutes. Set the tomato and onion mixture and the sausage aside.

Heat remaining 2 tablespoons of butter in a large heavy skillet. Season the eggs with salt and pepper and the thyme. Pour the mixture into the skillet and cook the omelet in the usual way, stirring the eggs with the flat of a fork. When the omelet is half cooked, add the sausage, ham, onion and tomato and finish cooking. Slide the omelet onto a flameproof round serving dish and pour the heavy cream over it. Sprinkle with the cheese and put it under a preheated broiler to brown the cheese. Sprinkle with a little paprika and serve.

OEUFS BOURGUIGNONS

(Eggs, Burgundy Style)

SERVES 4.

This is Marc Chevillot's own recipe from his Hôtel de la Poste in Beaune. For a grand meal it makes a wonderful first course, but it is also good as the main course of a light lunch or supper. A whole head of garlic will not be too much as cooking gentles the flavor.

1 large onion, coarsely chopped
6 tablespoons butter
1 thyme sprig
1 bay leaf
2 tablespoons flour
3 cups full-bodied young red Burgundy wine, or any dry red wine
1 head of garlic, peeled and chopped

1 pound Oignons Glacés à Brun (see Index)
1 cup Lardons (see Index)
1 tablespoon vegetable oil
½ pound small mushrooms
4 Croûtes à l'Ail (see Index)
1 tablespoon vinegar
8 eggs

Combine the onion, 4 tablespoons butter, thyme and bay leaf in a saucepan and sauté, stirring from time to time over low heat, until the onion is soft. Stir in the flour and cook for 1 or 2 minutes, stirring. Add the red wine, stirring to mix. Add the garlic, cover, and simmer over very low heat for 1½ hours. Stir from time to time. Strain the sauce and set it aside.

Prepare the onions and *lardons* and set them aside. In a large skillet heat remaining 2 tablespoons butter and the oil and sauté the mushrooms over moderately high heat for 4 to 5 minutes, or until they are lightly browned. Put into a bowl and set aside. Prepare the *croûtes à l'ail* and keep them warm.

(recipe continues)

Reheat the sauce and add the brown glazed onions, the *lardons* and mushrooms. Keep the sauce hot.

Heat 2 inches of water in a large skillet, add 1 tablespoon vinegar, and one by one slide in the eggs. Keep the water at a simmer, and poach the eggs until the whites are set but the yolks are still soft, about 4 minutes.

Place the toasted *croûtes* on 4 warmed plates, and put 2 eggs on each slice. Pour the sauce over the eggs.

SAUCISSON CHAUD POITEVIN

(Hot Sausage, Poitiers Style)

SERVES 8 AS A FIRST COURSE, 4 AS MAIN COURSE.

I like this robust and warming dish for lunch on a blustery winter day, although M. Robert of the Hôtel de France in Poitiers, who gave me his version of this very traditional recipe, serves it as a first course. I serve it as a first course for 8 or double the portions for 4 as a main course. It is a splendid way to serve garlic sausage, on a bed of mixed vegetables with hot potato salad on the side. The salad is also good with cold meats or poultry.

6 tablespoons butter
2 cups finely diced carrots
1 cup finely diced white turnips
2 leeks, well washed, white part only, finely chopped
1 cup finely chopped celery
½ medium-size onion, finely chopped
2 tomatoes, peeled and chopped

2 garlic cloves, minced
1 tarragon sprig, chopped
1 bay leaf
2 or 3 parsley sprigs, chopped
2 cups dry white wine
½ cup Veal or Chicken Stock (see Index)
Salt, freshly ground pepper
1 pound raw garlic sausage

74

In a heavy casserole heat the butter and add all the vegetables and herbs. Cover and cook over very low heat for 20 minutes. Pour in the wine and stock, season with salt and pepper, cover, and cook over low heat for 1 hour longer. Add the sausage and simmer for 30 minutes longer. Remove the sausage and cut it into 8 slices. Discard the bay leaf. Arrange the vegetables on a heated platter with the sausage slices on top. Serve accompanied by Salade de Pommes de Terre Chaude (Hot Potato Salad) (following recipe).

SALADE DE POMMES DE TERRE CHAUDE

(Hot Potato Salad)

2 pounds potatoes, unpeeled	2 tablespoons chopped parsley
½ cup Vinaigrette Dressing (recipe follows)	

Boil the potatoes in their skins until tender, about 20 minutes. As soon as they are cool enough to handle but still warm, peel them and cut them into ¼-inch slices. Place in a bowl and toss with the vinaigrette dressing. Sprinkle with chopped parsley and serve immediately.

VINAIGRETTE DRESSING

1 tablespoon Dijon mustard	Salt, freshly ground pepper
2 tablespoons red-wine vinegar	½ cup vegetable oil

In a bowl combine the mustard, vinegar and salt and pepper to taste. Beat in the oil. Pour over the hot potatoes.

SALADE BERTHELOTIÈRE

(Berthelotière Salad)

SERVES 4.

Chef Gérard Ryngel of Domaine de la Berthelotière in Nantes created this salad, which makes a great first course if followed by a main course of fish or a *soufflé*. It is an example of the unstructured nature of modern meals. Preceded by soup, it can be the main course of a light meal.

1 pound young tender spinach
1 whole chicken breast, poached and cooled
4 cooked artichoke hearts, quartered
8 small crayfish tails, or jumbo shrimps, cooked and peeled

½ cup Sauce Vinaigrette (see Index), made with 1 part olive oil, 3 parts peanut oil
Salt, freshly ground pepper

Wash and dry the spinach and remove the coarse stems. Chop leaves coarsely. Place in a large salad bowl. Cut the chicken breast into neat strips and add to the bowl, along with the artichoke hearts. Cut the crayfish tails or the jumbo shrimps lengthwise and add. Toss with the vinaigrette. Season if necessary with salt and freshly ground pepper.

SALADE DE PRINTEMPS

(Spring Salad)

SERVES 4.

Houard Hugues, chef at the hotel Aux Armes de Champagne at L'Épine, created this salad. It is robust enough to be served as a main course if the helpings are generous. It makes an attractive first course if served in smaller portions.

¼ pound fresh salmon, very thinly sliced
2 tablespoons lemon juice
Salt, freshly ground pepper
1 teaspoon herbes de Provence (use mixed herbs)
½ pound prepared veal sweetbreads (see Index)
2 tablespoons butter
¼ pound mushrooms, chopped, about 1 cup

Chicory, about ½ pound
1 small Boston lettuce
Red-leaf lettuce, about ½ pound
1 small endive, chopped
2 cups cooked green beans, cut into ½-inch pieces
Sauce Vinaigrette (see Index), made with peanut oil

Put the salmon in a flat dish and sprinkle with the lemon juice, salt and pepper to taste and the herbs. Set aside.

Cut the prepared sweetbreads into ½-inch diagonal slices. Heat the butter in a skillet and sauté the sweetbreads over moderate heat until they are tender, 8 to 10 minutes. Lift out the sweetbreads to a plate. Add the mushrooms and sauté for 3 or 4 minutes. Add mushrooms to the sweetbreads.

To assemble the salad, have all the lettuces washed, thoroughly dried and torn into pieces. On a large platter make a bed of chicory, top it with the Boston lettuce, arrange the red-leaf lettuce around the sides of the platter, and sprinkle the chopped endive over the Boston lettuce. Arrange the green beans round the edge of the platter. Lift out the salmon strips and pat off the herbs. Arrange the fish on top of the lettuce and place the sweetbread slices and mushrooms in and around the fish. Pour the Sauce Vinaigrette over the dish. Serve immediately.

Variation: Use smoked salmon instead of fresh.

SALADE CAPRICE GOURMAND

(Salad Gourmet's Fancy)

SERVES 2 OR 3.

This salad from the young chef Michel Loustau, of the restaurant Lou Païrol in the Montpelier Frantel, is an exciting example of what is happening in the kitchens of France today. It takes very little time to make, and offers one a large choice of variations. In place of French *langoustines* (lobsterettes, Dublin Bay prawns, Danish lobsters, Norway lobsters) the chef invites us to use crabs, scallops, mussels or clams. I used shrimps and found the salad delicious. Once I used mung bean sprouts instead of soybean sprouts, and ordinary mushrooms instead of fresh *cèpes,* which I couldn't get. The result was always good.

2 cups bean sprouts
⅔ cup ½-inch pieces of
   cooked shrimps
½ cup thinly sliced
   mushrooms
1 tablespoon each of
   chopped chives and
   scallions

⅓ cup Sauce Vinaigrette
   (see Index), made with
   olive oil, mustard,
   garlic and lemon juice,
   and using celery salt
   instead of ordinary salt
Croûtons (see Index)
   (optional)

Rinse the bean sprouts in cold water, drain, and remove the roots. Pat dry with paper towels, or use a salad dryer. Combine all the ingredients in a salad bowl and toss with the vinaigrette. Serve with croutons fried in oil or butter and rubbed with garlic, if liked.

Variation: If *cèpes* are available, use them in place of mushrooms. Cut them into julienne strips and sauté in olive oil for about 5 minutes. Add 1 garlic clove, finely chopped, and 1 tablespoon chopped parsley to the *cèpes* and toss into the salad hot, just before serving.

SALADE DE POIRE

(Pear Salad)

SERVES 2.

Paul Pauvert, the smiling young chef at the Nantes Frantel's restaurant Le Tillac, is full of original ideas, especially for salads which make excellent first courses.

1 cup julienne strips of scraped carrots
1 cup julienne strips of peeled white turnips
½ cup Sauce Vinaigrette (see Index), made with Sherry vinegar
2 medium-size pears, peeled, cored and cut into 4 slices

1 cup chopped celery
1 cup chopped white of leek
Pomegranate seeds (optional)

In a small saucepan cook the carrots in salted water for about 6 minutes, or until they are tender but still crisp. At the same time, in another small saucepan, cook the turnips in salted water until they are tender but still crisp, about 10 minutes. Drain the vegetables and set aside separately. Make the Sauce Vinaigrette and toss the pears in it as soon as they are peeled. Arrange the pears on 2 plates. Surround pears with small heaps of the carrots, turnips, celery and leeks. Moisten the vegetables with the vinaigrette. If liked, when making the vinaigrette, add some pomegranate seeds, about 2 tablespoons.

Variation: The vinaigrette may be varied by using different oils and vinegars, or lemon juice in place of vinegar, according to personal taste. Paul Pauvert uses cider vinegar with walnut oil, red-wine vinegar with olive oil, and vegetable oil with red- or white-wine vinegar and garlic.

SALADE DE CREVETTES AU PAMPLEMOUSSE

(Shrimp and Grapefruit Salad)

SERVES 4 AS A FIRST COURSE, 2 AS MAIN COURSE OF A LIGHT MEAL.

This is another of Nantes chef Paul Pauvert's salad ideas. Refreshingly unusual for a first course, this can, if served in generous quantities, make a main course.

2 cups cooked shrimps, coarsely chopped	2 tart apples, peeled, cored and chopped
1 grapefruit, peeled and sectioned	½ cup Sauce Vinaigrette (see Index)
2 cups finely shredded spinach leaves	

Combine all the ingredients in a large salad bowl and toss lightly.

SALADE BIGOUDEN

(Lettuce Salad)

SERVES 2 OR 3.

This salad, given me by François Laustriat of the Relais Gourmand Hôtel de Paris in Moulins, has an amusing history. M. Laustriat found it in a book of memoirs of a Breton from the Pays Bigouden. The Breton invented this for a Nicaraguan lady who didn't like oil in her salad dressing.

1 Boston lettuce, washed and dried	1 tablespoon sugar
3 tablespoons cider vinegar	

Tear up the lettuce and toss it with the vinegar. Sprinkle with the sugar and toss lightly again. Serve as a first course or salad course.

SALADE MIXTE AUX ANCHOIS

(Mixed Green Salad with Anchovies)

SERVES 4 TO 6.

The salad greens used for this dish can be varied according to personal taste and the market, varying the salad considerably.

2 hard-cooked eggs
2 teaspoons Dijon mustard
¼ cup mayonnaise
2 tablespoons peanut or similar oil
1 tablespoon lemon juice
Salt, freshly ground pepper
1 can (1¾ ounces) anchovy fillets, drained, rinsed and halved

Mixed greens the equivalent of 1 large Boston lettuce: lamb's lettuce, Boston, Bibb, watercress with thick stems removed, or dandelion greens

In a bowl mash the yolks of the hard-cooked eggs. Reserve the whites. Using a fork, beat in the mustard, mayonnaise, oil and lemon juice. Season lightly with salt as the anchovies are salty, and with pepper. Put the anchovy fillets and the greens into a salad bowl and toss with the dressing. Chop the reserved egg whites very finely and sprinkle on top of the salad.

SALADE VÉRONIQUE

(Veronica Salad)

SERVES 6 TO 8.

Christian Vignes, director of Le Toit de Bigorre, restaurant of the Mapotel Président at Tarbes, with its impressive view of the Pyrenees, and his chef, Yves Pinard, both believe in using recipes that rely on local products, as his Salade Véronique demonstrates. It makes a luxurious beginning to a festive meal. If *confit de canard* or *confit d'oie* are not available, substitute strips of roast duckling instead. With a little extra duckling the salad can be transformed into a light main course. A good *pâté de foie* can be used instead of the *foie gras*.

2 heads of chicory
½ cup Sauce Vinaigrette (see Index)
1 cup Croûtons (see Index)
1 cup Lardons (see Index)
1 tablespoon butter
1 cup walnut halves
2 ounces foie gras, cut into 6 to 8 pieces

¼ pound Confit de Canard or Confit d'Oie (see Index), cut into 12 to 16 little slices
12 to 16 cherry tomatoes, halved
Freshly ground pepper

Wash and dry the chicory and tear it into bite-size pieces. In a large salad bowl toss the chicory with the vinaigrette. Add the *croûtons* and *lardons*. In a small saucepan heat the butter and in it toss the walnut halves for 1 or 2 minutes. Let nuts cool and add them to the salad bowl. Toss the salad lightly. Arrange the salad in 6 to 8 individual bowls or on salad plates. Top each with a slice of *foie gras* and 2 slices of *confit de canard*. Arrange a halved cherry tomato on each serving. Grind a little pepper over each plate or bowl.

SALADE DE LAITUE AUX NOIX

(Lettuce and Walnut Salad)

SERVES 4.

This makes an attractive first course to a summer meal. It is equally good served after the main course, as a regular salad.

1 garlic clove, cut	1 large head of Boston or
6 tablespoons walnut oil	other soft-leaf lettuce,
2 tablespoons white-wine	torn into pieces
vinegar	12 walnuts, halved
Salt, freshly ground	
pepper	

Rub a wooden salad bowl with the garlic. Pour in the oil and vinegar and beat well with a fork. Season to taste with salt and pepper. Add the lettuce and the walnuts and toss lightly.

Variation: Cook 8 small broccoli florets and 8 cauliflowerets until tender but still crisp. Cool and chill lightly. Toss with 2 bunches of watercress and ⅓ cup shelled hazelnuts in ½ cup Sauce Vinaigrette (see Index), made with Dijon mustard.

SOUPS

The blender and the food processor have done much to revolutionize soup, making possible light delicate soups, such as celery, chervil and parsley. When vegetables had to be pounded in a mortar and then pushed through a sieve, involving hours of work and an inevitable loss of freshness of flavor, these soups seemed hardly worth the effort. Now with speedy modern methods we have the delicate soups, while the great old robust meal-in-itself soups are still with us, and so are the hearty warming winter soups. We are lucky. There has been a gain, and no loss.

PETITE MARMITE DU PÊCHEUR

(Fisherman's Soup)

SERVES 4 AS A MAIN COURSE, 6 AS FIRST COURSE.

Pierre Hiély of the Relais Gourmand restaurant Hiély-Lucullus in Avignon gave me the recipe for this delicious fish soup. I find it makes a most attractive main course for either lunch or dinner. Followed by salad, cheese and fruit, it is ideal for lunch, perhaps with a richer dessert for dinner. It can be served as a first course for those with robust appetites. I take liberties with the fish in this recipe. I once used rock lobster tails in place of the anglerfish, a splendid extravagance, and once when I couldn't get mussels I used Cherrystone clams and clam juice, most successfully.

1 garlic clove
2 tablespoons butter
1 medium-size carrot, scraped and minced
1 medium-size onion, finely chopped
1 thyme sprig
1 bay leaf
⅛ teaspoon whole saffron, crumbled
2½ cups Fish Stock (see Index), approximately

2 dozen mussels
½ cup dry white wine
1 pound anglerfish, cut into 1-inch pieces
1 pound filet of sole, cut into 1-inch pieces
¼ cup heavy cream
Salt, pepper
4 to 6 slices of French bread
Olive oil
4 to 6 tablespoons grated Parmesan cheese

Rub the inside of a flameproof casserole with the garlic. Heat the butter in the casserole and sauté the carrot and onion until soft. Add the thyme, bay leaf, saffron and fish stock, and set aside. Put the mussels and wine in a large saucepan. Cover and cook over high heat for 5 minutes, by which time the mussels will have opened. Discard any that remain closed. Remove the mussels from their shells and set

aside. Strain the liquid and measure it. Make up the quantity to 2½ cups with fish stock if necessary. Pour liquid into the casserole. Add the anglerfish and simmer for 10 minutes. Add the sole and simmer for 5 minutes longer. Add the shelled mussels and the cream, season to taste with salt and pepper, and cook just long enough to heat through. Brush the bread slices with olive oil, toast them, and sprinkle them with the cheese. Place a slice of bread on the bottom of each soup plate. Arrange the fish and mussels on top and pour the soup over.

SOUPE DE POISSON

(Strained Fish Soup)

SERVES 6 TO 8.

Fish soups from Provence are traditionally served with *rouille,* a mixture of sweet and hot chili peppers, garlic and other ingredients blended into a thick sauce with olive oil, which is stirred into the soup. The *rouille* that accompanies this soup from the Marseilles region is deliciously hot, but a milder version can be made by reducing the number of chili peppers. Fish heads and bones and trimmings as well as shellfish carcasses can all be used for the soup. If clam juice is used to replace some of the water, it is even more flavorful.

4 pounds mixed fish,
   including fish heads,
   small crabs and so on,
   using nonoily fish.
1 pound tomatoes,
   chopped
1 whole head of garlic,
   peeled and crushed
1 thyme sprig, or ½
   teaspoon dried thyme

1 bay leaf
⅛ teaspoon whole saffron
   Salt, freshly ground
   pepper
10 cups water, or half
   water half clam juice
   Rouille (recipe follows)

(recipe continues)

Combine all the ingredients except *rouille* in a large soup kettle and simmer, covered, for 1 hour. Strain through a sieve, pressing down hard to extract all the juices. Reheat the soup and serve with *rouille,* grated Parmesan or Gruyère cheese and toasted French bread.

ROUILLE

(Garlic, Tomato and Chili Pepper Sauce)

MAKES ABOUT 1½ CUPS.

1 tablespoon tomato paste
5 small fresh hot peppers, preferably red, seeded and chopped
1 freshly cooked medium-size potato, chopped
2 large garlic cloves, chopped

1 cup strained fish soup
2 tablespoons Mayonnaise (see Index), made with olive oil and lemon juice
Salt, freshly ground pepper

In a food processor fitted with the steel blade, or in a blender, combine tomato paste, peppers, potato and garlic, and reduce to a purée. Add a little of the fish soup if necessary. (Traditionally the ingredients are pounded in a mortar.) Transfer the purée to a bowl and beat in the mayonnaise bit by bit. Heat remaining fish soup and gradually beat it into the sauce. Taste for seasoning and add salt and pepper if necessary.

Variation: For a milder sauce reduce the number of chili peppers to 1. Seed and chop ½ medium-size red bell pepper and simmer it in salted water for 5 minutes. Drain and add to the ingredients in the food processor; or use 1 whole canned pimiento.

SOUPE DE CONGRE

(Conger Eel Soup)

SERVES 4 TO 6.

Although eel is not usually for sale in U.S. fishmarkets, it is worth looking for. Whenever it is available I buy it, as I enjoy it in many dishes. There is sometimes a bonus: if the head is available I ask for it and have it cut up to make this very fine soup. If there is no head I can always use 1½ pounds of eel. If I have leftover fish stock from other cooking, I use it instead of water as it enriches the soup; or I use a mixture of water and bottled clam juice, though water will do.

4 tablespoons butter
2 large onions, chopped
1 pound potatoes (about 3), peeled and cubed
1 garlic clove, chopped
1 head of conger eel, cut into 2 or 3 pieces
1 thyme sprig

2 or 3 parsley sprigs
1 bay leaf
  Salt, freshly ground white pepper
8 cups Fish Stock (see Index), or clam juice and water, or water

Heat the butter in a soup kettle or large heavy saucepan and sauté the onions until soft. Add the potatoes and garlic and sauté for a few minutes longer, stirring once or twice. Add the eel pieces, thyme, parsley, bay leaf, a little salt, a generous amount of pepper and the stock. There should be enough liquid to cover the eel completely. Add more water if necessary. Simmer gently, covered, for about 40 minutes. Allow to cool. Lift out the eel pieces; as soon as they are cool enough to handle, remove the pieces of fish and discard the bones, leaving the fish in fairly large pieces. Set aside.

Remove and discard the thyme, parsley and bay leaf. Measure the liquid. There should be about 6 cups.

If there is a great deal more, reserve the extra liquid as fish stock for another use, or reduce it over high heat to

(recipe continues)

intensify the flavor. Taste for seasoning and add more salt and pepper if liked. Return the fish to the saucepan and simmer just long enough to heat it through. The potato and onion will have thickened the soup a little. Ladle into large bowls, making sure each bowl has some of the fish. Crusty bread makes a perfect accompaniment.

SOUPE AU PISTOU

(Vegetable Soup with Basil and Garlic)

SERVES 3 OR 4.

M. Mayard, who with his wife presides over the Relais et Châteaux La Mayanelle, a sixteenth-century château on the ramparts of Gordes, is one of the most enthusiastic and generous chefs I have ever met. M. Mayard's own recipe for this traditional and robust soup is as generous and heart-warming as the chef himself.

½ cup (¼ pound) dried red kidney beans

½ cup (¼ pound) dried white beans such as Great Northern or Navy

2 quarts water

2 medium-size onions, chopped

3 medium-size carrots, scraped and finely sliced

3 medium-size potatoes, peeled and cubed

Bouquet garni: 1 small celery rib, 1 parsley sprig, 1 thyme sprig, 1 bay leaf, tied together with cotton

2 or 3 small zucchini, cut into ¼-inch slices

2 large tomatoes, peeled, seeded and chopped

Salt, freshly ground pepper

2 cups uncooked elbow macaroni

PISTOU

2 large garlic cloves

Salt, pepper

1 cup fresh basil leaves

4 tablespoons olive oil

Gruyére cheese, grated

90

Wash and pick over the beans and put them in a large saucepan or soup kettle with 2 quarts water. Bring to a boil and simmer, covered, for 30 minutes, or until the beans are half-cooked. The time will depend on the freshness of the beans. Add the onions, carrots, potatoes and *bouquet garni,* and cook until beans are tender. Add zucchini, tomatoes, salt and pepper to taste and macaroni. Simmer for 15 minutes longer, or until macaroni is tender.

While the soup is cooking make the *pistou.* In a large mortar crush the garlic with salt and pepper, then pound in the basil leaves. Add the oil. Do this in a blender or food processor if preferred. The traditional method is rewarding but time-consuming.

Serve the soup in a tureen. It should be very hot, with the *pistou* either in the mortar or in a bowl, and with the cheese served separately. Ladle the soup into large bowls and pass round the *pistou* and cheese to be added as liked.

Drink a chilled rosé or a light Provençal red wine. Dessert is probably all that will be needed to complete the meal.

SOUPE AUX DEUX LÉGUMES

(Soup with Two Vegetables)

SERVES 4 OR 5.

This fresh-tasting soup takes very little time to prepare and cook. It is fine hot and splendid lightly chilled, with the vegetable flavors coming through clearly.

2 tablespoons butter
1 shallot, finely chopped
½ pound zucchini,
    trimmed but unpeeled,
    coarsely grated
½ pound cucumber,
    preferably hothouse
    variety, unpeeled,
    coarsely grated

4 cups light Chicken
    Stock (see Index)
    Salt, freshly ground
    white pepper

In a saucepan heat the butter and sauté the shallot until it is very soft but not browned. Add the zucchini and cucumber and cook for 1 to 2 minutes. Add the stock, bring to a simmer and cook, covered, for 10 minutes. Drain, reserving liquid and solids. Purée the solids in a food processor fitted with the steel blade, or in a blender in batches, with a little of the stock. Pour through a sieve. Return to the saucepan with remaining stock, season to taste with salt and pepper, and reheat gently if serving hot. Otherwise chill in the refrigerator.

VELOUTÉ D'OSEILLE

(Cream of Sorrel Soup)

SERVES 6.

It is hard to translate this accurately as, strictly speaking, a cream soup is finished just with cream—eggs are not used. Sorrel, which gives this soup its special flavor, is often avail-

able in Italian markets and anyone with a garden can grow it easily. Sorrel is delicious in sauces, especially for fish, and in salads.

1 pound sorrel
1 tablespoon butter
3 medium-size tomatoes, peeled, seeded and chopped
4 cups Chicken Stock (see Index)

Salt, freshly ground pepper
2 whole eggs
2 extra egg yolks
1 cup heavy cream

Trim sorrel stalks and wash leaves thoroughly in cold water. Drain and cut into thin strips. Put the sorrel into a heavy saucepan without any additional water, cover, and cook over very low heat for 15 minutes, or until tender.

Heat the butter in a small saucepan. Add the tomatoes and simmer over moderate heat, stirring occasionally, until tomatoes are thick and smooth, about 5 minutes. Add tomatoes to the sorrel and stir in the stock. Season to taste with salt and pepper. Simmer gently over low heat.

Beat whole eggs and extra egg yolks in a bowl with the cream. Gradually beat in 1 cup of the hot soup, then pour the egg mixture into the soup and cook, stirring or whisking constantly over very low heat, until the soup has thickened, 2 or 3 minutes. Do not let soup boil after adding the liaison, as it will curdle.

POTAGE CRÈME DE CERFEUIL

(Cream of Chervil Soup)

SERVES 6.

Given a shady spot in a garden, or on a terrace or window ledge, chervil is easy to grow from seed. It is a favorite herb

(recipe continues)

of mine and I am particularly fond of this delicate, subtly flavored soup.

3 tablespoons butter
1 cup chopped chervil, plus 2 tablespoons for garnish
6 cups Chicken Stock (see Index)

½ cup heavy cream
Salt, freshly ground pepper

Heat the butter in a saucepan and add the cup of chopped chervil. Cover and cook over the lowest possible heat for 5 minutes. Add ½ cup of the stock, simmer for 1 or 2 minutes, then purée in a blender. Return the purée to the saucepan, add the rest of the stock and simmer, covered, over low heat. Strain through a sieve, then pour back into the saucepan. Stir in the cream and season to taste with salt and pepper. Garnish with the 2 tablespoons chopped chervil, and serve hot. The soup is also pleasant chilled.

SOUPE AUX CHAMPIGNONS

(Mushroom Soup)

SERVES 4.

This mushroom soup has a pure, delicate flavor. It is equally good hot or lightly chilled.

¾ pound mushrooms
2 tablespoons butter
4 cups Chicken or Veal Stock (see Index)

Salt, freshly ground pepper
¼ cup heavy cream
Mushrooms for garnish

Wipe the mushrooms with a damp cloth or paper towels to clean, then slice thinly. Combine mushrooms, butter and 1 cup of the stock in a saucepan. Bring to a boil, lower the heat and simmer, covered, for 5 minutes. Cool slightly, then purée the mushrooms with a little of the stock in a food

processor fitted with the steel blade, or in a blender, in batches if necessary. Strain the soup through a fine sieve, and return it to the saucepan. Add the rest of the stock, season to taste with salt and pepper, and simmer for 5 minutes to blend the flavors. Just before serving stir in the cream and heat through. Peel the mushrooms for garnish and slice thinly. Pour the soup into soup bowls and garnish with sliced mushrooms.

The recipe can be doubled or trebled successfully.

POTAGE DE CÉLERIS

(Celery Soup)

SERVES 4 TO 6.

This is another of the elegant light soups that are, thanks to the food processor and the blender, replacing the more robust traditional soups as first courses. This too may be served hot or cold.

4 tablespoons butter
¼ cup finely chopped
    shallots or scallions
6 cups chopped celery,
    about 2 bunches
4 cups Chicken Stock (see
    Index)
    Salt, freshly ground
    pepper

¼ cup heavy cream
2 tablespoons shredded
    sorrel, or chervil or
    parsley

In a large saucepan or soup kettle heat the butter and sauté the shallots until soft. Stir in the celery and sauté for 2 or 3 minutes. Pour in the chicken stock, bring to a simmer and simmer, covered, for 45 minutes. Drain, reserving liquid and solids. Purée the solids in a food processor or blender, using some of the liquid. Push the purée through a sieve, then return it to the saucepan. Season with salt and pepper, add the cream, and heat through. Garnish with the sorrel.

CRÈME DE CONCOMBRES

(Cream of Cucumber Soup)

SERVES 4 TO 6.

1 large or 2 medium-size
   cucumbers, preferably
   long hothouse type or
   seedless, about 1
   pound
1 leek, or medium-size
   onion
1 head of Boston lettuce

4 tablespoons butter
4 cups Chicken Stock (see
   Index)
   Salt, freshly ground
   pepper
¼ cup heavy cream

Grate the unpeeled cucumber. Thoroughly wash the leek and finely shred, using white part only, or finely chop the onion. Wash, drain, and shred the lettuce. In a saucepan heat the butter and sauté the leek or onion until soft but not brown. Add the lettuce and cucumber and sauté for about 2 minutes longer. Pour 1 cup of the stock into the saucepan and simmer, covered, for 5 minutes, or until cucumber is tender. In a food processor fitted with the steel blade, or in a blender in batches, purée the cucumber mixture. Strain purée through a sieve and return it to the saucepan with the rest of the stock. Season to taste with salt and pepper and bring to a simmer. Stir in the cream. The soup may also be served chilled.

POTAGE DE LAITUES

(Lettuce Soup)

SERVES 6.

This is a most delicate soup. It is useful for anyone with a garden when there are too many lettuces ready at the same time, or for anyone finding lettuce overabundant in a supermarket or greengrocery.

96

3 tablespoons butter
1 leek, white part only, or
   1 medium-size onion,
   finely chopped
3 heads of Boston lettuce
   or other soft lettuce,
   washed and shredded

6 cups Chicken Stock (see
   Index)
Salt, freshly ground
   pepper
½ cup heavy cream
Chopped parsley or
   other herb for garnish

Heat the butter in a large saucepan and sauté the leek or onion, without letting it brown, until it is very soft, about 5 minutes. Add the lettuce and sauté for 1 or 2 minutes, stirring to mix with a wooden spoon. When the lettuce has wilted, pour in the stock and simmer for 5 minutes. Drain the soup, reserving liquid and solids. In a food processor fitted with the steel blade, or in a blender, purée the lettuce mixture with a little of the stock. Push the purée through a fine sieve into a saucepan with the reserved stock. Heat through. Season to taste with salt and pepper and stir in the cream. Simmer just long enough to heat the cream through. Serve garnished with chopped herbs.

SOUPE AUX HARICOTS VERTS

(Green Bean Soup)

SERVES 4.

2 tablespoons butter
1 medium-size onion,
   finely chopped
¾ pound green beans,
   trimmed and washed
2 cups water
2 cups Chicken or Beef
   Stock (see Index),
   approximately

Salt, freshly ground
   pepper
¼ cup heavy cream,
   optional

(recipe continues)

Heat the butter in a saucepan. Add the onion and sauté until onion is very soft but not browned. Add beans and water. Bring to a simmer and cook for 10 minutes. Pour off and reserve the liquid. Purée the beans in a little of the reserved liquid in a food processor fitted with the steel blade, or in a blender, in batches if necessary. Rub the beans through a sieve for a finer texture and return purée to the saucepan. Add enough stock to the bean liquid to make a total of 4 cups and add to the beans. Season with salt and pepper. Simmer for 5 minutes to blend the flavors. If liked, stir in the cream.

Variation: For a slightly thicker soup add 4 chopped outside leaves of romaine lettuce to the onion.

SOUPE DE PERSIL

(Parsley Soup)

SERVES 6.

2 tablespoons butter
2 leeks, white part only, well washed and chopped
2 tightly packed cups flat-leaf (Italian) parsley, using some of the stems

2 or 3 outside leaves of romaine lettuce
Salt, freshly ground pepper
6 cups Chicken or Beef Stock (see Index)

Heat the butter in a heavy saucepan and sauté the leeks until soft but not browned. Drop the parsley and lettuce leaves into briskly boiling salted water for 1 minute. Drain and rinse immediately in cold water. Drain again, then gently squeeze out any remaining water. Chop parsley and lettuce coarsely and add to the saucepan with the leeks. Pour in the stock, cover, and simmer for 10 minutes. Pour

off and reserve the stock. Purée the solids, with a little of the stock if necessary, in a blender or food processor fitted with the steel blade. Push the purée through a sieve back into the stock. (There are usually quite a lot of stringy bits left from the parsley which would give the soup a coarse texture.) Season to taste with salt and pepper and heat through but do not boil.

POTAGE DE PETITS POIS

(Green Pea Soup)

SERVES 6.

4 cups shelled green peas
3 cups Chicken Stock (see Index)
2 tablespoons butter
½ head of Boston lettuce, shredded
6 scallions, both white and green parts, chopped

3 tablespoons mixed chopped fresh herbs (parsley, chervil, basil, mint, tarragon or whatever is available)
Salt, white pepper
½ cup heavy cream

In a saucepan combine the peas and stock and simmer until the peas are tender, about 10 minutes. Pour off and reserve the stock. In a food processor fitted with the steel blade, or in a blender, purée the peas using a little of the stock, then put the purée through a fine sieve. Add the rest of the stock. In a skillet heat the butter and sauté the lettuce, scallions and herbs until just wilted. Put into a blender or food processor with a little of the pea soup and reduce to a coarse purée; there should be flecks of herbs. Add herbs to the soup. Season soup to taste with salt and pepper and simmer for a few minutes to blend the flavors. Stir in the cream and cook just long enough to heat it through.

TOURIN AUX TOMATES

(Tomato Soup)

SERVES 4.

At the moment when tomatoes are at their ripest and best, and least expensive, I like to make this Provençal tomato soup. It is simplicity itself, with a wonderfully fresh flavor.

2 tablespoons butter
2 medium-size onions, finely chopped
1 small garlic clove, crushed
2 pounds tomatoes, peeled, seeded and chopped

Salt, freshly ground pepper
½ teaspoon sugar
4 cups Chicken Stock (see Index)

In a heavy saucepan heat the butter. Add the onions and garlic and cook over very low heat until onions are almost reduced to a purée; do not let them brown. Add the tomatoes, salt and pepper to taste and the sugar and cook, stirring, for 3 or 4 minutes. Stir in the chicken stock and simmer, covered, for 5 minutes to blend the flavors.

LA SOUPE AUX CHOUX

(Cabbage Soup)

SERVES 4 GENEROUSLY, OR 8 IN SMALLER PORTIONS.

This hearty cabbage soup was given me by M. François Laustriat of the Relais Gourmand Hôtel de Paris at Moulins. It is the sort of soup that comforts in wintry weather and is a meal in itself. I like the mellow flavor of Savoy cabbage and the interesting addition of walnut oil. If I have no chervil for the *fines herbes*, I double the amount of pars-

ley. The bread used in the soup is *pain de campagne* (country bread), very like the crusty round loaves that are sold in Italian bakeries. Any good, chewy, crusty bread will do. Or make your own (see Index).

½ pound fresh pork belly, cut into small strips
3 medium-size carrots, scraped and diced
3 medium-size white turnips, peeled and diced
2 leeks, white part only, thoroughly washed and sliced
1 medium-size onion, finely chopped
1 garlic clove, chopped
2 medium-size potatoes, peeled and diced

1 small Savoy cabbage, washed and shredded
8 cups Beef or Chicken Stock (see Index)
1 tablespoon walnut oil
2 tablespoons chopped fines herbes (parsley, chervil, chives)
8 slices of bread, ½ inch thick
8 slices of large garlic sausage
¼ pound grated Gruyère cheese
Cream

Drop the pieces of pork belly into rapidly boiling water, blanch for 1 minute, then drain. Transfer the pork strips to a large saucepan or soup kettle and let them brown in their own fat over low heat. If necessary, add a little oil or butter. Add the carrots, turnips, leeks, onion and garlic and sauté in the fat for about 5 minutes, stirring from time to time with a wooden spoon. Add potatoes and cabbage and cook for about 2 minutes longer. Pour in the stock, cover, and cook until all the vegetables are tender. Season to taste with salt and pepper. Stir the soup vigorously, then stir in the walnut oil and the herbs.

Just before serving prepare the croûtes. Cover the slices of bread with the slices of sausage. Mix the cheese with just enough cream to hold it together and spread it over the sausage. Broil croûtes just to brown the cheese lightly. Place 2 slices of bread in the bottom of each of 4 large soup plates and ladle the soup on top.

SOUPE DE POTIRON BASQUAISE

(Basque-Style Squash Soup)

SERVES 6.

3 tablespoons goose, duck or pork fat, or vegetable oil

4 ounces fresh pork belly, cut into small pieces

3 medium-size onions, finely chopped

3 garlic cloves, chopped

1½ pounds Hubbard or other winter squash, or West Indian pumpkin (calabaza), peeled and cubed

1 small Savoy cabbage, shredded

1 cup dried Great Northern or Navy beans, cooked, and the cooking water

5 cups Beef or Chicken Stock (see Index), approximately

Salt, freshly ground pepper

Heat the fat in a saucepan and sauté the pieces of pork belly until they have released all their fat and are lightly browned. Add the onions and sauté for a few minutes, then add the garlic and the squash and sauté, stirring with a wooden spoon, until the squash pieces are coated with fat. Add the cabbage and cook, stirring, over moderate heat until the cabbage is wilted. Drain the beans and add them to the soup. Measure the liquid in which they were cooked and add to the saucepan with enough stock to measure 6 cups. Season with salt and pepper and simmer for 30 minutes, or until the squash is beginning to disintegrate. Stir thoroughly and serve.

If liked, the quantity of beans can be increased to 2 cups. Serve with grated cheese and crusty bread.

POTAGE AU POTIRON

(Squash Soup)

SERVES 6 TO 8.

4 tablespoons butter
2 medium-size onions, finely chopped
1½ pounds Hubbard or other winter squash, or West Indian pumpkin (calabaza), peeled and cubed
2 medium-size potatoes, peeled and cubed

6 cups Chicken or Beef Stock (see Index)
Salt, freshly ground pepper
½ cup heavy cream
Mixed chopped herbs (parsley, chervil, fennel, hyssop, etc.), for garnish

In a large saucepan or soup kettle heat the butter and sauté the onions until soft. Add the squash and potatoes and sauté for a few minutes longer, stirring to mix. Add 2 cups of the stock and simmer, covered, until squash and potatoes are very soft, about 30 minutes. Purée the mixture in a food processor fitted with the steel blade, or in a blender in batches, and return to the saucepan. Add the rest of the stock, season with salt and pepper and simmer, covered, for 10 minutes to blend the flavors. Stir in the cream and heat through but do not let the soup boil. Serve garnished with the herbs.

Variation: Omit the potatoes. Reduce the stock to 5 cups and add 2 cups peeled, seeded and chopped tomatoes.

SOUPE AU LAPIN DE GARENNE

(Rabbit Soup)

SERVES 4.

I was searching for a rabbit soup with no great success when my search was ended by Pierre Duvauchelle of the Mapotel Hôtel de l'Aigle Noir in Fontainebleau. A marvelous soup for which I thank Chef Aubriet. Another thing to consider is that this is a splendid way to use up egg yolks after making meringues or angel-food cake.

2 tablespoons butter	Salt, freshly ground
1½ to 2 pounds rabbit, cut up	pepper
4 cups Beef Stock (see Index) or water	½ pound mushrooms, finely chopped
2 medium-size onions, chopped	8 egg yolks
2 garlic cloves, minced	4 tablespoons heavy cream
Bouquet garni of mixed herbs: rosemary, summer savory, basil	

Heat the butter in a heavy flameproof casserole and sauté the rabbit pieces lightly. Pour in the stock and add the onions, garlic and herbs. Season with salt and pepper, and simmer, covered, over low heat until the rabbit is very tender and falling off the bones, about 1½ hours. Lift out the rabbit pieces and let them cool. Remove the meat, cut it into small pieces, and set aside. Discard the bones.

Strain the stock and add three quarters of the mushrooms. Set the remaining quarter aside. Simmer the mushrooms and stock over low heat for 10 to 15 minutes. Remove from the heat. Beat the egg yolks with the cream.

Pour 1 cup of the hot soup into the mixture, mix well, then stir into the soup. Add the reserved rabbit meat and the reserved mushrooms and simmer until the soup is lightly thickened, stirring. Do not let the soup boil or it will curdle. The second lot of mushrooms should remain firm to the bite, *al dente*. Serve the soup very hot.

LE VELOUTÉ DE FÈVES

(Broad Bean Soup)

SERVES 6 TO 8.

1 tablespoon pork fat or vegetable oil
4 slices of bacon, coarsely chopped
2 leeks, well washed
1 medium-size onion, chopped
1 celery rib, chopped
1 medium-size head of lettuce, chopped

4 pounds fresh broad beans, shelled, about 4 cups
6 cups Chicken or Beef Stock (see Index)
1 bay leaf
1 thyme sprig
2 or 3 parsley sprigs
Salt, freshly ground pepper

In a large saucepan or soup kettle heat the pork fat or oil and sauté the bacon until it has released all its fat and is lightly browned. Chop the leeks, using the white parts and a little of the green. Add to the saucepan with the onion and celery. Sauté vegetables until onion is soft. Add the lettuce, beans, stock, bay leaf, thyme and parsley. Bring to a simmer over moderate heat and simmer for 30 to 45 minutes, or until the beans are very soft. Pour off and reserve the stock. Purée the vegetables in a blender or food processor with a little of the stock. Return purée and stock to the saucepan, season to taste with salt and pepper, and simmer until the soup is heated through.

Serve with bread cubes fried in pork fat or vegetable oil, if liked.

POTAGE DE PRINTEMPS

(Spring Soup)

SERVES 6.

3 tablespoons butter
2 leeks, white part and
   about 1 inch of the
   green, thoroughly
   washed and sliced
1 large head of romaine
   lettuce, shredded
2 large artichoke hearts,
   cooked and cubed

6 cups Beef or Chicken
   Stock (see Index)
   Salt, freshly ground
   pepper
⅓ cup heavy cream
   Chopped chervil or
   parsley for garnish

Heat the butter in a large saucepan and sauté the leeks, lettuce and artichoke hearts for about 5 minutes, stirring from time to time. Do not let the vegetables brown. Add the stock, cover, and simmer for 15 minutes. Lift out the solids and purée them in a food processor fitted with the steel blade, or in a blender in batches, using a little of the stock if necessary. For a finer texture pour the mixture through a sieve, though this step is not absolutely necessary. Return the mixture to the saucepan, season to taste with salt and pepper, stir in the cream, and heat through. Serve sprinkled with chervil or parsley.

CRÈME NIGNON

(Potato Soup)

SERVES 4 TO 6.

I love potatoes, so I was very pleased indeed when that great cook, Arthur Keller of the Hôtel-Restaurant Quincangrogne at Dampmart on the Marne, offered me this recipe for his own exquisite potato soup.

¼ pound (1 stick) butter
4 leeks, white part only,
    well washed and finely
    chopped
1 onion, finely chopped
  Salt
  Pinch of sugar

4 cups Chicken Stock (see
    Index)
2 large potatoes, about 1
    pound, peeled
1 cup heavy cream
1 tablespoon finely
    snipped chives

In a large, heavy flameproof casserole heat the butter and add the leeks, onion, salt to taste and the sugar. Sauté, stirring from time to time with a wooden spoon, for 5 minutes. Pour in the stock and add the potatoes. Bring to a simmer, cover, and cook for 1 hour. Lift out the potatoes and push them through a sieve. Return the sieved potato to the casserole. Bring the soup just to a boil, then stir in the cream. Taste for seasoning, adding a little more salt if necessary. Sprinkle with chives and serve.

PASTRY-TOPPED SOUPS

No innovation in the cooking world has been quite so charming as the Paul Bocuse idea of topping small soup bowls with puff pastry and having the diner break the pastry into the soup as bread. Paul Bocuse, with his usual generosity, sent me the recipe for his famous Soupe aux Truffes, with permission to use it. It was the recipe he created for the French President Valéry Giscard d'Estaing, and it is a lovely piece of luxury, a soup for once or twice in a lifetime. Paul Bocuse says it was inspired by his friend Paul Haeberlin of the Auberge de l'Ill at Illhaeusern. I have enjoyed exquisite food at Illhaeusern and am not surprised at Paul Haeberlin's involvement. The recipe has been published quite widely, and it is in M. Bocuse's own book, *La Cuisine du Marché*, but I think it merits repeating here together with some of the simpler, yet most appetizing soups it has inspired.

SOUPE AUX TRUFFES

(Truffle Soup)

SERVES 2.

BRUNOISE

1 tablespoon butter
4 mushrooms, finely diced
1 small carrot, scraped and finely diced
1 small celery rib, without leaves, finely diced
1 small onion, finely diced
4 ounces fresh truffles, sliced

3 tablespoons diced foie gras
¼ cup minced cooked chicken breast
1 cup rich chicken consommé
6 ounces puff pastry, approximately
1 egg yolk, lightly beaten

To make the *brunoise*, melt the butter in a small heavy saucepan over low heat. Add mushrooms, carrot, celery and onion, cover, and simmer until the vegetables are tender but still slightly crisp.

The French would use a type of terrine called a *soupière à gratinée lyonnaise*, but any small ovenproof terrine, holding about 1 cup, will do just as well. Divide the ingredients between 2 such terrines, putting half of the *brunoise* into each, then add the truffles, *foie gras* and chicken breast. Pour in the consommé.

Roll out the pastry into 2 circles each large enough to cover a soup terrine and overhang by about 1 inch all round, a circle about 7 inches and ⅛ inch thick. Brush the inside of the pastry with the egg yolk and place over the bowl. Press the pastry gently to the sides of the bowl; do *not* press it to the rim. Refrigerate the little terrines until the pastry is firm, at least 30 minutes. The soup bowls can be covered with plastic wrap and refrigerated overnight.

Bake the soup in the lower third of a preheated hot oven (425°F.) for about 10 minutes, or until the pastry is puffed and golden. Using a spatula, slide the soup bowls onto plates and serve. To eat, break the crust into the soup.

Variations: **SOUPE DE CRABE** (*CRAB SOUP*), an invention by Paul Pauvert of the Nantes Frantel: Simmer 2 cups Fish Stock (see Index) with ¼ cup crab meat, picked over and any cartilage removed, uncovered for 15 minutes. Cool, purée, and push through a sieve. Taste for seasoning and add salt and pepper if necessary. Add ⅛ teaspoon ground coriander. Stir in ¼ cup picked-over crab meat. Divide the soup between 2 soup terrines, cover with pastry, and bake in the lower third of a preheated hot oven (425°F.) until the tops are puffed and browned.

SOUPE DE MORILLES (*MOREL SOUP*): Soak ¼ cup dried morels in 2 cups Brown (Beef) Stock (see Index) for 30 minutes. Simmer, uncovered, over very low heat for another 30 minutes. Lift out the morels, chop them finely, and return to the liquid. Pour in ¼ cup dry Madeira. Divide between 2 soup bowls, cover with pastry as above, and bake.

Pour 1½ cups Soupe de Poisson (see Index) into two 1-cup terrines. Stir into each terrine 1 tablespoon Rouille (see Index). Cover with pastry and bake as above.

Use any chicken, meat, fish or vegetable leftovers, combined with the appropriate stock, as the basis for pastry-topped soups. Or use any soup such as onion or tomato. Creamed mixtures are less successful than clear soups.

FISH AND SHELLFISH

Nowhere in the French kitchen is there more exciting innovation than in the fish and shellfish dishes. We are lucky in having a wonderful variety of fish in our waters and fortunately our fish markets are stocking an increasing variety of them. It is a pleasure to discover that many of the fish that were thought of as exclusively French, or at least exclusively European, swim in our waters too. A lot of the confusion over fish and their multiplicity of names has been sorted out recently in excellent reference books such as Alan Davidson's *North Atlantic Seafood.* Fish that are not transatlantic often have close cousins across the water so that suitable substitutes can be found, and I have given these in the recipe text. Fish is good for us; it is slimming as well as being delicious. It takes little time to cook and presents few kitchen difficulties. The sauce it comes with may be a rich one, but there will not be much of it. The small flat spoon (we would use a teaspoon) that today is part of the French table setting makes it possible to enjoy the sauce to the last drop without resorting to bread to mop it up, though bread lovers and the skinny can of course ignore the spoon.

111

TRUITE NANO

(Trout Stuffed with Sorrel and Spinach)

SERVES 2.

This is a prize-winning recipe from M. Roussel, chef of Monique Moitry's Relais et Chatêaux Hostellerie Claire-Fontaine at Remiremont in the Vosges. The sorrel needed can usually be found in Italian markets. For those with gardens it is extremely easy to grow, and comes up by itself every spring.

2 rainbow trout, each 8 to 10 ounces
1 cup finely chopped spinach
1 cup finely chopped sorrel
Salt, freshly ground pepper
1 tablespoon finely chopped mint leaves
½ tablespoon finely chopped fresh tarragon, or ½ teaspoon dried tarragon

3 tablespoons butter, approximately
¾ cup Fish Stock (see Index)
¾ cup dry white wine
¼ cup chopped shallots
½ cup heavy cream
1 tablespoon Dijon mustard
1 tablespoon lemon juice
1 tablespoon finely chopped mixed herbs (parsley, chives, chervil, or whatever is available)

Have the fishmonger dress the trout through the gills, leaving on the heads and tails, and remove the backbones through the back; or do this last part yourself as it is not difficult. In a bowl mix together the spinach, sorrel, ½ teaspoon salt, ⅛ teaspoon pepper, the mint and tarragon. Stuff the trout with the mixture. Put the fish into a buttered skillet and pour in the fish stock and wine; add a little salt and pepper and dot the fish with 1 tablespoon butter. Cover and poach over low heat for 15 minutes, or until the fish flakes easily when tested with a fork. Pour off the cooking liquid and strain it through a fine sieve to remove any bits of spinach or sorrel that may have escaped from the fish. Cover the fish and keep them warm.

Heat 1 tablespoon butter in a small saucepan and sauté the shallots until soft. Add the strained fish cooking liquid and reduce over high heat to ½ cup. Stir in the cream and reduce the mixture to ⅔ cup. Stir in mustard and lemon juice, taste for seasoning, and add salt and pepper if necessary. Cook over very low heat just to heat the sauce through. Stir in the herbs. Nap the trout with the sauce. Serve with boiled potatoes tossed with butter and sprinkled with chopped parsley.

TRUITE AUX FINES HERBES
(Trout with Mixed Herbs)

SERVES 6.

Five generations of the Rieux family have run the Mapotel Hostellerie Saint-Antoine in Albi, founded in 1734. They serve lovely food and I am grateful to M. Rieux for giving me this splendid recipe of chef Roger Chaîne's.

6 trout, each about 7 ounces, boned	2 cups freshly made bread crumbs
Salt, freshly ground pepper	12 tablespoons (1½ sticks) butter
3 eggs, lightly beaten	6 small tomatoes
1 cup mixed finely chopped parsley, chives and chervil	2 cups dry white wine

If possible, have the fishmonger open and bone the trout through the back. Salt and pepper the fish. Dip the fish into beaten eggs, then into the mixed herbs and lastly into the bread crumbs. Butter an ovenproof baking dish large enough to hold the trout and arrange them on it. Cut a slice from each tomato and gently squeeze out the seeds. Place a

(recipe continues)

tomato slice on the head of each trout. Dot the fish with remaining butter and pour wine over carefully. Bake in a preheated moderate oven (375°F.) for about 10 minutes, or until done. Serve from the baking dish.

Drink a dry white wine.

TRUITE AUX HERBES

(Trout with Herbs)

SERVES 4.

Trout is usually available, so when fresh tarragon and other herbs are around this is an uncomplicated dish I enjoy. It was given me by M. Leyssalles of the Mapotel Cro-Magnon in the Périgord.

4 trout, each 7 to 8 ounces, boned

STUFFING

1 cup fresh bread crumbs
½ cup finely chopped parsley
¼ cup chopped tarragon leaves
1 teaspoon chopped fresh thyme, or ¼ teaspoon dried

¼ cup finely chopped shallots
Salt, freshly ground pepper
2 tablespoons olive oil
1 cup dry white wine

Dress the trout and pat them dry. Mix together the crumbs, herbs and shallots, and use to stuff the trout. Secure the openings in the trout with toothpicks and arrange fish on an oiled flameproof baking dish. Season with salt and pepper and brush with oil. Bake in a preheated moderate oven (375°F.) for about 10 minutes, or until done. Transfer the trout to a serving dish and keep warm. Pour the wine into the baking dish and bring to a boil on top of the stove. Stir and pour over the fish.

Drink a dry white wine.

TRUITE FARCIE AUX ÉPINARDS

(Trout Stuffed with Spinach)

SERVES 2.

Paul Pauvert, young chef of the Frantel restaurant Le Tillac in Nantes, also has a stuffed trout recipe, and since trout is usually available I'm pleased to have several recipes for it. When I find young, tender spinach in the market I change my cooking plans and buy trout.

2 trout, each about 8 ounces
½ pound spinach, about 4 cups tightly packed
Salt
2 tablespoons butter
¼ cup chopped shallots
1 cup slivered almonds
Freshly ground pepper
3 tablespoons heavy cream
1 tablespoon oil
6 tablespoons butter
Additional cream (optional)
1 lemon
Chopped parsley

If possible have the fish store open and bone the trout through the back; otherwise bone them from the front. Wash the spinach, remove any wilted leaves, and cut off the stems. Drop the spinach into a large saucepan of briskly boiling salted water, bring back to a boil over high heat, and simmer for 5 minutes. Plunge the spinach into cold water, drain, and squeeze out the moisture. An easy way to do this is to place the spinach on a bamboo mat and roll up the mat, squeezing the bamboo cylinder gently; or roll the spinach in a kitchen towel. Chop the spinach, and set it aside.

In a small skillet heat the butter and sauté the shallots until soft but not browned. Add half the almonds and sauté until they are golden. Add the spinach, stir to mix, season with salt and pepper, and stir in the cream. Cook for 1 min-

(recipe continues)

115

ute. Cool the stuffing, then stuff the trout with the mixture. Secure the opening with toothpicks.

In a large skillet heat the oil and butter. Add more butter to the skillet if necessary, as the butter should be about ¼ inch deep. When the butter is hot add the trout and sauté until golden brown on both sides, 12 to 15 minutes. Arrange the trout on a serving dish on which, if liked, just enough cream has been poured to coat the surface. Keep trout warm. Add the remaining almonds to the butter in the skillet and sauté until golden, about 1 minute. Add a squeeze of lemon juice to the pan and pour the mixture over the trout. Garnish with slices of peeled lemon dipped into chopped parsley.

Drink a dry white wine, preferably Muscadet or Gros Plant.

Variation: Add 1 cup chopped flat-leaf (Italian) parsley to the saucepan with the spinach. Omit the almonds. Stuff the trout with the spinach-parsley mixture prepared as above. Cook in the same way but omit the almonds from the butter sauce. Increase the amount of lemon juice in the butter from a squeeze to 1 tablespoon. Sprinkle the trout with a little ground coriander.

PETIT SAUMON SAINT-PATRICK

(Small Salmon St. Patrick)

SERVES 2.

Nowhere in modern French cooking is there such originality as in fish recipes. Yves Pinard, of the Mapotel Président's restaurant Le Toit de Bigorre, gave me his recipe for small stuffed salmon. It is versatile, as it can be made successfully with trout or with a larger fish such as salmon (sea) trout, or even, with a little ingenuity, with a large slice of salmon, boned and stuffed in the middle. Yves Pinard is specially gifted with fish; he has worked at Prunier, in both Paris and London, and with the brilliant André Daguin at the Hôtel de France at Auch. As small salmon are not usually available in the United States, use a 1¼ pound piece of salmon and divide it in two when serving. Or use trout.

2 small salmon or trout, about 9 ounces each
¼ pound fillets of any white fish—halibut, cod, haddock, etc.
Salt, freshly ground pepper
½ teaspoon sweet paprika
1 large egg white, lightly beaten
¾ cup heavy cream
4 cups Fish Stock (see Index), approximately
¼ cup finely chopped shallots
½ cup very dry vermouth, preferably Noilly Prat

Bone the salmon or have the fish store do it. Set the salmon aside. Chop the white fish coarsely and put it into a blender or food processor with the salt and pepper to taste and the paprika. Reduce fish to a purée. Scrape fish out into a bowl and set the bowl over a larger bowl filled with cracked ice. Gradually beat in the egg white, then beat in ¼ cup cream. The mixture should be light and fluffy. Stuff the salmon with the mixture and secure the openings with toothpicks. Pour the fish stock, which should be well seasoned, into a large heavy skillet with a lid. Arrange the fish in the skillet, bring the liquid to a simmer, and cover; poach the fish until it is tender, about 10 minutes, turning carefully halfway through. Simmer a little longer if necessary.

Carefully lift out the fish to a serving dish and keep warm. While the fish is cooking, combine shallots and vermouth in a small heavy saucepan and reduce over low heat until the shallots are just a moist purée. Pour in remaining ½ cup heavy cream and reduce the mixture, stirring from time to time until the sauce coats a spoon. Season with salt and pepper. Nap the fish with the sauce and serve it surrounded by a julienne of vegetables—leeks, carrots, small white turnips, cooked in plain salted water—and accompanied by plain boiled potatoes.

Drink a dry white wine.

ESCALOPES DE SAUMON EN PAPILLOTE

(Salmon Baked in Cooking Parchment)

SERVES 4.

Gérard Ryngel, chef de cuisine of the Mapotel Domaine de la Berthelotière in Nantes, uses scallops of Loire salmon baked in kitchen parchment for this dish. Traditionally the parchment, about 8 by 11 inches, is cut into double heart shapes, then folded over to seal in the contents. The paper is oiled on both sides. The fish is served on individual plates and eaten from the paper cases. If you have good hands and don't mind taking the trouble, this can be quite fun to do. I have found that salmon steaks do as well as salmon scallops, and that foil, which is far easier to handle, does as well as parchment paper. I package salmon for 4 in 1 aluminum-foil parcel, and serve the finished fish and sauce onto individual plates.

¼ pound (1 stick) butter
2 leeks, well washed, using only the white part, cut into julienne
2 medium-size carrots, scraped and cut into julienne
1 medium-size onion, finely chopped
1 celery rib, cut into julienne, or add 1 small rib to the bouquet garni

1 thyme sprig
2 parsley sprigs
1 bay leaf
Salt, freshly ground pepper
1½ cups Muscadet or other dry white wine
4 salmon scallops or steaks, each ¼ pound
Vegetable oil

Heat 4 tablespoons of the butter in a skillet and sauté the leeks, carrots, onion and celery over low heat until the vegetables are soft. Make a *bouquet garni* of the thyme, parsley

118

and bay leaf; add the celery if using it as part of the *bouquet garni*. Add the *bouquet* to the vegetables, and season the mixture with salt and pepper. Pour in the wine. Simmer, uncovered, over very low heat until almost all of the wine has evaporated. Remove and discard the *bouquet garni*.

Oil a piece of aluminum foil large enough to hold the salmon comfortably, and spread on it half of the vegetable mixture. Arrange the salmon on top, cover with the rest of the vegetables, and dot with the rest of the butter. Fold up into a parcel. Put on a baking sheet and bake in a preheated hot oven (425°F.) for 10 minutes. Lift out, open the parcel, and serve onto 4 heated plates.

TRUITE DE MER À L'OSEILLE ET CRESSON

(Salmon [Sea] Trout with Sorrel and Watercress)

SERVES 4.

Chef Michel Devauchelle of the Frantel Hotel's restaurant La Rétirade in Clermont-Ferrand is the inspiration behind this recipe. He is an enthusiastic believer in food based on the freshest of ingredients, never overcooked, and served with airy sauces. The dish is splendid with salmon (sea) trout and very good with any firm-fleshed nonoily white fish. With fresh salmon it is very special indeed.

½ pound sorrel, about 6
   cups tightly packed
   Salt
1 bunch of watercress
   Butter
2 pounds salmon (sea)
   trout fillets, cut into 4
   portions

   Freshly ground pepper
1 recipe Beurre Blanc
   (see Index), made with
   dry white wine and no
   vinegar

(recipe continues)

Wash sorrel thoroughly. Cut away the stems and central veins of the leaves. Stack the leaves, roll them up, and shred them. Drop into a saucepan of briskly boiling salted water and blanch for about 15 seconds. Drain immediately and set aside. Thoroughly wash the watercress and pick it over; remove any yellowish leaves and cut off any coarse stems. Blanch in briskly boiling salted water for 3 minutes. Drain, refresh in cold water, drain again, and squeeze out the moisture. Chop coarsely. Reserve ¼ cup of the sorrel. Purée the rest of the sorrel and the watercress in a blender or food processor. Butter a shallow baking dish and spread it with the sorrel-watercress purée.

Season the fish with salt and pepper and arrange the portions on top of the vegetable purée. Put the dish in a steamer, or *couscoussière,* cover, and steam until fish has lost its translucent look and flakes easily when tested with a fork, for 4 to 5 minutes. Cook for a little longer if necessary but be careful not to overcook.

While the fish is steaming, make the *beurre blanc*. Stir the reserved sorrel into the butter sauce and nap the fish with a little of it. Serve the rest of the sauce separately.

Plain boiled potatoes are a perfect accompaniment. Drink a dry white wine.

TOURTE DE SAUMON

(Salmon Pie)

SERVES 6 TO 8.

This is a luxurious dish. When made with fresh salmon as it was served to me by chef Bernard Passevent of the Relais Gourmand Hôtel de Paris at Moulins-sur-Allier, it is a dish for festive occasions. I've also found it very good made with firm-fleshed nonoily white fish such as halibut or sole, or with red snapper or other fish less costly than fresh salmon. It is a recipe that invites the cook to improvise and innovate.

1 recipe Pâte Feuilletée
  (see Index)
2 pounds fresh salmon,
  or other fish, skinned
  and boned
4 egg whites
1½ cups heavy cream
  Salt, freshly ground
  pepper, cayenne
  pepper

2 tablespoons mixed
  chopped chives,
  chervil and tarragon,
  or other fresh herbs
  such as parsley
2 tablespoons butter
1 whole egg

Make the *pâte feuilletée* and give the dough 2 extra turns. Roll out two thirds of the dough on a floured surface. Drape it over the rolling pin and fit it into a 10-inch pie pan. Trim the pastry and turn the overhang back on the edge of the pan. Roll remaining dough into a ball and refrigerate it, covered. Refrigerate the pie pan, covered.

Halve the salmon. Chop half coarsely and purée it in a blender or food processor or pound it in a mortar. Scrape salmon into a bowl and set the bowl over a larger bowl filled with ice. Beat in 4 egg whites, then the cream, and salt, pepper and cayenne to taste. Fold in the herbs, mixing thoroughly but gently. Take the pie pan from the refrigerator and prick the pastry with a fork all over the bottom. Line with half of the salmon mousse.

Cut remaining salmon into enough small scallops to cover the bottom of the pan. Heat the butter in a skillet and sauté the salmon scallops for about 30 seconds on each side. Cool, and arrange on top of the mousse. Cover with the rest of the mousse. Roll out remaining pastry into a round. Beat the whole egg with 1 tablespoon water and brush the edges of the pastry in the pie pan with the egg wash. Cover with the pastry round. Trim the pastry and crimp the edges together. Brush the top with remaining egg wash. Bake the pie in a preheated moderate oven (350°F.) for 45 minutes, or until golden.

FILET DE SOLE EN COURT-BOUILLON AU TOMATE

(Fillet of Sole Poached in Tomato Stock)

SERVES 4.

This delicate and simple dish can be adapted to fish other than sole. Fillets of any nonoily firm white-fleshed fish can be used.

1 cup Fish Stock (see Index), or clam juice	Salt, freshly ground pepper
½ cup dry white wine	¼ pound (1 stick) butter
½ cup tomato purée	2 tablespoons heavy cream
3 garlic cloves, chopped	1 cup small raw shrimps, peeled
1 pound fillets of sole or other firm, white-fleshed nonoily fish	

In a saucepan combine the fish stock, wine, tomato purée and garlic, and simmer over low heat, uncovered, for 15 to 20 minutes, or until the mixture is reduced to half its volume. Strain and cool.

Season the fish with salt and pepper and fold the fillets in half. Using 1 tablespoon of the butter, generously butter a skillet large enough to hold the fish comfortably. Arrange the fish in the skillet and pour the strained stock over them. Bring to a simmer over moderate heat, and simmer, covered, for about 8 minutes. Lift the fillets to a serving platter and keep warm.

Over moderate heat whisk remaining butter into the sauce, adding each new piece as the previous one is incorporated. Whisk in the cream. Taste, and season with salt and pepper. Add the shrimps and cook for 1 minute longer. Nap the sole with the sauce.

Serve with rice, noodles or boiled potatoes; or serve with a green salad.

SOLE AU VERMOUTH

(Sole with Vermouth)

SERVES 2.

The French have a way with sole that makes this delicious fish into something special. I enjoy this simple dish, perfect for two, though it can easily be doubled. The fish is covered with a velvety sauce lightly flavored with vermouth.

Butter	¼ cup dry white wine
1 tablespoon finely chopped shallot	½ cup reduced Fish Stock (see Index), made from head and bones of sole
2 sole fillets, each about 8 ounces	
Salt, white pepper	¼ pound butter (1 stick), cut into bits
¼ cup dry vermouth	

Butter a flameproof baking dish just large enough to hold the sole fillets comfortably. Sprinkle the dish with the shallot, arrange the fillets on top, and season them lightly with salt and pepper. Pour in the vermouth, wine and fish stock. Bring to a simmer on top of the stove, cover with aluminum foil, and cook in a preheated moderate oven (300°F.) for 10 minutes. Remove dish from the oven and pour the cooking liquid into a small heavy saucepan. Cover the fish and keep it warm (the turned-off oven with the door slightly ajar will do quite well). Reduce the cooking liquid over high heat to ½ cup, then over low heat beat in the butter with a wire whisk. The sauce will be slightly thickened and creamy. Arrange the fish on plates and nap with the sauce.

Serve with plain boiled potatoes, rice or noodles, which may be tossed with a little butter or cream if liked. Green beans or a baked tomato are also good accompaniments. Drink a dry white wine such as Chablis, Pouilly-Fuissé, Pouilly-Fumé, or Muscadet.

DÉLICE DE SOLE Á LA MOUSSE DE TOMATE FRAÎCHE

(Fillets of Sole with Fresh Tomato Mousse)

SERVES 4.

Georges Paineau, who owns and runs the Relais Gourmand Hotel and Michelin two-starred restaurant Le Bretagne at Questembert, is an original and gifted chef. It seems niggly to translate his *délice de sole* simply as fillets when it is really "a deliciousness of sole" in both words and taste.

4 medium-size tomatoes, peeled, seeded and chopped	2 tablespoons finely chopped shallots
Salt, freshly ground pepper	4 large fillets of sole, each about 8 ounces
3 egg whites, lightly beaten	½ cup dry white wine
3 tablespoons butter, approximately	6 tablespoons heavy cream

Put the tomatoes in a small heavy saucepan, preferably enameled cast-iron, and cook uncovered, stirring from time to time, until the mixture is very thick with almost all the moisture evaporated. Do this over low heat ahead of time while doing something else in the kitchen. It does not require much attention. Let the tomatoes cool, season with salt and pepper, and scrape into a bowl set over a larger bowl of crushed ice. Gradually beat in the egg whites, to a mousselike consistency. Refrigerate until ready to use.

Butter an ovenproof dish and sprinkle it with the shallots. Spread half of each fillet of sole with the mousse, then fold over lightly. Arrange fillets in the baking dish. Pour the white wine and cream over the fish. Bake in a preheated moderate oven (350°F.) for 12 to 15 minutes, depending on the thickness of the fillets, or until a fork pierces the flesh easily. Be careful not to overcook. Lift out the fish to a serving platter and keep warm. Pour the liquid into a small saucepan and reduce it over high heat until it is thick, then beat in 2 tablespoons butter, cut into bits. Nap the fish with the sauce.

Serve garnished with small vegetables such as little new potatoes, tiny carrots or turnips, tiny green beans or snow peas. The potatoes, carrots and turnips may be glazed.

BROCHET AUX NOIX

(Pike with Walnuts)

SERVES 6.

Bernard Passevent, gifted chef of the Relais Gourmand Hôtel de Paris at Moulins, gave me this marvelous dish. When I've had trouble getting pike, I've substituted a nonoily firm-fleshed white fish with considerable success.

2½ pounds boneless pike fillets, or fillets of any nonoily white fish
Salt, freshly ground pepper
¼ pound (1 stick) plus 4 tablespoons butter

2 cups heavy cream
¼ cup lemon juice
¾ cup ground walnuts (use shelled green walnuts if available)

(recipe continues)

Pat the fish dry with paper towels and season with salt and pepper. In a large heavy skillet heat ¼ pound butter and sauté the fish until it is golden on both sides, 4 to 5 minutes a side. Lift out the fish and keep it warm. Discard the fat in the skillet. Pour in the cream and let it reduce over moderate heat to half its volume. Cut the 4 tablespoons butter into small bits and whisk them into the cream, adding a new piece as the previous one is incorporated into the sauce. Stir in the lemon juice. Taste the sauce and season with salt and pepper. Stir in the walnuts and cook for a minute to heat through. Pour some of the sauce onto a serving dish and arrange the fillets on top. Nap with the rest of the sauce, or serve the sauce separately in a sauceboat.

Drink a dry white wine.

SANDRE DE LA LOIRE BRAISÉ À LA TOURANGELLE

(Braised Pike Tourangelle)

SERVES 4.

That great chef, and most charming of men, Charles Barrier of Tours, gave me this original recipe. I had some difficulty tracking down the fish but fortunately could call on Alan Davidson's expertise for help. *Sandre* is a pike-perch, a freshwater fish that is found in both European and North American waters. Use the blue pike or its close relative, the walleye. The recipe is so delicious that I'd break all the rules and use any firm-fleshed white fish.

1 blue pike or walleye, 2
    pounds
Salt, freshly ground
    pepper
10 tablespoons butter
2 cups diced carrots
1 cup diced small white
    turnips

1 cup finely chopped
    leeks or onions
½ cup diced celery
1 cup dry white wine
1 cup heavy cream
1 pound cooked green
    beans, tossed in butter

If possible have the fishmonger bone the fish through the back to remove as many bones as possible, otherwise simply remove the backbone. Season the fish with salt and pepper and set it aside.

In a saucepan heat 2 tablespoons of the butter and sauté the carrots, turnips, leeks and celery until the vegetables are soft; cool. Stuff the fish with half of the vegetable mixture and secure the opening with toothpicks. Reserve the remaining vegetables. Place the fish in an ovenproof baking dish. Dot with 4 tablespoons butter and pour the wine over the fish. Bake in a preheated moderate oven (375°F.) for about 30 minutes, basting frequently with the pan juices. Transfer the fish to a serving platter and keep it warm.

Pour the pan juices into a saucepan; add remaining 4 tablespoons butter and the cream. Stir to mix and reduce over high heat to 1½ cups. Nap the fish with the sauce and surround it with the reserved vegetable mixture in small heaps, alternating with small bundles of green beans. Serve remaining sauce in a sauceboat.

Drink a white Sancerre, a Pouilly-Fumé or other dry white wine.

FILET DE TURBOT À L'OSEILLE

(Fish Fillets with Sorrel)

SERVES 4.

The pleasant, slightly acid flavor of sorrel has inspired a number of fish recipes, each one considerably different. I've chosen four of the ones I've most enjoyed. Turbot is not a fish of American waters, but halibut makes an excellent substitute.

We had the great good fortune to be the guests of Hubert Trimbach of the Trimbach Winery when we dined at Le Clos Saint Vincent where the Michelin-starred Relais de Campagne at Ribeauvillé, Alsace, is presided over by chef Bertrand F. Chapotin. It was a memorable experience. M. Chapotin was kind enough to give me two recipes for this book; one for a delicious *rillettes de lapin,* and this one.

1½ pounds halibut fillets, and the head and bones

2 cups dry white wine

3 large onions, finely chopped

2 leeks, well washed, chopped, using white part only

1 head of garlic, unpeeled and halved

Bouquet garni: 6 parsley stalks, 1 thyme sprig, 1 bay leaf and 1 small celery rib

⅛ teaspoon freshly ground white pepper

3 cups water

2 cups heavy cream

Salt

2 cups shredded sorrel

Set the fillets aside. In a large saucepan combine the head and bones of the fish with the wine, onions, leeks, garlic, *bouquet garni* and white pepper. Bring to a boil, and boil uncovered for 5 minutes. Add the water, bring back to a simmer, cover, and simmer over low heat for 45 minutes. Cool the stock slightly and strain through a fine sieve lined with a double layer of dampened cheesecloth. Discard the bones and vegetables.

Pour the fish stock into a heavy flameproof casserole with 1 cup of the cream and simmer, uncovered, until the sauce has thickened slightly. Season the fish with salt and add it to the casserole. Simmer for about 15 minutes. Lift the fish out to a serving dish and keep warm. Add the rest of the cream to the sauce and reduce it over high heat until it is smooth and thickened. Taste for seasoning, adding more salt if necessary. Stir in the sorrel and pour the sauce over the fish.

Plainly boiled potatoes are perfect with this, or serve noodles or rice. Drink a Riesling.

SUPRÊME DE TURBOT À L'OSEILLE

(Fish with Sorrel Sauce)
SERVES 6.

Jean-Claude Leterme of the restaurant Au Bon Vieux Temps in Sedan created this variation on the turbot-sorrel theme. It is subtle and delicious. The sauce can be used successfully with any white fish. I use halibut.

4 tablespoons butter, approximately
½ pound mushrooms, sliced, about 2½ cups
2 cups julienne carrot strips
1 cup julienne celeriac strips
1 leek, well washed, halved and sliced, using white part only
1 cup coarsely chopped mixed parsley, chervil and chives
1½ cups Fish Stock (see Index), made with head and bones of fish
¼ cup chopped shallots
2½ to 3 pounds halibut fillets
Salt, freshly ground pepper
1 cup dry white wine
¾ cup heavy cream
1 tablespoon lemon juice
2 teaspoons cornstarch
2 recipes Sorrel Chiffonade (see Index)

(recipe continues)

Heat 3 tablespoons butter in a skillet and sauté the mush-rooms, carrots, celeriac, leek and mixed herbs over very low heat, covered, for 3 minutes. Pour in the fish stock and sim-mer for 5 minutes. Strain the stock, set the vegetables aside, and reserve the liquid.

Butter a large flameproof baking dish and sprinkle it with the shallots. Arrange the fish fillets on top in overlap-ping layers. Season lightly with salt and pepper and pour in the white wine mixed with ½ cup heavy cream. Cover fish with buttered wax paper and cook at a bare simmer—the liquid should hardly move—for 10 to 15 minutes, or until fish is no longer translucent and is pierced easily with a fork. Be careful not to overcook. Drain off and reserve the cooking liquid; cover the fish and keep it warm.

Pour the liquid from the fish and the reserved liquid from the vegetables into a saucepan and reduce over high heat to 2 cups. Stir in the lemon juice. Mix the cornstarch with ¼ cup cream and stir it into the sauce. Add reserved vegetables to the sauce and simmer just long enough to heat them through, about 1 minute. Place a little sorrel on each of the fillets and arrange the rest of the sorrel round the dish. Nap the fish with the sauce.

Serve with plainly boiled potatoes. If liked, garnish with triangles of fried bread. Drink Riesling, or other dry white wine.

Variations: **FILET DE SOLE À L'OSEILLE** (*SOLE FILLETS WITH SORREL*): Butter a flameproof dish and sprinkle it with 2

tablespoons chopped shallots. Layer the dish with 1 to 1¼ pounds fillets of sole, season fish with salt and pepper, dot with butter, and pour in ¾ to 1 cup dry white wine. The liquid should just reach the top of the fish. Bring the liquid to a simmer on top of the stove, cover with buttered wax paper, and cook in a preheated moderate oven (325°F.) for 10 minutes. Lift the fish to a serving dish, cover, and keep warm. Pour the liquid into a saucepan, add ¼ cup heavy cream, and reduce over high heat until the sauce is quite thick, about 3 minutes. Reduce the heat and whisk in 4 tablespoons butter cut into bits, adding each piece of butter when the previous one has melted into the sauce. Taste for seasoning and add salt and pepper if necessary. Stir in ½ cup sorrel chiffonade and simmer for 1 minute longer. Nap the sole with the sauce and serve with sautéed button mushrooms. Serves 2 or 3.

Bruno Fava, of the luxurious and lovely Bas-Bréau at Barbizon, has an elegant way with fillets of John Dory. I find the recipe works equally well with sole or any firm-fleshed white fish. Butter a skillet and sprinkle it with ¼ cup chopped shallots. Arrange 1½ pounds fillets in the skillet and pour in 1½ cups fish stock, or enough to barely cover the fish. Cover with buttered wax paper and the skillet lid and simmer very gently for 10 minutes. Transfer fish to a serving dish and keep it warm. Add ½ cup dry white wine, ¼ cup dry vermouth and ½ cup heavy cream to the fish stock and reduce it over high heat until it is lightly thickened. Add 1 cup raw sorrel leaves, stems and veins removed and leaves finely shredded, to the sauce. Season with salt and pepper and a little lemon juice and nap the fish with the sauce. Serves 3 or 4.

FILETS DE TURBOTIN À LA MOUTARDE

(Fish Fillets with Mustard)

SERVES 4.

We are lucky to have that splendid fish, the halibut, as a substitute for turbot and turbotin (chicken, or small, turbot). Daniel Léron of Daniel et Denise, an elegant small husband-and-wife restaurant in Lyon, gave me this delicious recipe.

4 halibut fillets, about 2 pounds altogether	4 medium-size tomatoes, peeled, seeded and chopped
Salt, freshly ground pepper	1½ cups dry bread crumbs
2 tablespoons Dijon mustard	¾ cup Fish Stock (see Index)
¼ pound butter (1 stick), approximately	¾ cup dry white wine

Season the fillets with salt and pepper and spread them with the mustard. Butter a flameproof baking dish and arrange the fillets in it. Cover the fish with tomatoes and bread crumbs. Melt 3 tablespoons butter and pour over the fish. Pour in the fish stock and white wine and bring to a bare simmer. Put the dish into a preheated hot oven (425°F.) and cook for 15 minutes, or until the fish flakes easily with a fork. Transfer fish to a serving platter and keep warm.

Pour the cooking liquid into a saucepan and reduce quickly over high heat to 1 cup. Beat in 4 tablespoons butter, cut into bits. Nap the fish with the sauce. If liked, omit the extra butter and nap the fish with the reduced sauce.

Plain boiled potatoes or rice are good with this, and a dry white wine enhances one's pleasure in the dish.

FILETS DE BARBUE "ROSA BONHEUR"

(Fish Fillets, Rosa Bonheur)

SERVES 2.

M. Aubriet, chef at Pierre Duvauchelle's Mapotel Hôtel de l'Aigle Noir in Fontainebleau, is a great teacher as well as a great chef. I find this one of the most attractive of the recipes he gave me. *Barbue,* brill, a smaller, shallow-water version of turbot, does not cross the Atlantic. Fortunately halibut makes a more than adequate substitute.

7 tablespoons butter
¼ cup chopped shallots
1 pound halibut fillets
Salt, freshly ground
pepper
½ cup dry white wine
½ cup Fish Stock (see Index)

2 medium-size carrots, cut into julienne
2 medium-size leeks, well washed, cut into julienne, using white part only

Butter a skillet large enough to hold the fish comfortably. Sprinkle it with the shallots. Arrange the fish in the skillet and season with salt and pepper. Pour in the wine and stock, bring to a bare simmer, cover, and cook over very low heat for 10 minutes.

While the fish is cooking blanch the carrots in boiling salted water for 6 minutes; drain. Heat 1 tablespoon butter

(recipe continues)

in a skillet and sauté the carrots for 2 or 3 minutes. They should still be crisp. Blanch the leeks in boiling salted water for 4 minutes; drain. Sauté leeks in 1 tablespoon butter for 2 or 3 minutes. Set the carrots and leeks aside.

When the fish is cooked, transfer it to a serving platter, cover, and keep warm. Reduce the poaching liquid over high heat to ½ cup. Beat in 4 tablespoons butter, cut into bits, then stir in the carrots and leeks and cook just long enough to heat them through. Pour any liquid that has accumulated on the serving dish into the sauce. Taste for seasoning and add more salt and pepper if necessary. Nap the fish with the sauce.

Variations: If liked, scrape and slice 2 medium-size carrots and boil in salted weater until tender. Drain and purée in a blender, then reheat with 2 tablespoons butter. Make a bed of the carrot purée on the serving platter and top it with the fish and the sauce.

Instead of the leeks I sometimes use a fennel bulb, or young white turnips.

BLANC DE TURBOT AU MIEL ET AUX ORANGES

(Fish Fillets with Honey and Oranges)

SERVES 2.

Chef Truchetet of the Relais et Châteaux Château d'Isenbourg in Rouffach has traveled a great deal to extend his culinary horizons, and his lively interest in food from other cultures gives his own creations a new dimension. This beautifully simple but unusual dish, with its Moroccan influence in the use of honey and oranges, shows this. The small amount of honey adds a subtle flavor to the sauce as well as neutralizing the acid of the orange juice. Halibut makes an admirable substitute for turbot, but fillets of any nonoily white fish may be used.

4 tablespoons butter, approximately
2 tablespoons very finely chopped shallots, or scallions using white part only
2 fillets of halibut or any nonoily white fish, each about ½ pound
Salt, freshly ground pepper

⅓ cup orange juice
1 teaspoon honey
1 cup Sylvaner or other dry white wine
⅓ cup Fish Stock (see Index)
8 segments of peeled and seeded orange
2 tablespoons heavy cream

Butter a flameproof dish just large enough to hold the fish comfortably and sprinkle it with the shallots. Season the fish with salt and pepper and arrange it on top of the shallots. Pour in the orange juice mixed with the honey, wine and fish stock. Bring to a simmer on top of the stove, cover with foil, and bake in a preheated moderate oven (350°F.) for 10 to 15 minutes, or until the fish flakes easily with a fork. Put the fish on a warmed serving dish, surround it with the orange segments, cover, and keep warm in the turned-off oven.

Over high heat reduce the liquid in the baking dish to 1 cup. It will be slightly syrupy. Reduce the heat and beat in 3 tablespoons butter, bit by bit, adding each new piece as the previous one is absorbed into the sauce. Stir in the cream. Season with salt and pepper if necessary. Pour the sauce over the fish and serve it immediately.

Accompany with rice or noodles. An Alsatian Sylvaner is very good with this, or drink any pleasant dry white wine.

TURBOT AVEC D'ORANGE

(Fish with Orange)

SERVES 2.

Jacques Le Divellec of the Relais Gourmand restaurant Le Yachtman in La Rochelle has created an exciting dish with fish and orange. Fillets of halibut or any nonoily white fish are fine for this.

2 fillets of halibut or any nonoily white fish, each about ½ pound
Salt, freshly ground pepper
½ cup orange juice
½ cup Muscadet or other dry white wine
2 slices of orange
6 tiny baby carrots, scraped and boiled
4 baby turnips, peeled and boiled, or 1 large white turnip, peeled, quartered and boiled

2 tablespoons young green peas, cooked
1 leek, white part only, washed and thinly sliced
1 medium-size carrot, scraped and cut into julienne strips
1 tablespoon butter

Season the fish with salt and pepper. In a skillet large enough to hold them comfortably, poach the fish in the orange juice and white wine for 10 minutes, or until the fish flakes easily when tested with a fork. Drain; reserve the cooking liquid. Cover the fish and keep it warm.

Pour the liquid into a saucepan and reduce it over high heat to ½ cup. Pour this sauce onto 2 plates. Arrange the fish on the plates and garnish each with a slice of orange. Divide the carrots, turnips and peas between the plates. While the fish is cooking, combine the leek and julienne of carrot in a small saucepan with the butter and cook, covered, over low heat until they are tender, about 15 minutes. Garnish each plate with a heap of the leek-carrot mixture.

The result is not only appetizing, but extremely pretty.
Drink a Muscadet, Gros Plant, or other dry white wine.

FILETS DE SAINT-PIERRE À L'ESTRAGON

(Fillets of John Dory with Tarragon)

SERVES 4.

I was pleased when M. Renardias of the Hôtel de la Paix in Reims helped me work out this version of one of his restaurant's splendid fish dishes. It is worth searching for fresh tarragon for its subtle flavor, but the dried herb will do.

5 tablespoons butter, approximately

2 pounds fillets of John Dory, or other nonoily white fish

¾ cup dry white wine, preferably a still Champagne

¾ cup Fish Stock (see Index)

Salt, freshly ground pepper

1 tablespoon fresh tarragon leaves, finely chopped, or 1 teaspoon crumbled dried tarragon

1 tablespoon heavy cream

2 teaspoons lemon juice

Butter a flameproof baking dish and arrange the fish in it. Pour the wine and fish stock over the fillets, season with salt and pepper, add the tarragon and the cream, and bring to a simmer on top of the stove. Transfer to a preheated moderate oven (350°F.), cover, and cook for 8 to 10 minutes, or until the fish flakes easily when tested with a fork. Pour the liquid from the fish into a heavy saucepan. Cover the fish and keep it warm.

Reduce the liquid over high heat to half its volume. Stir in the lemon juice, then whisk in 4 tablespoons butter, bit by bit. Nap the fish with the sauce and serve with plainly boiled potatoes.

FLÉTAN AUX NOIX

(Halibut with Walnut Sauce)

SERVES 6.

2½ pounds halibut fillets,
    cut into 6 pieces, or
    use flounder, sole or
    similar fish
    Clarified butter or
    vegetable oil
2 cups heavy cream
    Salt, freshly ground
    pepper

4 tablespoons butter, cut
    into bits
6 tablespoons lemon
    juice
¾ cup shelled walnuts,
    finely ground

Pat the fish dry. Heat enough clarified butter or vegetable oil to cover the bottom of a heavy skillet by about ⅛ inch. Sauté the fish until it is golden on both sides, about 10 minutes. Lift the fish to a warmed serving platter; keep warm. Pour the fat out of the skillet. Pour in the cream and reduce over high heat to 1 cup, about 3 minutes. Season to taste with salt and pepper, then beat in the butter. Add the lemon juice, stir to mix, then add the ground walnuts and cook just long enough to heat the sauce through. Nap the fish with the sauce.

Serve with boiled potatoes, rice or noodles.

FILETS DE FLÉTAN INTERALLIÉ

(Stuffed Halibut Fillets)

SERVES 4.

This is a delicious domestic version of a recipe generously given me by René Lasserre of the Michelin three-star Lasserre in Paris—Suprême de Barbue Interallié. "Stuffed Fillets of Brill" is rather a pedestrian translation of the title, which has more the sense of fillets of brill united by a stuffing. Brill, which is a smaller, shallow-water version of turbot, is not found in American waters, but halibut is a good substitute.

2 pounds halibut fillets, cut into 8 pieces, 4 ounces each
Salt, freshly ground pepper
½ pound scallops, coarsely chopped
1 egg white
2 tablespoons plus 1 cup heavy cream
½ teaspoon minced chervil
1½ cups Fish Stock (see Index)
½ teaspoon lemon juice
¾ cup dry white wine
8 large mushrooms
8 large shrimps
Chopped chervil

Lightly flatten the fillets and season them with salt and pepper. Put the scallops, egg white, 2 tablespoons cream and ½ teaspoon chervil into a food processor fitted with the steel blade, or into a blender, and reduce to a coarse purée. Spread the mixture over half of the fillets and top with the other half. Butter 4 sheets of parchment cooking paper, about 8½ by 11 inches, and parcel up each pair of fillets. Arrange the wrapped fillets in a baking dish and pour in the fish stock, lemon juice and wine. Cook in a preheated moderate oven (350°F.) for 20 minutes. Carefully lift out the fish and unwrap it. Arrange on a platter and keep warm.

Pour the poaching liquid into a saucepan and reduce it over high heat to half. Add remaining 1 cup cream and reduce again over high heat for 2 minutes, or until sauce coats a spoon. Cook the mushrooms in salted and peppered water for 5 minutes and the shrimps for 3 minutes. Arrange mushrooms and shrimps over the fish and pour the sauce over both fish and garnish. Sprinkle with chopped chervil. Serve hot.

SUPRÈME DE TURBOT AUX ASPERGES

(Fish Fillets with Asparagus)

SERVES 6.

Halibut makes a fine substitute for the turbot used in France. This attractive recipe is the creation of Pierre Hiély of the Relais Gourmand restaurant Hiély-Lucullus at Avignon.

2½ pounds halibut fillets	1 medium-size leek, washed, white part thinly sliced
5 tablespoons butter	
2 pounds cooked asparagus	½ cup dry white wine
1 medium-size carrot, peeled and cut into julienne strips	1 cup heavy cream
	Salt, white pepper
1 medium-size white turnip, peeled and cut into julienne strips	

Butter an ovenproof dish and arrange the fish in it. Cut asparagus into tips and stalks, and arrange the tips among the fish fillets. Cook the carrot in boiling salted water until tender but still crisp, about 5 minutes. Cook the turnip in boiling salted water until tender but still crisp, about 3 minutes. Cook the leek in the same way, for about 5 minutes. Drain the vegetables and sprinkle them over the fish. Finely chop the asparagus stalks and set aside.

In a small saucepan reduce the wine and cream over high heat until it is slightly thickened. Stir in the chopped asparagus, then beat in 4 tablespoons butter, bit by bit. Season with salt and white pepper. Cover the fish with the sauce. Cook in a preheated moderate oven (375°F.) for 10 minutes, or until the fish is done. It is important not to overcook the fish.

140

FILET DE BAR AU BASILIC

(Striped Bass Fillets with Fresh Basil)

SERVES 4.

This is another of Jean-Pierre Vullin's recipes from Auberge Bressane. The fresh basil gives it an unusual flavor. Basil is such an easy herb to grow and so rewarding in the kitchen that I always have a pot of it growing.

¼ pound (1 stick) unsalted butter plus butter for skillet
2 pounds fillets of striped bass
Salt, freshly ground white pepper
2 tablespoons chopped shallots
3 tablespoons chopped fresh basil
1 cup Fish Stock (see Index)

1 cup dry white wine
¼ cup white-wine vinegar
8 medium-size mushrooms, sautéed in butter
4 medium-size tomatoes, peeled, seeded, coarsely chopped, and seasoned with salt and pepper

Butter a skillet large enough to hold the fish fillets comfortably. Season the fish with salt and pepper and arrange in the skillet. Sprinkle with the shallots and 1 tablespoon of the basil. Combine fish stock and wine and pour over the fish. Bring the liquid to a simmer over moderate heat, cover, and cook until the fish flakes when tested with a fork, about 4 minutes. Transfer the fish to a platter and keep it warm.

Reduce the cooking liquid over high heat to 1 cup. It will be slightly syrupy. Strain it into a saucepan and add the vinegar. Simmer for a minute or 2, then whisk in the butter, cut into 6 pieces, 1 piece at a time, until the sauce is thick and creamy. Season with salt and pepper and stir in remaining 2 tablespoons of basil. Spoon the sauce over the fish. Surround the fish with the mushrooms, alternating with tablespoons of chopped tomato.

FILET DE RASCASSE AUX CONCOMBRES

(Rascasse Fillets with Cucumber)

SERVES 4.

There are times when, having eaten an exquisite fish in France, I despair at ever reproducing the dish elsewhere. But the ocean is a kinder provider than most of us realize. I went looking for a substitute for the rascasse in this recipe and found a close cousin swimming in North American waters, a member of the Scorpaenidae family. It is not quite as great as its famous relative, the scarlet rascasse used in bouillabaisse, but is worth looking for in fish markets. It is called "blue mouth" and is red with a mouth the color of lead blue. Other useful members of the family are the ocean perch or red perch. The original recipe was given me by the two very gifted young chefs, Jean-Louis Paul and Marc Beaujeu, who with their wives run the Hôtel and Restaurant Bérard at Saint-André-de-Corcy near Lyon.

4 blue mouth fillets, or
    similar firm-fleshed
    white fish, each about
    ½ pound
Salt, freshly ground
    pepper
1 tablespoon finely
    chopped shallot

1 cup dry white wine
1 cup heavy cream
¾ cup strips of unpeeled
    cucumber, about ½ by
    ⅛ inch

Arrange the fillets in a skillet large enough to hold them comfortably and season them with salt and pepper. Sprinkle them with the shallot and pour the wine over them. Bring the liquid to a simmer over moderate heat, reduce the heat to low, and poach the fish until it is just cooked, about 4 minutes. Lift the fish out carefully onto a serving platter

and keep warm. Over high heat reduce the cooking liquid to about 2 tablespoons, then pour in the cream and cucumber strips and bring almost to a boil. Taste for seasoning and add more salt and pepper if necessary. Nap the fish with the sauce.

Serve accompanied by rice or potatoes.

MULET GRILLÉ AU FENOUIL

(Grilled Striped Mullet with Fennel)

SERVES 2.

Striped mullet, also called grey mullet, occurs, fortunately, on both sides of the Atlantic. Ask the fishmonger not to fillet it but to sell it whole. This is a beautifully simple dish that can be broiled or cooked on a charcoal grill. It needs only a green salad as an accompaniment.

Dried fennel stalks, about 10	Salt, freshly ground pepper
1½ pounds striped mullet	1 teaspoon fennel seeds
2 tablespoons Pastis (Pernod, Ricard)	¼ cup olive oil

Line a broiling pan with aluminum foil, brush lightly with oil, and add half of the fennel stalks. Lay the fish on top. Pour half of the Pastis inside the fish and season inside with salt and pepper and the fennel seeds. Pour the rest of the Pastis over the fish, and sprinkle with salt and pepper. Pour half of the olive oil over the fish and top with remaining fennel stalks. Broil about 5 inches from the source of heat for 5 minutes. Turn carefully, pour the remaining oil over fish, and broil for a further 5 minutes.

Drink a Provence wine such as Bandol, or any dry white wine.

ROUGET GRILLÉ AU FENOUIL

(Red Mullet Broiled with Fennel)

SERVES 6.

This is a fine way to use the green feathery fronds of fennel. Though the famous *rouget* of the Mediterranean does not swim all the way to U.S. waters, there are closely related fish that make near equivalents—red mullet, bass and the porgies.

8 or more fennel stalks, fresh or dried	Salt, freshly ground pepper
6 small fish, each 8 to 10 ounces	3 tablespoons Pastis (Pernod, Ricard)
Olive oil	

Make a bed of the fennel in the broiling pan and place a grill over it. Brush the fish with olive oil and season with salt and pepper. Oil the grill and arrange the fish on it. Broil the fish, turning once, for 5 minutes on each side. Remove the broiling pan with its contents from the stove. Set it on a work surface. Warm the Pastis, pour it over the fish, and ignite it. Stand well back as this liqueur can flame quite fiercely. When the flames die down, remove the fish to a serving dish and keep warm.

Strain the liquid in the broiling pan and pour it over the fish. The fish will be perfumed by both the fennel and the Pastis.

Serve, if liked, with Sauce Vert de Martigues (recipe follows).

SAUCE VERT DE MARTIGUES

(Provençal Fish Sauce)

SERVES 6 TO 8.

6 anchovy fillets
1 pound spinach, cooked
  and coarsely chopped
4 tablespoons capers
1 cup cornichons, coarsely
  chopped
2 hard-cooked egg yolks,
  chopped

4 garlic cloves, chopped
⅓ cup Mayonnaise (see
  Index), made with
  olive oil and lemon
  juice
Salt, freshly ground
  pepper

Combine all the ingredients in a food processor, or in a blender in batches, and reduce to a purée. The sauce is also good with any grilled fish, especially red mullet, bass and the porgies.

DAURADE À LA PROVENÇALE

(Red Porgy Provençal Style)

SERVES 6.

Strictly speaking *daurade* should be translated as gilt-head bream but alas, this beautiful fish, which ranges from the Mediterranean to the Bay of Biscay, is not found on the United States side of the Atlantic. However, its very close relative the red porgy does exist on both sides of the ocean. While not as handsome as the *daurade,* which has a golden

(recipe continues)

145

spot on each cheek and a gold crescent between the eyes, the red porgy makes a satisfactory substitute. Chef Lucien Mennetret of the hotel Le Pigonnet in Aix-en-Provence let me have his own recipe for this excellent dish.

3 to 3½ pounds red porgy
  Extra fish bones
  Butter
2 tablespoons finely
  chopped shallots
1 lemon, peeled, thinly
  sliced and seeded
1 cup finely chopped
  mushrooms
4 medium-size tomatoes,
  peeled, seeded and
  chopped
1 small celery heart, finely
  chopped, about 2 cups

2 bay leaves
1 thyme sprig
4 garlic cloves, crushed
  Salt, freshly ground
  pepper
1 cup dry white wine
¼ pound (1 stick) butter,
  cut into bits
2 tablespoons mixed
  chopped fresh herbs
  (parsley, chives,
  tarragon, chervil), or
  use parsley

Have the fish store cut off the head of the porgy and with extra bones make 1 cup fish *fumet* (see Index). Butter an ovenproof dish large enough to hold the fish comfortably. Sprinkle the dish with the shallots, make a layer with the lemon slices, then the mushrooms, tomatoes and celery. On top place the bay leaves and thyme and the crushed garlic. Season with salt and pepper. Lay the fish on top and season it with salt and pepper. Pour the fish *fumet* and the wine over the fish and cover with aluminum foil. Bake in a preheated moderate oven (350°F.) for 30 to 40 minutes. Lift the fish carefully onto a serving platter; 2 spatulas are useful for this. Keep the fish warm.

Remove and discard the thyme and bay leaves from the baking dish. Pour the contents of the dish into a saucepan and reduce over high heat until syrupy, about 4 minutes. Reduce the heat and whisk in the butter. Pour the sauce over the fish and garnish with the herbs.

Serve with rice, noodles or plain boiled potatoes.

POISSON AU FOUR PROVENÇALE

(Baked Fish, Provençal Style)

SERVES 2 OR 3.

1½ pounds bass or similar fish, dressed, but left whole with head and tail on
Salt, freshly ground pepper
Fennel stalks, about 6
1 medium-size onion, finely chopped
1 lemon, peeled and thinly sliced
2 medium-size tomatoes, thinly sliced

2 tablespoons olive oil
½ cup dry white wine
1 cup Fish Stock (see Index), or ½ cup clam juice and ½ cup water
1 tablespoon lemon juice
1 cup Coulis de Tomates Fraîches (see Index)
Chopped parsley

Season the fish with salt and pepper, inside and out. Arrange it in an oiled baking dish and cover with the fennel stalks. Sprinkle with the onion and place the lemon slices down the length of the fish, topped with the sliced tomatoes. Sprinkle with the olive oil and pour the wine over fish. Bake in a preheated moderate oven (350°F.) for 30 minutes, or until the fish is done. During the cooking baste the fish with the fish stock. Lift out the fish to a serving platter and keep warm. Scrape the fennel and lemon and tomato garnish into the pan liquids.

Push the pan liquids through a sieve and transfer to a small saucepan. Pour in the lemon juice and the tomato purée and simmer over moderate heat until the sauce has reduced and thickened slightly. Taste for seasoning; add salt and pepper and a pinch of sugar if necessary. Spoon the sauce over the fish, or serve the sauce separately in a sauceboat.

Serve with boiled potatoes. If liked, sprinkle the fish with chopped parsley.

EMBEURRÉE AUX POISSONS

(Steamed Fish with Cabbage)

SERVES 6 GENEROUSLY.

The translation fails to convey the delicious originality of
this dish created by Serge Coulon, an enthusiastic lover of
fish cookery, at his Michelin-starred restaurant, Chez Serge,
at La Rochelle. There is a splendid bonus as leftovers make
a magnificently satisfying soup for the following day.

3 pounds Savoy cabbage
Salt
½ pound (2 sticks) butter
2 medium-size carrots,
  scraped and chopped
1 medium-size onion,
  finely chopped
5 garlic cloves, minced
½ pound unsmoked
  bacon, chopped
2 cups dry white wine
8 cups Chicken or Beef
  Stock (see Index)
Freshly ground pepper

1 pound each of cod,
  haddock and eel, cut
  into 1-inch pieces (If
  eel is not available,
  increase the cod and
  haddock to 1½
  pounds each.)
10 ounces anglerfish, cut
  into 1-inch pieces
6 scallops
½ cup finely chopped
  parsley
½ pound smoked salmon,
  chopped

Drop the cabbage into a large saucepan filled with boiling
salted water, bring back to a boil over high heat, drain, and
plunge immediately into cold water. Drain and set aside. In
a flameproof casserole large enough to hold the cabbage
comfortably, heat 2 tablespoons of the butter. Add the carrots, onion, 3 garlic cloves and the chopped *unsmoked* bacon
and cook, stirring, for 2 or 3 minutes. Cut the cabbage into
6 wedges and arrange it on top of the other vegetables.
Pour in the wine and the stock, season with salt and pepper,
and bring to a simmer. Cover and transfer to a preheated
slow oven (325°F.) for 2 hours.

About 20 minutes before the cabbage is ready, arrange

the fish, except the smoked salmon, for steaming. First put in the eel and the anglerfish and steam for 10 minutes. Add the cod and haddock to the steamer and steam for 10 minutes longer. Add the scallops and steam for 1 minute. Remove the fish from the steamer. Lift out the cabbage wedges from the casserole and arrange in a serving dish. Place the fish on top of the cabbage, cover, and keep warm.

Pour 1½ cups of the cooking liquid from the cabbage into a small heavy saucepan and reduce it over high heat to half its volume, ¾ cup. Cut the rest of the butter into bits and whisk into the liquid. Stir in the parsley and remaining 2 garlic cloves. Pour the sauce over the fish and cabbage and garnish with the smoked salmon.

For the Soup: If there is enough fish left over to make 2 servings of soup, pour 1 cup of the cooking liquid from the cabbage, adding stock if necessary, into a saucepan. Add ½ cup peeled and coarsely chopped tomatoes, with their juice, or use canned tomatoes, ½ teaspoon whole saffron steeped in a little hot water, and ½ cup dry white wine. Season to taste with salt and pepper and simmer for a minute or 2 to blend the flavors. Add the leftover fish and any sauce and cook just long enough to heat the fish through. Lift the fish out into 2 deep soup bowls and pour the liquid over it. Serve with crusty bread and butter.

GIGOT DE LOTTE AU MOGETTES

(Anglerfish with White Beans)

SERVES 6.

This is one of the inspired dishes that draws people to Chez Serge in La Rochelle where Serge Coulon presides. Innovative and enthusiastic, he is eager to share his recipes. Anglerfish, also called goosefish or monkfish, is becoming increasingly available.

(recipe continues)

6 slices of anglerfish, each
  about 8 ounces
¼ cup Pastis
  Bouquet garni: thyme,
  bay leaf, parsley sprigs
2 cups dried white beans,
  Great Northern or pea
  beans
1 onion, coarsely chopped

1 medium-size carrot,
  scraped and sliced
¼ pound lean salt pork
3 whole heads of garlic,
  peeled
1 cup heavy cream
  Salt, freshly ground
  pepper
4 tablespoons butter

Put the slices of fish in a bowl, pour the Pastis over them, add the *bouquet garni,* and set aside.

In a large saucepan or casserole combine the beans with the onion, carrot and salt pork and enough cold water to cover by about 2 inches. Bring to a simmer, cover, and cook over moderate heat until the beans are tender, about 1½ hours. The time will vary according to how fresh the beans are. Add a little hot water to the beans during the cooking time if necessary. During the last half hour cook uncovered. There should not be a great deal of liquid when the beans are done.

Drop the garlic cloves into briskly boiling water, drain, and repeat the process twice, leaving the garlic just long enough to cook; drain thoroughly. Purée garlic with the cream in a blender or food processor. Season with salt and pepper and set aside.

Lift the fish out of the marinade and pat dry. Heat the butter in a skillet and sauté the fish until it is tender, about 15 minutes. Arrange the fish on a warmed platter, surround it with the drained beans, and nap the fish with the garlic sauce.

BAUDROIE AUX CHAMPIGNONS

(Anglerfish with Mushrooms)

SERVES 2 OR 3.

Gérard Ryngel of the Mapotel Domaine de la Berthelotière is a chef of great originality and, from my point of view, of great generosity since he has shared several of his recipes with me. This is a favorite of mine when anglerfish (goosefish or monkfish) is available. The firm white flesh is perfect with the sharp flavor of anchovy and the mushroom-enriched sauce.

1 anglerfish, head removed, about 1 pound
1 can (1¾ ounces) anchovy fillets, drained and rinsed
Salt, freshly ground pepper
2 tablespoons vegetable oil
1 cup Muscadet or other dry white wine
2 tablespoons and ¼ pound (1 stick) butter
¼ pound button mushrooms, sliced, about 1¼ cups

Skin the anglerfish tail and remove the dorsal fin, or have the fish store do it. Bone the fish, if liked, for easier serving. This is easy to do; the bone can be pulled out with little difficulty. Lard the fish at 1-inch intervals with halved anchovy fillets. Season the fish with salt and pepper. Heat the oil in a flameproof baking dish and sauté the fish over moderately high heat until it is lightly browned on both sides. Pour off and discard the oil. Pour the wine into the baking dish and bring to a simmer. Put the fish into a preheated moderately hot oven (375°F.) and cook for 15 minutes.

While the fish is cooking, heat 2 tablespoons butter in a skillet and sauté the mushrooms over moderate heat for 5 minutes. Set aside.

(recipe continues)

151

Lift the fish out of the baking dish and keep warm. Over high heat reduce the cooking liquid to ⅓ cup. Beat in ¼ pound butter, cut into bits. Stir in the mushrooms and nap the fish with the sauce.

Serve with boiled potatoes or rice and a green vegetable. Drink Muscadet or any dry white wine.

LE RÔTI DE LOTTE TORTINIÈRE

(Braised Anglerfish Tortinière)

SERVES 3 OR 4.

Mme Denise Olivereau-Capron of the Domaine de la Tortinière in Montbazon gave me this interesting and original anglerfish recipe. The fish is also called monkfish or goosefish.

DUXELLES
2 tablespoons butter
1 shallot, finely chopped
½ cup chopped
   mushrooms

Salt, freshly ground
   pepper
2 teaspoons finely
   chopped parsley

MOUSSE
¼ pound salmon, sea
   trout, red mullet or
   similar fish, coarsely
   chopped
1 whole small egg

1 extra egg white
2 tablespoons butter, cut
   into bits
2 tablespoons heavy
   cream

1 anglerfish tail, about 1
   pound
1 cup Fish Stock (see
   Index)

4 tablespoons butter, cut
   into bits
2 tablespoons cream

Make the *duxelles:* In a small saucepan heat the butter and sauté the shallot until soft. Add the mushrooms and cook, stirring, over moderate heat until the mixture is quite dry, about 5 minutes. Season with salt and pepper. Stir in the parsley. Set aside.

Have all the ingredients for the mousse thoroughly chilled. Put the fish into a food processor fitted with the steel blade and reduce it to a purée. With the machine running add the whole egg and the egg white. When eggs are incorporated in the mixture, add 2 tablespoons butter, bit by bit. Add 2 tablespoons cream. Season with salt and pepper. Transfer the mousse to a bowl and chill in the refrigerator. (If not using a food processor, purée the fish in a blender, transfer to a bowl, set the bowl in a larger bowl of cracked ice, and beat in the egg, then the butter, then the cream. Season with salt and pepper and chill.)

Skin the anglerfish, remove the fins and tail, and bone the fish, or have the fish store do it. There will be 2 fillets. Butterfly each by cutting open the fillet lengthwise but do not cut them right through; stop about ⅛ inch from the other side. Open the fillets. Cover with wax paper and flatten the fillets gently with the blade of a large knife. Season with salt and pepper. Spread one of the fillets with the *duxelles,* then top with the mousse. Cover with the other fillet, then tie up as for a roast. Pour the fish stock into a flameproof baking dish. Add the fish and bring to a simmer on top of the stove. Cover with foil and bake in a preheated moderate oven (375°F.) for 20 minutes, or until the fish is tender. Lift out the fish, remove the string it has been trussed with, and keep fish warm on a serving dish.

Pour the liquid into a saucepan and reduce it over high heat to half its volume. Over moderate heat beat in 4 tablespoons butter, bit by bit, adding a new piece as the previous piece is incorporated into the sauce, then beat in 2 tablespoons cream. Taste for seasoning and add salt and pepper if necessary. Slice the fish into serving pieces and nap with the sauce.

Drink a dry white wine.

LOTTE AU MUSCADET

(Anglerfish in Dry White Wine)

SERVES 6.

This is a versatile yet simple dish. It can be dressed up with a garnish of cooked mussels or clams (about 1 pound in the shell), and other fish can be used. Anglerfish is also called monkfish or goosefish.

4 tablespoons butter
2 to 2½ pounds anglerfish, boned and cut into 6 pieces
Salt, freshly ground pepper
1 cup finely chopped shallots or spring onions
4 leeks, well washed, white part only, sliced

1 cup cubed ham
1 cup Muscadet or other dry white wine
1 cup Fish Stock (see Index), or use mussel or clam juice
Lemon juice
2 tablespoons chopped parsley
6 bread triangles, fried in butter (optional)

Heat 2 tablespoons of the butter in a skillet large enough to hold the fish in a single layer. Season the fish with salt and pepper and sauté lightly on both sides. Lift out and reserve. Add remaining 2 tablespoons of butter to the skillet and sauté the shallots and leeks until they are soft but not browned. Return the fish to the skillet, add the ham, pour in the wine and stock, and bring liquid to a gentle simmer. The liquid should barely move. Cover and simmer until the fish is tender, about 15 minutes. Transfer the fish and the ham to a serving dish, cover, and keep warm.

Reduce the liquid in the skillet over high heat to 1½ cups. Taste for seasoning. Add a squeeze or 2 of lemon juice, and salt and pepper if necessary. Nap the fish with the sauce, sprinkle with the parsley, and garnish with the triangles of fried bread, if liked, or serve with potatoes, rice or noodles.

Drink Muscadet, or other dry white wine.

Variations: Use eel or conger eel, sliced, instead of anglerfish and increase the cooking time to 20 to 30 minutes.

Omit the ham and leeks. Butter a baking dish and sprinkle it with 1 cup finely chopped shallots or spring onions and 2 cups finely chopped mushrooms. Add the fish. Pour in ½ cup each of dry white wine and fish stock, or mussel or clam juice, and dot with about 1½ tablespoons butter, cut into bits. Cover, and cook in a preheated moderate oven (375°F.) until the fish is tender when pierced with a fork, 15 to 20 minutes. Sprinkle with parsley and serve with plain boiled potatoes.

Cook the fish as in the master recipe but reduce the liquid in the skillet to 1 instead of 1½ cups. Add ½ cup heavy cream and 2 cups finely chopped mushrooms sautéed in 1 tablespoon butter to the skillet. Stir in 1 tablespoon lemon juice, heat through, and nap the fish with the sauce.

LOTTE AUX MOULES

(Anglerfish with Mussels)

SERVES 4.

3 pounds mussels	1½ pounds anglerfish, cut
4 tablespoons butter	into 4 slices
½ cup finely chopped	Salt, freshly ground
shallots	pepper
1 garlic clove, minced	3 tablespoons lemon
3 tablespoons finely	juice
chopped parsley	⅓ cup heavy cream
1 cup Muscadet or other	
dry white wine	

Thoroughly scrub the mussels, changing the water several times. Scrape off the beards and rinse the mussels, then put them to soak in water to cover for 2 or 3 hours to disgorge any sand. Lift out and rinse again in fresh water. They are now ready to cook.

(recipe continues)

In a large flameproof casserole or heavy saucepan heat 2 tablespoons of the butter and sauté half of the shallots and the garlic over moderate heat until the shallots are soft. Add 2 tablespoons of the parsley, the mussels and the wine. Bring the liquid to a boil, cover, and simmer over moderate heat for 6 minutes, shaking the pan once or twice. Uncover and remove and discard any unopened mussels. Take the opened mussels out of their shells and reserve them. Discard the shells. Strain the liquid through a sieve lined with a double thickness of dampened cheesecloth. Set aside.

Rinse out the casserole or saucepan and dry it. Heat remaining 2 tablespoons of butter in the saucepan, and sauté remaining ¼ cup shallots over moderate heat until soft. Add the fish and sauté for 2 or 3 minutes on both sides. Season with salt and pepper. Pour in the reserved liquid from the mussels, cover, and cook over low heat for 15 to 20 minutes, or until the fish is tender. Lift the fish out to a serving dish and keep it warm.

Over high heat reduce the liquid in the saucepan to 1 cup. Stir in the lemon juice and cream. Taste and add more salt and pepper if necessary. Add the reserved mussels and cook just long enough to heat them through. Pour the sauce over the fish and sprinkle with remaining tablespoon of parsley.

Serve with rice and drink Muscadet, or a dry white wine like Pouilly Fumé.

LOTTE AU CIDRE

(Anglerfish in Cider)

SERVES 2.

Anglerfish tail with its firm lobsterlike texture makes a satisfying main-course dish when cooked in cider with bacon and tiny onions. The fish is also sold as monkfish or goosefish.

1 pound anglerfish tail
1 large garlic clove,
  slivered
  Salt, freshly ground
  pepper
12 small white onions
 6 tablespoons butter
¼ pound (8 slices,
  medium thickness)
  unsmoked bacon

1 thyme sprig
1 bay leaf
1 cup dry cider
2 tablespoons chopped
  parsley

Skin and bone the anglerfish tail and remove the fins, or have the fish store do it. It is very easy to do as there is just a single central bone. Cut the tail into 2 lengthwise fillets. Make small incisions all over the fish and stuff with the garlic slivers. Season with salt and pepper. Set aside.

Drop the onions into briskly boiling water and blanch them for 3 minutes. Drain and remove the skins. Heat 4 tablespoons of the butter in a heavy flameproof casserole or skillet with a lid. (If unsmoked bacon is not available, simmer smoked bacon for 10 minutes, drain, and pat dry before using.) Chop the bacon and add it to the casserole with the onions. Sauté, stirring from time to time, until the onions are lightly browned and the bacon has released its fat. Add the fish and sauté lightly on both sides. Add the thyme, bay leaf and cider, cover, and simmer for about 10 minutes, or until the onions and fish are both tender. Lift out the fish to a serving platter. Using a slotted spoon lift out the onions and bacon bits and arrange them around the fish.

Reduce the cooking liquid over high heat for about 2 minutes, then whisk in remaining 2 tablespoons of butter, cut into bits, adding a new piece of butter as the last one is incorporated into the sauce. Cover the fish with the sauce. Sprinkle with the parsley.

Serve with a green vegetable. If liked, serve with plain boiled potatoes. Drink either a dry white wine such as a Muscadet, or dry cider.

BAUDROIE À L'AÏGO SAU

(Anglerfish Stew)

SERVES 4.

Roland Petrini started his career at 15 working at the Royal Hôtel in Évian, at the Carlton in Cannes and then, at the same time as Paul Bocuse, at the Pyramide in Vienne, before becoming chef de cuisine at the Relais et Châteaux Hôtel Jules César in Arles. I love his cooking and feel privileged that he has helped me with recipes for this book. *Aïgo sau* is Provençal for saltwater, which hardly does justice to this truly splendid dish, but perhaps stew doesn't either. Anglerfish is also called goosefish and monkfish.

3 medium-size potatoes, peeled and cubed	Salt, freshly ground pepper
12 small white onions	2 medium-size tomatoes, peeled, seeded and chopped
12 button mushrooms	
2 garlic cloves, finely chopped	1 pound anglerfish, boned and cut into 4 slices
3 large artichoke hearts, cooked and quartered	1 cup olive oil, plus a little more
Bouquet garni: 2 small pieces of orange peel, 1 bay leaf, 1 fennel sprig, parsley	4 slices of bread
	2 garlic cloves, crushed

In a casserole or heavy saucepan combine the potatoes, onions, mushrooms, chopped garlic, artichoke hearts, *bouquet garni*, salt and pepper to taste, tomatoes, fish, olive oil and enough water barely to cover. Cook at a brisk simmer, uncovered, for 20 minutes and skim as necessary. Remove and discard the *bouquet garni*. Transfer the stew to a tureen.

While the fish is cooking, toast the bread on one side, then rub the untoasted side with crushed garlic and sprinkle each slice with about 1 teaspoon of olive oil, and toast. Serve the garlic toast separately.

Though it flies in the face of tradition I use fish stock instead of water when I have any on hand.

BLANQUETTE DE LOTTE

(Anglerfish Stew)

SERVES 6.

This delicate dish is easy to cook and takes very little time. Serve with Riz Créole (see Index) and drink a dry white wine. Muscadet would be pleasant. A green vegetable such as peas, green beans or artichoke hearts could be served with the fish, or could substitute for the rice. Anglerfish is also called monkfish or goosefish.

3 tablespoons butter	Salt, freshly ground
¼ cup chopped shallots	pepper
½ pound mushrooms,	1 thyme sprig
sliced	2 or 3 parsley stalks
2½ pounds anglerfish,	1 cup heavy cream
boned and cut into 6	Chopped chives,
pieces	parsley or chervil
1 cup wine	

In a skillet large enough to hold all the fish comfortably, heat the butter. Sauté the shallots and mushrooms over moderate heat until shallots are soft but not browned. Add the fish and sauté for 1 minute on each side. Pour in the wine, season with salt and pepper, and add the thyme and parsley stalks. Cover and simmer over low heat for 15 minutes, or until the fish is tender. Arrange the fish on a serving platter and keep warm.

Remove and discard the thyme and parsley stalks. Pour the cream into the skillet and reduce the sauce over high heat until it coats a spoon, about 3 minutes. Nap the fish with the sauce and sprinkle with chopped chives, parsley or chervil.

LA PETITE MARMITE DU PÊCHEUR

(Fisherman's Stew)

SERVES 6 TO 8.

This is one of the happiest creations of M. Aubriet, whom I met when he was chef at the Mapotel Hôtel de l'Aigle Noir in Fontainebleau. It is a family version of a traditional recipe.

1 cup dried pinto beans or dried white beans (Great Northern, Navy or pea)

8 cups Fish Stock, including mussel stock if using fresh or canned mussels (see Index)

4 tablespoons olive oil

1 red and 1 green bell pepper, seeded and cut into julienne

1 large fennel bulb, trimmed and cut into julienne

2 pounds assorted fillets of any firm-fleshed fish, preferably sole, eel, anglerfish, cut into 2-inch pieces

2 squids, dressed and cut into 1-inch slices

Salt, freshly ground pepper

¾ pound cooked fresh mussels, or canned or frozen

¾ pound sea scallops, sliced into halves

Wash and pick over the beans. Put into a saucepan with enough boiling water to cover by about 2 inches and bring back to a boil. Remove from the heat and let the beans stand for 40 minutes to 1 hour. Drain, replace the soaking water with fish stock, and simmer until tender, about 1 hour.

While the beans are cooking, heat the oil in a large skillet with a lid, or in a flameproof casserole. Add the peppers and the fennel. Arrange the pieces of fish and squid on top of the vegetables and sauté over very low heat for 5 minutes. Season to taste with salt and pepper. Pour in 6 cups of fish stock and simmer over low heat for 10 minutes. Add the mussels, scallops and drained beans, and simmer just long enough to cook the scallops, about 2 minutes, and to heat the beans and mussels.

Serve hot with crusty bread; drink a dry white wine. A green salad, cheese and/or fruit is all that is needed to complete the meal.

POISSONS AUX POIREAUX

(Mixed Fish with Leeks)

SERVES 6.

This dish is splendid whether made with an assortment of fish and shellfish, or with a single fish. Choose firm-fleshed white fish fillets and mussels, scallops, clams or large shrimps for the shellfish, using one or two kinds.

3½ pounds leeks
½ pound butter (2 sticks), plus 2 tablespoons
Salt, freshly ground pepper
3 pounds mixed fish fillets such as sole, grey mullet, John Dory, striped bass, tilefish, red snapper

1 pound shucked shellfish such as mussels, clams, scallops, shrimps
1 cup dry white wine

Wash the leeks thoroughly and chop coarsely, using about 2 inches of the green part. In a heavy flameproof casserole melt ½ pound butter; stir in the leeks, season with salt and

(recipe continues)

pepper, and cook over very low heat for 30 minutes, or until leeks are very soft. Stir once or twice to make sure they are not sticking on the bottom of the pan. Roll up the fish fillets or cut them into convenient-size pieces. Arrange the fish on top of the leeks, dot with 2 tablespoons butter, and season lightly with salt and pepper. Pour in the wine. Cover and simmer over low heat for 10 to 15 minutes, or until the fish is almost done. Add the shellfish and cook briefly, just until the shrimps turn pink and the scallops lose their translucent look, 2 or 3 minutes. (Shellfish toughen very quickly if overcooked.)

Serve with boiled potatoes or any starchy vegetable, or with crusty bread and butter.

PETITE MARMITE DIEPPOISE

(Fish Stew, Dieppe Style)

SERVES 6 AS A FIRST COURSE OR THE MAIN COURSE OF A LIGHT MEAL.

3 tablespoons butter
1 medium-size onion, finely chopped
1 leek, well washed, using white part only, chopped
2 medium-size tomatoes, peeled, seeded and chopped
6 cups Fish Stock (see Index)
3 pounds assorted fish, halibut, sole, anglerfish (or substitute bass, haddock or cod), cut into pieces

Salt, freshly ground pepper
½ teaspoon curry powder
½ cup heavy cream
½ pound small shrimps, shelled
1 pound mussels, cooked and shelled

In a large heavy saucepan or flameproof casserole, heat the butter and sauté onion and leek until both are soft. Add the tomatoes and sauté for 1 or 2 minutes longer. Add the fish stock and the fish. Do not add the shrimps or mussels. Season to taste with salt, pepper and curry powder, cover, and simmer over low heat for 10 to 15 minutes, or until the fish is tender. Stir in the cream, add the shrimps and mussels, and cook just long enough to heat them through.

Drink a dry white wine, Muscadet or any white from the Loire.

ASSIETTE DES PÊCHEURS

(Mixed Fish Stew)

SERVES 6.

In no other place is fish cooked with such imagination and subtlety as in France. This deceptively simple dish, the creation of Gérard Ryngel of the Mapotel Domaine de la Berthelotière is a splendid example. I like to serve it as the main course of a leisurely luncheon party.

3 pounds assorted fish such as striped bass, salmon, salmon trout, John Dory, halibut, anglerfish, swordfish, etc., using 6 kinds of fish

1 pound sea scallops

1 pound medium-size shrimps

6 tablespoons butter

2 medium-size carrots, scraped and cut into julienne

2 medium-size leeks, well washed and sliced, using a little of the green part

2 medium-size onions, chopped

2 celery ribs, sliced

1½ cups dry white wine, preferably Muscadet

Salt, freshly ground pepper

2 tablespoons chopped chervil or parsley

(recipe continues)

Have the fishmonger dress and fillet the fish. Keep heads and bones for stock. Rinse the scallops and halve them if they are large. Peel the shrimps and add the heads and shells to the fish heads and bones. Make a stock. Strain the stock and reduce it to 1½ cups. Set the stock and the fish aside.

Heat 2 tablespoons butter in a heavy flameproof casserole large enough to hold all the ingredients. Add the carrots, leeks, onions and celery, and sauté over very low heat until vegetables are soft. Pour in the wine and the reserved fish stock. Season with salt and pepper. Add the fish, cut into 2-inch pieces. If using anglerfish add it 10 minutes before the rest of the fish and let it simmer in the wine and stock mixture; then add the rest of the fish and simmer for about 10 minutes longer, or until the fish is almost done. Add the scallops and the shrimps and cook for 2 or 3 minutes, just until they turn pink. Be careful not to overcook the fish. Transfer the fish, shrimps and scallops to a warmed large tureen, cover, and keep warm.

Measure the liquid in the casserole and reduce it over high heat to 2 cups. Beat in 4 tablespoons butter, cut into bits. Taste for seasoning and add salt and pepper if necessary. Pour the sauce over the fish and sprinkle with the chervil or parsley.

Serve with crusty bread or with boiled potatoes, and drink a dry white wine, preferably Muscadet.

COQUILLES SAINT-JACQUES AU SAFRAN

(Scallops in Saffron Sauce)

SERVES 4 AS A MAIN COURSE, 8 AS A FIRST COURSE.

I am indebted to Jean-Pierre Fava of the Relais et Châteaux Hôtellerie du Bas-Bréau, once Robert Louis Stevenson's house in Barbizon, for this recipe which is as exquisite as it is easy. French scallops, which are larger than ours, are sold with the roe, or coral. In the United States only the edible muscle, the white part, is sold. I find this dish delicious with or without the coral. The important thing to remember is that scallops toughen very quickly if overcooked. Reduce the cooking time for smaller ones. Tiny ones need less than a minute of cooking time.

I also owe Jean-Pierre a debt for his patience in listening to my ideas in the early days of this book, and for his critical comments, help and encouragement.

2 tablespoons finely chopped shallot	Salt, freshly ground pepper
1 medium-size tomato, peeled, seeded and chopped	½ cup dry white wine
	2 pounds scallops
2 tablespoons finely chopped parsley	1 cup heavy cream
	3 tablespoons butter, cut into bits
½ teaspoon whole saffron, crumbled	

In a skillet combine the shallot, tomato, parsley, saffron, salt and pepper to taste and the wine. Bring the mixture to a boil over moderate heat. Add the scallops and cook for 2 minutes, turning the scallops once. Lift out the scallops and place in a serving dish; keep them warm.

Reduce the cooking liquid over high heat to half its volume. Pour in the cream, bring to a boil, and reduce until the mixture is thick, 2 or 3 minutes. Reduce the heat to moderate and whisk in the butter, bit by bit. Pour the sauce over the scallops.

Serve with rice. Accompany with a dry white wine.

To serve 8 as a first course, serve the scallops on triangles of white bread sautéed in clarified butter.

COQUILLES SAINT-JACQUES GEORGES BLANC

(Georges Blanc's Scallops)

SERVES 6.

Georges Blanc who, with his wife Jacqueline, owns the Relais et Châteaux La Mère Blanc in Vonnas (where if you are lucky you can hear nightingales), is a young, gifted, innovative and most generous chef. He gave me a lot of his time for which I am deeply grateful. He also gave me recipes, like this one, delectable and able to be prepared in very little time.

1½ pounds scallops, rinsed and dried	½ cup heavy cream
6 tablespoons butter	1 tablespoon peeled, seeded and chopped tomato
¼ cup finely chopped shallots	Salt, freshly ground pepper
1½ cups dry red wine, preferably a Beaujolais	2 tablespoons finely chopped parsley

If any of the scallops are very large, cut them into halves. In a heavy skillet heat 4 tablespoons of the butter and sauté the scallops over moderate heat for ½ minute a side. Lift out the scallops and keep them warm. In the butter remaining in the skillet sauté the shallots over moderate heat until they are soft but not browned. Pour in the wine and simmer until it is reduced to 1 cup. Stir in the cream and the tomato and season with salt and pepper. Simmer over moderate heat until the sauce is again reduced to 1 cup. Beat in remaining 2 tablespoons butter, cut into bits. Return the scallops to the skillet for just long enough to warm them through. Serve on a hot platter, sprinkled with parsley and surrounded with rice.

MOUCLADE

(Curried Mussels)

SERVES 6.

This is a famous mussel dish from Brittany and the Côte Atlantique. My recipe comes from Jacques Le Divellec of the Relais Gourmand Le Yachtman in La Rochelle, with the unmistakable marks of this chef's originality. I sometimes like to serve the mussels out of the shells in small bowls, and in half the usual quantity, as a first course.

1 recipe Moules à la Marinière (see Index)	1 teaspoon Dijon mustard White wine, if needed
4 tablespoons butter	2 egg yolks
4 tablespoons flour	¼ cup heavy cream
2 teaspoons curry powder	Salt, freshly ground
½ teaspoon cayenne pepper	pepper
	1 tablespoon lemon juice

Make the Moules à la Marinière (Steamed Mussels). Transfer the mussels to a dish; remove and discard the top shells. Keep mussels warm. Strain the liquid through a sieve lined with a double layer of dampened cheesecloth and set aside.

In a heavy saucepan melt the butter and stir in the flour. Cook over low heat, stirring constantly with a wooden spoon, for 2 minutes without letting the mixture take on any color. Stir in the curry powder, cayenne pepper and mustard. Stir in the reserved mussel liquid. There should be 2 cups. Make up the quantity, if necessary, with a little white wine. Cook over low heat, stirring, until the mixture is smooth and thick. Beat the egg yolks and the cream together and stir into the sauce. Cook for 1 or 2 minutes longer. Remove from the heat, taste for seasoning, and add salt and pepper if necessary. Stir in the lemon juice. Nap the mussels with the sauce.

Serve with crusty bread and butter and drink a dry white wine such as Muscadet or Graves.

MEURETTE D'ANGUILLE VIGNERONNE

(Eel in Red Wine)

SERVES 4 TO 6.

I spent a rewarding time in the little Beaujolais village of Pruzilly in an old stone farmhouse lent us by our friends Elizabeth and Tony Curnow. I had the good fortune to meet Gérard Cortembert and his wife who run the Auberge du Cep in nearby Fleurie. I am grateful to this creative chef for his help with this recipe.

3 tablespoons butter	6 peppercorns
2 pounds eel, dressed, skinned and sliced	Salt
	5 garlic cloves
2 tablespoons Cognac or other brandy	½ pound bacon, chopped
	½ pound button mushrooms
3 cups dry red wine, preferably a Beaujolais	½ pound small white onions
1 thyme sprig	4 slices of bread
2 or 3 parsley sprigs	4 teaspoons olive oil
1 small celery rib	½ pound seedless white grapes (optional)
1 carrot, scraped and sliced	

In a large skillet heat 1 tablespoon butter and sauté the eel pieces until they are lightly colored on both sides. Pour off the fat. Warm the Cognac and flame the eel pieces. In a saucepan or flameproof casserole combine the wine, thyme, parsley, celery, carrot and peppercorns. Season to taste with salt. Add the eel and any liquid from the skillet, bring to a simmer, and cook until the eel is tender, about 30 minutes. Crush 4 garlic cloves and stir into the saucepan. Simmer for a few minutes longer. Lift out the eel pieces and keep them warm. Strain the sauce and reduce it over high heat to 1½ cups.

While the eel is cooking, sauté the bacon until crisp. Drain and set aside. Heat 1 tablespoon butter in a small skillet and sauté the mushrooms over moderately high heat until they are lightly browned; set aside. Simmer the onions in salted water to cover in a small saucepan until they are tender. Drain onions and return to the saucepan with 1 tablespoon butter; sauté until onions are golden. Add onions to the sauce with the bacon, mushrooms and eel pieces, and simmer over very low heat for 5 minutes. Taste for seasoning and add salt and pepper if necessary.

Toast the bread on one side. Rub the untoasted side with the remaining garlic clove, halved, and the olive oil and toast until lightly browned. (The bread may be baked in a preheated slow oven (325°F.) for about 30 minutes; season by rubbing the surface with a cut garlic clove and brush with olive oil about halfway through the baking.) Serve toasts with the eel.

If liked, poach the grapes for a few minutes and add to the sauce just before serving.

Variation: For a simpler dish, using conger eel, **DAUBE DE CONGRE** (*EEL STEW*), sauté the eel slices in 2 tablespoons butter in a flameproof casserole until lightly colored on both sides. Lift out and reserve. In the butter remaining sauté 1 medium-size onion, finely chopped. Return the eel to the casserole. Season with salt and freshly ground pepper, and add a thyme sprig, parsley sprig and a bay leaf. Pour in 2 cups dry red wine and simmer until the eel is tender, about 30 minutes. Lift out the eel pieces to a warmed serving platter and reduce the sauce over high heat to 1 cup. The sauce may be enriched by beating in 2 or more tablespoons of butter. Nap the eel with the sauce and serve accompanied by boiled potatoes.

ANGUILLE DES ABBAYES

(Eel, Abbey Style)

SERVES 6.

I'm fond of eel, but it isn't available very often. I have favorite recipes handy and buy it whenever I can. I'm indebted to M. Robert of the Hôtel de France in Poitiers for
giving me this recipe from his kitchens. It makes a grand
party dish for eel-loving friends.

2 pounds eel, dressed, skinned, cut into 6 slices	1 cup dry red wine
	1 cup heavy cream
Salt, freshly ground pepper	1 tablespoon Glace de Viande (see Index)
Flour	18 small white onions, peeled
5 tablespoons butter	2 to 3 tablespoons clarified butter
2½ tablespoons vegetable oil	3 slices of bread, cut into triangles
6 shallots, finely chopped	3 hard-cooked eggs, peeled and halved
2 garlic cloves, minced	2 tablespoons finely chopped parsley
1 pound mushrooms, chopped, reserving 6 for garnish	
2 tablespoons Cognac	
Bouquet garni: 1 thyme sprig, 1 parsley sprig, 1 bay leaf, tied together	

Pat the eel slices dry, season with salt and pepper, and flour
them lightly, shaking to remove the excess. In a flameproof

casserole heat 2 tablespoons butter and 2 tablespoons oil and sauté the eel lightly on both sides. Lift out and set aside. Add shallots, garlic and mushrooms to the casserole and sauté until shallots are soft. Return eel to the casserole and flame with the Cognac. Add the *bouquet garni,* the wine, cream and *glace de viande.* Bring to a simmer, cover, and cook in a preheated moderate oven (350°F.) for 15 to 20 minutes, or until the eel is tender.

Drop the onions into boiling salted water and simmer for 5 minutes. Drain, add 2 tablespoons butter, cover and cook, shaking the saucepan from time to time, until onions are glazed. Add them to the casserole in the oven about halfway through the cooking time.

Heat 1 tablespoon butter and ½ tablespoon vegetable oil in a skillet and sauté the reserved 6 mushrooms until they are lightly browned, about 3 minutes. Set aside.

Heat 2 to 3 tablespoons clarified butter in a skillet and sauté the bread triangles until lightly browned, adding more butter as necessary.

Remove the casserole from the oven. Remove and discard the *bouquet garni.* Arrange the eel slices on a warmed serving platter and spoon a little of the sauce over them. Dip the halved eggs into the sauce and place one on top of each of the slices of eel. Top each egg with a mushroom. Pour the remaining sauce around the eel slices and sprinkle with chopped parsley. Arrange the bread triangles round the dish.

Variation: For a simpler, but no less well-flavored dish, omit the bread, egg and mushroom garnish. Do not cook the onions separately but add them to the casserole and sauté at the same time as the shallots, garlic and chopped mushrooms. Add the 6 mushrooms reserved for the garnish to the casserole, chopped, with the others. Serve with rice or boiled potatoes.

171

LANGOUSTINES AU CHOU

(Rock Lobster Tails with Cabbage)

SERVES 4.

Lunching with Jean-Pierre Billoux at the Relais Gourmand restaurant Bonnevay-Billoux in Digoin was sheer pleasure. There was nothing routine in the tastes that delighted one's palate; so much was fresh and new. When Jean-Pierre gave me recipes to try out at home for this book I found them uncomplicated, their secret lying in the balance of flavors. I cooked this one with rock lobster tails and then again with large shrimps as a substitute. I found 4 large or 3 jumbo shrimps for each lobster tail about right.

1 Savoy cabbage, about 1 pound	1 cup dry red wine
Salt	½ cup red-wine vinegar
½ pound (2 sticks) butter	Freshly ground pepper
¼ cup finely chopped shallots	4 rock lobster tails, or 12 to 16 large shrimps, peeled

Trim the cabbage and cut it into 4 wedges. Drop the cabbage pieces into a large saucepan filled with boiling salted water and blanch for 10 minutes. Drain, refresh quickly with cold water, and drain thoroughly, gently squeezing out any excess water. In the same saucepan heat 4 tablespoons of the butter, add the blanched cabbage, and cook for a few minutes, turning the pieces to absorb all the butter. Keep the cabbage warm.

In a small saucepan heat 2 tablespoons of the butter and sauté the shallots until soft but not browned. Pour in the wine and vinegar and reduce over high heat to ¾ cup. Whisk in 8 tablespoons of the butter, bit by bit, over moderate heat. Season with salt and pepper and keep warm.

Heat remaining 2 tablespoons butter in a skillet and sauté the rock lobster tails or shrimps until done, about 5 minutes for the lobster, 3 or 4 minutes for the shrimps, or just until they turn pink. Arrange the cabbage on a warmed serving platter. Place the lobster tails or shrimps on top, and nap with the sauce.

CALAMARS

(Squids)

SERVES 4.

Jean-Pierre Billoux of the Relais Gourmand restaurant Bonnevay-Billoux in Digoin is a young chef, talented and original. An exquisite dish of his, which I find particularly pleasing for lunch, appears simply as *Calamars,* which gives no notion of how good it is. A word is necessary about the cephalopods, the head-footed sea creatures we know as octopus, cuttlefish and squid. Octopuses are tough and require a lot of cooking to tenderize them, about 3 hours; squids and cuttlefishes mercifully are tender, but they all taste about the same—delicious. Until one is used to squid, it is a good idea to have the fish store dress it.

2 pounds squids, dressed
2 medium-size carrots, scraped and cut into julienne strips
1 leek, well washed, white part coarsely chopped
Salt
1 cup Veal or Chicken Stock (see Index)
1½ cups Fish Stock (see Index)
Freshly ground pepper
½ pound (2 sticks) butter, cut into small bits
4 medium-size tomatoes, peeled, seeded and coarsely chopped

Drop the squids into boiling water and blanch for 1 or 2 minutes. Drain, cool, and cut into thin slices. Put the carrots

(recipe continues)

and leek into a saucepan, cover with salted water, and simmer over moderate heat until they are tender but still crisp, about 8 minutes. Drain. Pour the veal stock and the fish stock into an enameled saucepan and reduce over moderate heat to 1¼ cups. Season with salt and pepper, then whisk in the butter to thicken the sauce. Add the carrots, leek and tomato and bring to a boil over moderate heat. Reduce the heat to low, add the squids, stir, cover, and keep warm until ready to serve.

Serve with rice and a full-bodied red wine.

POULTRY

Nothing surely can ever be as useful in the kitchen as poultry. It is readily available all year round, it is always tender and fresh, and it is reasonably priced. It is easy to cook, and often takes little time; when it needs longer time, it usually does not need watching. Surely no bird is as friendly as the domestic chicken, which welcomes an astonishing variety of garnishes to its stewpot or skillet, grill or broiler pan. It can appear at table as the most elegant, or as the simplest, of dishes and does as well for a dinner party as it does for a simple family meal. I am enchanted to have found new chicken and other poultry dishes, the creations of both gifted chefs and innovative home cooks.

POULET AU CHAMPAGNE

(Chicken in Still Champagne)

SERVES 6.

Chicken is useful either as a standby or a special dish, able to appear in many culinary guises. I'm always glad to have a new chicken dish like this one which I enjoyed at the Hôtel des Berceaux in Épernay. The recipe was given me by chef Jacques Courgnaud, whose family has run the hotel since 1889.

1 chicken, 3 to 3½ pounds, cut into serving pieces
Salt, freshly ground pepper
4 tablespoons clarified butter
2 tablespoons Cognac or other brandy

2 cups dry white wine, preferably a still Champagne
½ cup heavy cream
1 tablespoon tomato purée
Sliced truffles (optional)

Season the chicken pieces with salt and pepper. Heat the clarified butter in a heavy flameproof casserole and sauté the chicken without letting it brown. Cover the casserole and cook chicken over low heat for 20 minutes, or until it is half done. Warm the Cognac, pour it into the casserole, and ignite it. Lift out the chicken and set it aside. Pour the wine into the casserole and reduce it over high heat to half its volume. Add cream and tomato purée; stir to mix. Return chicken to the casserole, cover, and simmer over low heat for 20 minutes longer, or until chicken is tender.

Lift out the chicken pieces to a serving dish and keep warm. The sauce should be quite thick. If necessary, reduce it a little over high heat. Taste for seasoning and add salt and pepper if necessary. Nap the chicken with the sauce and garnish, if liked, with thin slices of truffle.

Serve with Riz Créole (see Index). Drink a still Champagne or any dry white wine.

GOURMAND DE VOLAILLE

(Chicken Stuffed with Pâté de Foie)

SERVES 2 GENEROUSLY.

This elegant dish for two was created by chef Roussel of the Hostellerie Claire-Fontaine at Remiremont. It makes a perfect main course for a meal that starts with a jellied light soup and ends with fresh fruit. Ideally *foie gras* is used for the stuffing and the bird is garnished with slices of truffle, but I have found a really good *pâté de foie* makes a fine stuffing and the truffles are not essential to the success of the dish.

1 whole broiler-fryer, 2½ pounds	2 tablespoons Madeira wine
¾ pound good pâté de foie	2 tablespoons Cognac or other brandy
2 tablespoons butter	Salt, freshly ground pepper
¼ cups chopped shallots or scallions	¼ cup heavy cream
1 cup Brown Stock (see Index)	

Partially bone the chicken: Using poultry shears, cut out the backbone; flatten the bird slightly and lay it skin side down; using a small sharp knife cut away the breast bone and pull out the rib cage; cut off the wing tips. Cut the chicken into halves. Use the backbone, wing tips and rib cage for stock. Stuff each chicken half with some of the *pâté de foie*. Put the chicken halves into a baking pan, stuffed side up, cover loosely with foil, and bake in a preheated moderate oven (350°F.) for 45 minutes. While the chicken is roasting, make the sauce.

In a small saucepan heat the butter. Add the shallots and sauté until soft. Pour in the brown stock, Madeira and Cognac, season to taste with salt and pepper, and simmer over very low heat for 5 minutes. Stir in the cream. Set aside.

(recipe continues)

Take the baking pan from the oven and pour the pan juices into a bowl. Skim off the fat and add the juices to the sauce. Pour the sauce over the chicken halves, cover loosely with foil, and return to the oven for 15 minutes. Serve chicken with the sauce.

Serve with shoestring potatoes, and drink a full-bodied young red wine.

CURRY DE VOLAILLE À L'INDIENNE

(Chicken Curry)

SERVES 4.

French cooks have always embraced any new cooking coming from afar, and this curry is a good example of the process. Though Indian cooks don't care for prepared curry powder, preferring to grind their spices individually, and though tomatoes didn't reach India from Mexico until the 16th century, making them newcomers to Indian classic cuisine, the origin of the dish is clear—Indian and French by adoption. It is a beautiful dish and I am very happy that Jean-Pierre and Bruno Fava of the Relais et Châteaux Hôtellerie du Bas-Bréau at Barbizon understood my interest in the dish and were kind enough to give me the recipe.

2 tablespoons vegetable oil
3 medium-size onions, finely chopped
3 medium-size tomatoes, about 1 pound, peeled, seeded and chopped
1 whole head of garlic, peeled and chopped
2 tablespoons curry powder

1 cup water
2 apples, peeled, cored and cut into dice
1 chicken, 3 to 3½ pounds, quartered
Salt, freshly ground pepper
2 tablespoons clarified butter
1 cup heavy cream

178

In a skillet heat the oil and sauté the onions, tomatoes and garlic until onions are soft. Stir in the curry powder and cook for 2 or 3 minutes, then add 1 cup water and stir to mix. Add the diced apples and bring to a simmer, stirring. Cover and cook over low heat for 30 minutes, stirring from time to time.

Season the chicken pieces with salt and pepper. Heat the clarified butter in a large heavy skillet and sauté chicken pieces until golden brown on both sides. Do this in 2 lots if necessary. Arrange chicken pieces with the legs underneath and the breasts on top, cover, and cook over low heat until chicken is tender, about 30 minutes.

Stir the cream into the curry sauce and simmer for 1 or 2 minutes. Transfer the chicken pieces to a warmed serving platter and cover with the curry sauce. Serve with rice (recipe follows).

RICE WITH ALMONDS AND RAISINS

Sauté 1 medium-size onion, finely chopped, in 2 tablespoons butter over low heat until onion is soft. Combine onion and 1 cup raw rice in a saucepan with ½ teaspoon salt and 2 cups water. Bring to a boil and simmer, covered, over very low heat until the rice is tender and all the liquid absorbed, about 20 minutes for long-grain rice. In a small skillet sauté ½ cup sliced or slivered almonds in 1 tablespoon butter until they are golden brown. Fold the almonds and ½ cup golden raisins into the rice. Serve with the curry.

POULET EN ALICOTTE

(Chicken in White Wine)

SERVES 4 TO 6.

André Rémy and his wife have a delightful small restaurant, Au Bon Pasteur, in Carcassonne. I much enjoyed their cooking, which is typical of the cuisine of Languedoc, and the happy moments I spent in their kitchen. They both studied cooking before their marriage and spent ten years after that working in restaurants in Paris before they felt they were ready to have their own place, cooking the dishes of their own region. In giving me a selection of their favorite recipes, of which this is one, they wish the readers of this book *bon appétit*.

3 tablespoons olive or vegetable oil
4 ounces lean bacon, coarsely chopped
1 chicken, 3 to 3½ pounds, cut into serving pieces
2 tablespoons Cognac or Armagnac
1 medium-size carrot, scraped and thinly sliced

8 garlic cloves, peeled and left whole
¼ cup finely chopped parsley
1½ cups dry white wine
Salt, freshly ground pepper

Heat the oil in a large flameproof casserole and sauté the bacon until lightly browned. Add the chicken pieces and sauté until they are golden brown on both sides. Warm the brandy, pour it over the chicken, and ignite it. Add the carrot, garlic and parsley. Pour in the white wine, season to taste with salt and pepper, and cover. Simmer over low heat until the chicken is tender, about 45 minutes.

FRICASSÉE DE VOLAILLE AU VINAIGRE

(Chicken Fricassee with Vinegar)

SERVES 4.

Many French chefs, very great ones, have their own version of this chicken dish. Two gifted young chefs, Jean-Louis Paul and Marc Beaujeu, who run the Hôtel Bérard restaurant at St.-André-de-Corcy near Lyon gave me their version. It is easy to cook and is delicious. It is a favorite of mine for guests at short notice.

1 chicken, 3½ to 4 pounds, quartered	1 tablespoon finely chopped shallot
Salt, freshly ground pepper	¾ cup red-wine vinegar
6 tablespoons butter	¼ cup peeled, seeded and chopped tomatoes
1 sprig of fresh tarragon, or ¼ teaspoon dried	1 cup Chicken Stock (see Index)

Season the chicken pieces with salt and pepper. Heat 4 tablespoons of the butter in a large heavy skillet with a lid and sauté the chicken pieces until lightly colored on both sides. Pour out and discard the fat in the pan. Add remaining 2 tablespoons of butter, the tarragon and shallot, and cook the chicken over very low heat for about 5 minutes. Raise the heat a little and pour in the vinegar. Let the vinegar reduce for a minute or 2, then add tomatoes and chicken stock. Cover and simmer until the chicken is tender, 30 to 40 minutes. Lift out the chicken pieces to a serving platter. Taste the sauce and add more salt and pepper if necessary. Pour the sauce over the chicken.

Serve with Épinards en Branches au Beurre Noisette (see Index).

POULET AU RIESLING

(Chicken in White Wine)

SERVES 4.

This is one of those dishes that rewards the diners richly for very little work. I think it is the mushroom *fumet* that does it.

½ pound mushrooms, quartered if large, halved if medium, left whole if small
1 tablespoon lemon juice
6 tablespoons butter
¾ cup water
1 chicken, 3 to 3½ pounds, quartered
Salt, freshly ground pepper

1 medium-size onion, finely chopped
1 garlic clove, chopped
1 thyme sprig
1 bay leaf
1 cup Riesling or other dry white wine
½ cup rich Veal or Chicken Stock (see Index)
½ cup heavy cream

In a saucepan combine the mushrooms, lemon juice, 2 tablespoons of the butter and ¾ cup water. Bring to a boil over moderate heat, then simmer, covered, for 5 minutes. Lift out the mushrooms and set them aside. Over high heat, uncovered, reduce the liquid in the saucepan to ½ cup. Set this *fumet* aside.

Season the chicken pieces with salt and pepper. Heat remaining butter in a heavy flameproof casserole and sauté the chicken pieces until they are golden on both sides. Do the chicken in batches; do not crowd the casserole. Set the chicken pieces aside. In the fat remaining in the casserole sauté the onion and garlic until onion is soft but not brown. Return the chicken to the casserole, putting the legs in first, the breasts on top. Add the thyme, bay leaf, Riesling or other white wine, the veal or chicken stock and the reserved mushroom *fumet*. Cover, bring to a simmer, and cook over low heat until chicken is tender, about 45 minutes. Lift the chicken pieces into a serving dish and keep warm.

Reduce the liquid in the casserole over high heat to half its volume. Add the reserved mushrooms and cook just long enough to heat them through. Stir in the cream and warm the sauce, then pour it over the chicken.

Serve with noodles. Drink a Riesling wine or a Sylvaner, or if preferred a young, full-bodied red wine.

POULET AUX CONCOMBRES

(Chicken with Cucumbers)

SERVES 6.

1 chicken, 3 to 3½ pounds, cut into serving pieces
Salt, freshly ground pepper
4 tablespoons clarified butter
¾ cup dry white wine

¾ cup Chicken Stock (see Index)
2 standard medium-size cucumbers, or 1 long hothouse cucumber, about 1 pound
1 cup Coulis de Tomates Fraîches (see Index)

Season the chicken pieces with salt and pepper. Heat the butter in a heavy flameproof casserole and sauté chicken pieces until they are lightly colored. Pour in the wine and stock, bring to a simmer, cover, and simmer for about 30 minutes. Peel the cucumbers and halve them lengthwise. If they have a lot of coarse seeds, scoop them out; otherwise do not seed them. Cut the cucumber halves crosswise into ¼-inch slices. Add the cucumber to the chicken and continue cooking until the chicken is tender, 10 to 15 minutes. Transfer chicken pieces to a serving dish. Using a slotted spoon lift out the cucumber and add it to the chicken. Keep warm.

Over high heat reduce the liquid in the casserole to half its volume. Reduce the heat and stir in the fresh tomato purée. Taste for seasoning and add salt and pepper if necessary. Simmer for 1 or 2 minutes. Nap the chicken with the sauce.

Serve with rice or noodles.

POULET AUX NOISETTES

(Chicken with Hazelnuts)

SERVES 6.

This simple attractive recipe for chicken is the inspiration of Jean Lenoir of the 2-Michelin star Hostellerie Lenoir at Auvillers-les-Forges, where the cooking has elegance wedded to simplicity.

1 chicken, 3 to 3½ pounds, cut into serving pieces
Salt, freshly ground pepper
4 tablespoons clarified butter
½ pound small mushrooms, quartered
1 cup Chicken Stock (see Index)

½ cup Tawny Port
¼ cup heavy cream
1 cup coarsely chopped hazelnuts (filberts), tossed in butter
1 tablespoon chopped parsley

Pat the chicken pieces dry with paper towels and season them with salt and pepper. In a large heavy skillet or flame-proof casserole heat the butter and sauté chicken pieces over moderate heat until they are golden on both sides, about 10 minutes. Add the mushrooms and sauté for a few minutes longer. Pour in the chicken stock and the Port, cover, and simmer until the chicken is tender, about 30 minutes.

Lift the chicken pieces out to a serving dish. Keep warm. Stir the cream into the skillet, taste sauce for seasoning, and add a little salt and pepper if necessary. Add hazelnuts, stir to mix, and spoon the sauce over the chicken. Sprinkle with parsley.

Serve with French fried potatoes. Drink Bouzy red wine, lightly chilled, or chilled white Burgundy.

POULET AUX RAISINS

(Chicken with Grapes)

SERVES 6.

Nothing could be more attractive than this chicken dish, when tender seedless green grapes are in season.

1 chicken, 3 to 3½ pounds, cut into serving pieces
Salt, freshly ground pepper
3 tablespoons clarified butter
2 tablespoons Cognac or any brandy

1½ cups Chicken Stock (see Index), or 1 cup stock and ½ cup dry white wine
¾ pound seedless green grapes
½ cup heavy cream

Season the chicken pieces with salt and pepper. Heat the clarified butter in a skillet and sauté chicken pieces until golden on both sides. As they are done lift them out into a flameproof casserole. Pour the Cognac into the skillet and simmer over low heat, stirring with a wooden spoon to scrape up any brown bits. Pour the skillet contents into the casserole. Add the chicken stock, or mixture of stock and wine, bring to a simmer and simmer, covered, over low heat for about 30 minutes, or until the chicken is almost done. Add the grapes and simmer until chicken is tender, about another 15 minutes. Lift out the chicken to a serving platter. Using a slotted spoon, lift out the grapes and arrange them around the chicken. Keep warm.

Reduce the cooking liquid over high heat to 1 cup. Lower the heat and stir in the cream. Taste for seasoning, adding salt and pepper if necessary. Heat the sauce through over low heat and spoon over the chicken.

Serve with rice, potatoes or noodles.

POULET AU BLANCS DE POIREAUX

(Chicken with Leeks)

SERVES 4.

This deliciously different chicken recipe was given me by the young chef Jean-Paul Bossée, of the Relais et Châteaux Hostellerie La Cheneaudière at Colroy-la-Roche in the Bas-Rhin, not a great distance from Strasbourg. When Jean-Paul does the cooking, he uses young cockerels from a nearby farm; he calls his dish *Coq de Ferme au Blancs de Poireaux.* He agrees with me that broilers are more practical for the average U.S. kitchen.

2 tablespoons vegetable oil
2 broilers, each 2 to 2½ pounds, split
4 tablespoons butter
2 leeks, thoroughly washed, using white part only, thinly sliced
¼ cup chopped shallots
¼ cup Cognac or other brandy
1 cup dry white wine
1 cup heavy cream
Salt, freshly ground pepper

Heat the oil in a large heavy skillet and sauté the chicken halves until golden brown on both sides, about 15 minutes. Do in 2 lots if necessary. Lift out chicken and transfer to a flameproof casserole. Discard any oil remaining in the skillet and wipe it with paper towels. Heat 2 tablespoons of the butter in the skillet, add the leeks and the shallots and cook, covered, over very low heat until they are soft, about 20 minutes. Pour in the Cognac, wine and cream. Season with salt and pepper. Stir to mix and simmer for about a minute. Pour the mixture over the chicken in the casserole, cover, and simmer over low heat until chickens are tender, 15 to 20 minutes. Lift the chicken pieces out to a serving dish and keep warm.

Taste the sauce for seasoning and add salt and pepper if necessary. Beat in remaining 2 tablespoon of butter, bit by bit. Pour the sauce over the chickens and garnish, if liked, with a few slices of leek blanched in salted water.

Serve with plainly cooked baby carrots, baby turnips and green peas. Drink a light fruity red wine.

POULET AU THYM

(Chicken with Thyme)

SERVES 4.

A *couscoussière* is no longer the exotic piece of cookware it once was, but for those without one a colander set into a large deep saucepan makes a good substitute, or a steamer can be used. This recipe from chef Gérard Ryngel of the Mapotel Domaine de la Berthelotière in Nantes-Orvault is beautifully flavored.

6 or more thyme sprigs	1 recipe Beurre Blanc (see
1 chicken, 3 to 3½	Index)
pounds, quartered	2 tablespoons finely
Salt, freshly ground	snipped chives
pepper	
1 cup chopped fresh	
thyme, or ¼ cup dried	

In the top of a *couscoussière* filled with boiling salted water, or in the bottom of a colander or a steamer, put the sprigs of thyme. Season the chicken pieces with salt and pepper and put into the *couscoussière*. Cover chicken with the chopped thyme. Cover the pot and steam the chicken until tender, about 1½ hours. Make the white butter sauce and stir the snipped chives into it. Transfer the chicken pieces to a warm serving dish and nap with the sauce.

POULET À L'ARLÉSIENNE

(Chicken, Arles Style)

SERVES 4.

Chicken is still one of the best buys; since the number of chicken dishes is almost infinite, one can never tire of it. Chef Roland Petrini of the Relais et Châteaux Hôtel Jules César in Arles gave me this recipe, which I had much enjoyed at the hotel one summer. I wait until tomatoes are at their ripest and best, and usually then least expensive, before cooking this.

½ cup olive oil
6 tablespoons butter
1 chicken, 3½ pounds, quartered
2 large onions, finely chopped
4 large garlic cloves, chopped
Salt, freshly ground pepper
1 teaspoon herbes de Provence (summer savory, thyme and marjoram)
1 cup dry white wine
3 pounds tomatoes, peeled, seeded and chopped
2 tablespoons tomato purée
2 tablespoons chopped parsley

In a heavy flameproof casserole heat the oil and butter and sauté the chicken pieces until they are very lightly golden on both sides. Lift chicken out and set aside. Add the onions to the casserole with the garlic and sauté until the onions are soft. Return the chicken pieces to the casserole; season with salt and pepper and the herbs. Pour in the wine and simmer for 1 or 2 minutes. Add tomatoes and tomato purée, cover, and cook for 40 minutes, or until the chicken is tender. Lift out the chicken to a serving dish and keep warm.

Skim any excess fat from the sauce and reduce it over high heat until it is quite thick. Taste for seasoning and add

salt and pepper if necessary. Spoon the sauce over the chicken and sprinkle with the chopped parsley.

Serve with rice or boiled potatoes.

POULET AU POIVRE VERT

(Chicken with Green Peppercorns)

SERVES 4.

Jean Lenoir, the gifted chef of the Hostellerie Lenoir at Au-villers-les-Forges in the Ardennes, with 2 Michelin stars, created this splendid dish.

2 medium-size tomatoes, peeled, seeded and chopped	2 tablespoons Cognac
	¾ cup dry white wine
	¾ cup rich Chicken Stock
Salt	(see Index)
2 tablespoons vegetable oil	1 tablespoon green peppercorns
5 tablespoons butter	
1 chicken, 3 to 3½ pounds, cut into serving pieces	

Put the tomatoes into a small saucepan and simmer over low heat until reduced to ¼ cup. Season with salt. Set aside.

In a heavy flameproof casserole heat the oil and 2 table-spoons butter and sauté the chicken pieces until golden on both sides. Warm the Cognac and flame the chicken. Pour in the wine and stock, the reduced tomato and the green peppercorns, and bring to a simmer on top of the stove. Cover and cook in a preheated moderate oven (350°F.) for 45 minutes, or until the chicken is tender. Lift out the chicken pieces and keep warm.

Over high heat reduce the sauce until it is lightly thickened. Taste and add a little more salt if necessary. For a richer sauce whisk in remaining 3 tablespoons butter, cut into bits. Pour the sauce over the chicken.

Serve with fried potatoes. Bouzy rouge, very lightly chilled, is delicious with this, or drink a Beaujolais-Villages or any similar red wine.

SUPRÊMES DE POULET AUX OIGNONS NOUVEAUX

(Chicken Breasts with Scallions)

SERVES 2.

When I see very fat, fresh green scallions in the market I remember, and then enjoy, this simple and quick-cooking chicken dish which can, of course, be adapted for a quartered chicken. It is also successful made with sour cream instead of sweet cream.

1 whole chicken breast,
   boned and halved
   Salt, freshly ground
    pepper
4 tablespoons butter
2 bunches of scallions,
   about 20, trimmed,
   keeping 2 inches of the
   green part

½ cup dry white wine
½ cup Chicken or Veal
   Stock (see Index)
¼ cup heavy cream

Season the chicken breasts with salt and pepper. In a heavy skillet with a lid, heat 2 tablespoons of the butter and sauté chicken breasts until they are lightly colored on both sides, about 4 minutes. Add the scallions and sauté for about 2 minutes longer. Pour in the white wine and stock, cover, and simmer until chicken is done, about 10 minutes. The breasts are done when they are firm and springy to the touch. It is important not to overcook them as they lose their juiciness.

Lift chicken breasts and scallions to a serving dish and keep warm. Reduce the pan juices over high heat to half. Beat in remaining butter, cut into bits, and stir in the cream. Heat through. Spoon the sauce over the chicken.

Serve with rice.

Variations: After lifting out the chicken breasts and scallions, do *not* reduce the pan juices. Omit the enrichment of butter and cream. Stir in 1 teaspoon Glace de Viande (see Index) and thicken the sauce with 2 teaspoons arrowroot mixed with ¼ cup water. Simmer the sauce for 1 or 2 minutes until it is lightly thickened. Spoon the sauce over the chicken.

Or try this: After lifting out the chicken breasts and scallions, reduce the pan juices over high heat to half their volume. Omit the enrichment of butter and cream. Stir in ½ cup Coulis de Tomates Fraîches (see Index) and simmer just long enough to heat through.

SUPRÈMES DE POULET SAINT-ANTOINE

(Chicken Breasts St. Antoine)

SERVES 6.

This is an opulent dish if truffles are used, but it is very good without them. It is the creation of chef Roger Chaîne of the Mapotel Hostellerie Saint-Antoine at Albi, who says of adding the truffles, "if possible."

4 tablespoons butter	1 cup heavy cream
3 whole chicken breasts, skinned, boned and halved	¾ pound cooked tongue, cut into julienne strips
1½ cups sliced mushrooms	2 ounces truffles, thinly
4 ounces Scotch whisky	sliced (optional)

Heat the butter in a large heavy skillet and sauté the chicken breasts over moderate heat for 10 minutes, turning once. Add the mushrooms, whisky and cream, and cook for 5 minutes longer. Add the tongue, and if possible the truffles, and cook just long enough to heat through.

Serve with rice or noodles. Drink a young, full-bodied red wine.

VOLAILLE À LA CRÈME D'ESTRAGON

(Chicken in Cream Sauce with Tarragon)

SERVES 4.

Nothing could be simpler or more delicious than this poached chicken from Jean-Pierre Vullin of the Auberge Bressane in Bourg-en-Bresse. I like to cook it when there are four of us for dinner, or when we are alone and I want to serve cold chicken breast for lunch the following day.

1 chicken, 3 to 3½ pounds, trussed	Chicken giblets
2 tablespoons whole fresh tarragon leaves	8 cups Chicken Stock (see Index), approximately
Salt, freshly ground pepper	6 tablespoons butter, cut into bits
	1 cup heavy cream

Stuff the cavity of the chicken with 1 tablespoon of the tarragon. Season chicken with salt and pepper. Put the chicken, breast side uppermost, in a heavy flameproof oval casserole large enough to hold it comfortably. Add the chicken giblets to the casserole and pour in the chicken stock, almost to cover. Bring to a simmer over moderate heat, then cover and poach over very low heat so that the cooking liquid barely moves for 45 minutes, or until the chicken is tender. Pour off 3 cups of the stock into a saucepan. Off the heat partially cover the casserole so the chicken will keep warm without cooking further.

Bring the stock in the saucepan to a boil over high heat and reduce it to 1 cup. Lower the heat and whisk in the butter, bit by bit, until the sauce is thick and creamy. Stir in the cream. Taste for seasoning, adding salt and pepper if necessary. Lift the chicken to a warmed serving platter and remove the trussing strings. Nap with a little of the sauce and sprinkle with a few of the tarragon leaves. Stir the remaining leaves into the sauce and serve it separately.

Serve with Riz Créole (see Index).

Variation: Cook 8 baby carrots with the chicken and serve with the chicken.

Strain the remaining stock and refrigerate it. It will have a fine flavor, ideal for soup or sauce.

POULET SAUTÉ À LA CRÈME D'AIL ET AU SYLVANER

(Chicken Sautéed with Garlic and White Alsatian Wine)

SERVES 4.

I am indebted to Chef Gérard Truchetet of the Relais et Châteaux hotel Château d'Isenbourg in Rouffach for this simple but subtly flavored chicken dish and its accompanying potato dish. It is the sort of food that reflects the cooking mood in France today.

2 tablespoons butter
2 tablespoons vegetable oil
1 chicken, 3½ pounds, cut
   into 8 pieces
   Salt, freshly ground
   pepper
1 large garlic clove,
   minced

1 cup Sylvaner or other
   light dry white wine
1 cup heavy cream
2 tablespoons finely
   chopped parsley

In a heavy flameproof casserole heat the butter and oil. Season the chicken pieces with salt and pepper and add to the casserole. Cover and cook for 30 minutes, turning the pieces once. Add the garlic, increase the heat, and cook for 1 or 2 minutes. Add wine and cream and cook, uncovered, over moderate heat until the sauce has reduced and thickened. Sprinkle the chicken with parsley.

Serve accompanied by Gâteau de Pommes au Münster Fermier (see Index). Drink Sylvaner or other light dry white wine.

POULET SAUTÉ GRENOBLOISE

(Chicken Sauté, Grenoble Style)

SERVES 4.

M. Lucien Ogier, a maître-cuisinier for more than 45 years, worked at the Ritz in Paris and at Lucas-Carton, and once, to use his own words, "was under the orders of M. Escoffier." He opened L'Aubergade, a charming restaurant with a lovely garden, at Pontchartrain in 1934. He was kind enough to let me have recipes for dishes I especially enjoyed and which I felt could be successfully cooked at home. This is one that seems to me to fit very well into the modern pattern of living even though it is traditional.

1 chicken, 3 to 3½ pounds, cut into serving pieces Salt, freshly ground pepper 4 tablespoons clarified butter 8 large garlic cloves, unpeeled	½ cup dry white wine 2 medium-size tomatoes, peeled, seeded and chopped ¼ cup Veal or Chicken Stock (see Index) 2 tablespoons butter, cut into bits

Season the chicken pieces with salt and pepper. Heat the clarified butter in a flameproof casserole and sauté the chicken pieces until golden on both sides. Add the garlic cloves. Cover the casserole and cook over moderate heat until the chicken is almost done, about 30 minutes. Pour off most of the fat and deglaze the casserole with the wine. Add the tomatoes, cover the casserole, and cook until the chicken is tender, about 5 minutes. Arrange the chicken pieces on a platter and keep warm.

Pour the veal or chicken stock into the casserole, stir to mix, and add more salt and pepper if necessary. Beat in the raw butter, piece by piece, until the sauce is slightly thick-

ened. Pour the sauce over the chicken and serve. The purée from the garlic cloves is delicious spread on pieces of crusty bread.

Serve with rice or French fries and a green vegetable.

POULET NANTAISE

(Chicken, Nantes Style)

SERVES 4.

1 chicken, 3 to 3½ pounds, cut into serving pieces
Salt, freshly ground pepper
1¾ cups dry white wine, preferably Muscadet
¼ cup dry Madeira wine
4 ounces lean slab bacon, cut into ¼-inch cubes
2 tablespoons butter
½ cup chopped shallots, or 1 medium-size onion, finely chopped
1 garlic clove, chopped

GARNISH
12 small new potatoes, freshly cooked
12 mushroom caps, sautéed in butter
12 cherry tomatoes, sautéed in butter
12 small white onions, sautéed in butter
4 cooked artichoke hearts
12 asparagus stalks, freshly cooked

Season the chicken pieces with salt and pepper and put into a large bowl. Pour in the white wine and Madeira. Marinate the chicken at room temperature for 4 hours, turning once or twice. Lift out the chicken pieces; pat dry with paper towels. Reserve the marinade. Drop the bacon cubes into a saucepan full of briskly boiling water and blanch for 1 minute. Drain. Heat the butter in a flameproof casserole and sauté the bacon cubes until they have released all their fat and are lightly browned. Lift out with a slotted spoon and set aside. In the fat remaining in the casserole sauté the

(recipe continues)

195

chicken pieces lightly on both sides. Lift out and set aside. In the same fat sauté the shallots or onion, and the garlic. Arrange the chicken pieces in the casserole with the legs on the bottom and the breasts on top. Add the bacon cubes. Pour in the marinade, bring to a simmer, cover, and cook over low heat for about 45 minutes, or until the chicken is tender.

Arrange the chicken pieces on a serving platter and surround with the garnish. Keep warm. Reduce the cooking liquid over high heat to 2 cups. Nap the chicken pieces with a little of the sauce and serve the rest in a sauceboat.

POULET BRAISÉ AU SAUCE CRESSON

(Braised Chicken with Watercress Sauce)

SERVES 6.

The watercress sauce with its fresh taste and attractive color makes this braised chicken into something special.

3 slices of bacon,
   unsmoked if possible,
   coarsely chopped
3 tablespoons vegetable oil
2 medium-size carrots,
   scraped and coarsely
   chopped
1 medium-size onion,
   coarsely chopped
1 chicken, 3 to 3½ pounds,
   cut into serving pieces
   Salt, freshly ground
   pepper
1 cup dry white wine
1 cup Chicken Stock (see
   Index)

WATERCRESS SAUCE
2 tablespoons finely
   chopped shallots
4 tablespoons dry white
   wine
1 tablespoon lemon juice
2 bunches of watercress
1 tablespoon snipped
   chives
1 cup heavy cream
   Salt, freshly ground
   pepper

If the bacon is smoked and strongly flavored, blanch it in boiling water for 10 minutes, drain it, and pat dry with paper towels before chopping it. The strong flavor may otherwise overwhelm the dish.

In a skillet heat the oil and sauté the bacon over moderate heat until lightly browned. Using a slotted spoon remove the bacon bits to a flameproof casserole. Add the carrots and the onion to the skillet and sauté over moderate heat, stirring frequently, until onion is soft but not browned. Using a slotted spoon transfer the onion mixture to the casserole. Pat the chicken pieces dry. Season with salt and pepper and sauté, a few pieces at a time, in the fat remaining in the skillet until they are lightly browned all over. Add the chicken to the casserole. Pour off all the fat from the skillet. Pour in the wine and simmer for a minute, scraping to loosen any brown bits. Pour wine deglazing into the casserole. Add the chicken stock and bring to a simmer. Cover the casserole and transfer it to a preheated slow oven (325°F.) for 45 minutes, or until chicken is tender. Lift out chicken pieces to a serving dish, cover, and keep warm. Strain the cooking liquid and set it aside.

Make the watercress sauce: In a small saucepan combine the shallots and white wine. Simmer over low heat until the moisture has almost evaporated, leaving a moist purée. Stir in the lemon juice. Set aside.

Wash and trim the watercress. Drop the cress into boiling salted water and blanch for ½ minute. Drain cress and plunge it into cold water. Drain and cool. In a blender purée watercress with the chives and reduced shallot mixture. Set aside.

Into a saucepan pour 1½ cups of the reserved liquid from cooking the chicken, add the cream, and reduce over high heat to 1½ cups. Stir in 1 cup of the watercress purée. Taste for seasoning, and add salt and pepper if necessary. Do not let the sauce boil. Pour it over the chicken.

Serve with rice, noodles, or boiled potatoes.

Any leftover watercress purée can be frozen, to be used in soups or added to the reduced liquid in which fish has been cooked or added to mashed potatoes.

DINDE FARCIE AUX OEUFS BROUILLÉS ET MARRONS

(Turkey Stuffed with Scrambled Eggs and Chestnuts)

SERVES 8 TO 10.

Although Serge Coulon of the restaurant Chez Serge in La Rochelle is mainly interested in fish and shellfish, he gave me this recipe, his own, for turkey. The stuffing reminds me of South American cooking. It is a useful dish for serving a fairly large group.

1 turkey, 6 to 8 pounds
6 tablespoons butter
½ cup finely chopped shallots
1 tablespoon Cognac
3 eggs, lightly beaten
½ pound cooked chestnuts, coarsely chopped
2 cups freshly made bread crumbs

1 tablespoon finely chopped parsley
1 tablespoon snipped chives
1 teaspoon chopped thyme
1 whole egg
Salt, freshly ground pepper
1 cup dry white wine
½ cup heavy cream

Let the turkey come to room temperature. Chop the liver, heart and gizzard together. In a skillet heat 2 tablespoons of the butter and sauté the giblet mixture with the shallots until the meat is lightly browned and the shallots soft. Warm the Cognac and flame the mixture. In another skillet heat another 2 tablespoons of the butter and scramble the eggs with the chestnuts. In a bowl combine the giblet mixture, the eggs, bread crumbs, parsley, chives, thyme, whole egg, and salt and pepper to taste.

Stuff the turkey with this mixture. Truss the bird and place on a rack in a baking pan. Spread the bird with remaining butter, softened at room temperature. Tent with foil and roast in a preheated moderate oven (325°F.) for between 2 and 2½ hours. Baste every half hour, using the

butter in the baking pan or adding additional butter. When the turkey is done, lift it out onto a hot platter and let it rest for 10 to 15 minutes before carving. Pour the wine into the baking pan and over moderate heat scrape up all the brown bits. Beat in the cream, season to taste with salt and pepper, and pour into a gravy boat.

DINDONNEAU À LA BASQUAISE

(Turkey, Basque Style)

SERVES 4.

4 tablespoons olive oil
　Breast of a small (6- to 8-pound) turkey, cut into 4, or 4 turkey thighs
　Salt, freshly ground pepper
2 medium-size onions, finely chopped
2 garlic cloves, minced

2 large ripe red bell peppers, seeded and coarsely chopped
4 medium-size tomatoes, peeled and chopped
1 bay leaf
1 thyme sprig
2 or 3 parsley sprigs
1 cup dry white wine

Heat the oil in a flameproof casserole. Season the turkey pieces with salt and pepper and sauté in the oil until browned on both sides. Lift out and set aside. Add the onions, garlic and peppers to the casserole, stir to mix, cover, and cook over low heat until onions are soft, about 5 minutes. Add all remaining ingredients, and simmer for a minute or 2. Return the turkey pieces and cook, covered, over low heat until the turkey is tender, about 1½ hours, turning the pieces once during the cooking. Arrange the turkey pieces on a serving dish. If the sauce is very abundant, reduce it over high heat for 3 or 4 minutes.

Serve with Riz Créole (see Index).

199

SALMIS DE PINTADE

(Ragout of Guinea Fowl)

SERVES 4.

This is another of the simple, flavorful dishes Rémy André and his wife of Au Bon Pasteur restaurant in Carcassonne were kind enough to give me. Though the dish is traditional it has evolved in the Andrés' kitchen. When I can't get a guinea fowl, I use a chicken with good results.

1 tablespoon olive or vegetable oil
4 ounces lean bacon or ham, cut into dice
1 guinea fowl or chicken, 2½ to 3 pounds, cut into serving pieces
1 medium-size carrot, scraped and sliced
1 endive, sliced
1 small celery rib, sliced
1 small onion, chopped
1 garlic clove, chopped
1 leaf of Swiss chard, shredded, or use 2 or 3 leaves of spinach

3 cloves
⅛ teaspoon grated nutmeg
3 or 4 parsley sprigs, chopped
Neck, liver and giblets of guinea fowl or chicken, chopped
2 cups dry white wine
1 cup water
Salt, freshly ground pepper
4 slices of bread, fried in olive or vegetable oil

Heat the oil in a flameproof casserole and sauté the bacon or ham until lightly browned. Lift out the meat with a slotted spoon and set aside. In the fat remaining in the pan sauté the guinea fowl or chicken pieces until they are lightly browned on both sides. Lift out and set aside. Return the bacon or ham bits to the casserole and add the carrot, endive, celery, onion, garlic, Swiss chard or spinach, cloves, nutmeg, parsley, and the neck, liver and giblets. Sauté, stirring from time to time, over moderate heat for 3 or 4 minutes. Add the wine, 1 cup water, and salt and pepper to taste. Cook, covered, over low heat for 1 hour.

Remove and discard the cloves. Strain the sauce. Purée the solids with a little of the liquid in a blender or food processor. Pour purée and liquid into the casserole. Add the poultry pieces, cover, and cook over low heat until the bird is tender, about 30 minutes. Arrange the fried bread on plates, with a piece of poultry on top, and pour the sauce over them.

CANARD DUCHAMBAIS

(Duck with Vinegar and Mustard)

SERVES 4 OR 5.

I have to thank François Laustriat and his chef Bernard Passevent of the Hôtel de Paris, a Relais Gourmand, at Moulins-sur-Allier for this and other recipes. They were generosity itself in helping to illuminate for me today's French cooking.

4 slices of unsmoked fat bacon, chopped
¼ cup chopped shallots
1 duckling, 4½ to 5 pounds, cut into serving pieces
2 tablespoons flour
½ cup red-wine vinegar
4 cups dry red wine

Salt, freshly ground pepper
2 tablespoons butter
½ pound pork liver
2 teaspoons prepared mustard, preferably Dijon type
1 cup heavy cream

In a flameproof casserole over moderate heat sauté the bacon until it has released all its fat and is lightly browned. Add the shallots, stir to mix, then add the duckling pieces, in several batches, and sauté until lightly browned on both sides. Remove duckling to a plate. Stir in the flour, then the vinegar, and mix well. Return the duckling pieces to the casserole and pour in the red wine. There should be enough just to cover. Season with salt and pepper. Bring to

(recipe continues)

201

a simmer on top of the stove. Cover and cook in a preheated moderate oven (350°F.) for about 1½ hours, or until duckling is tender. Lift the pieces out of the casserole into a covered serving dish and keep warm. Skim the fat from the casserole and reserve it for another use. Reduce the liquid in the casserole over high heat to half its volume. Set aside.

While the liquid is reducing, heat the butter in a skillet and sauté the liver quickly on both sides. Cover and cook until the liver is done, about 5 minutes or less. Be careful not to overcook it as it should still be pink inside. Purée the liver with any juices in the skillet in a blender or food processor, or pound it in a mortar. Put the puréed liver through a sieve and mix it with the mustard and cream.

When ready to serve the duckling, whisk the liver mixture into the reduced wine mixture in the casserole. Season with a little salt and pepper if necessary. Mask the duckling with some of the sauce and serve the rest in a sauceboat. Serve with sautéed apples (recipe follows).

Sautéed Apples

Peel and core 4 medium-size tart apples and cut them into ¼-inch slices. In a skillet heat 2 tablespoons butter and sauté the apple slices until they are lightly browned on both sides. Sprinkle with a very little cinnamon.

FAISAN BRAISÉ AU PORTO

(Braised Pheasant with Port)

SERVES 4.

This is an interesting way of cooking a pheasant, which is not a bird one eats every day of the week. It makes a most elegant and festive meal for four.

1 pheasant, 2½ pounds
  Salt, freshly ground
    pepper
3 chicken livers, chopped
1 cup fresh bread crumbs
¼ pound finely diced
    unsmoked bacon,
    about ⅔ cup
2 tablespoons finely
    chopped shallots
¼ teaspoon each of dried
    thyme and summer
    savory

½ bay leaf, crumbled
1 large egg, lightly beaten
2 tablespoons clarified
    butter
1 cup Chicken Stock (see
    Index)
⅓ cup Tawny Port
⅔ cup heavy cream
2 tablespoons butter, cut
    into bits

Season the pheasant inside and out with salt and pepper. In a bowl combine the liver of the pheasant, chopped, and the chicken livers with the bread crumbs, bacon dice, shallots, herbs and the egg. Season with salt and pepper and mix thoroughly. Stuff the pheasant with the mixture and truss the bird.

In a heavy skillet heat the clarified butter and sauté the pheasant over moderate heat until it is lightly browned all over. Transfer the bird to a flameproof casserole large enough to hold it comfortably. Pour in the stock, bring it to a simmer over moderate heat, and cover the casserole with buttered wax paper and the lid. Braise pheasant over low heat for about 1 hour, or until it is tender. Lift the pheasant out to a heated serving dish, remove the trussing strings, cover, and keep warm.

Skim any fat from the liquid in the casserole and reduce the liquid over high heat to half its volume. Add the Port and cream and reduce it again to about 1 cup. Whisk in the butter, bit by bit. Taste the sauce and add salt and pepper if necessary. Pour the sauce into a sauceboat and serve with the pheasant.

Serve with rice.

CANETON AU POIVRE VERT

(Duckling with Green Peppercorns)

SERVES 4.

1 duckling, 4½ pounds
  Salt, freshly ground
  pepper
  Giblets, neck and wing
  tips of duckling
1 onion, chopped
1 small carrot, scraped
  and chopped

Bouquet garni: 1 thyme
  sprig, 1 bay leaf, 2
  parsley sprigs
1 cup dry white wine
1 tablespoon green
  peppercorns

Pat the duckling dry with paper towels and prick the fatty parts with a fork. Season inside and out with salt and pepper. Roast in a preheated moderate oven (350°F.) for 1 hour and 20 minutes for a medium rare bird. Lift out to a serving platter and let it stand for 10 minutes before carving.

While the duckling is cooking, make a stock with the giblets, neck, wing tips, onion, carrot and *bouquet garni.* Add salt and pepper to taste and water to cover. Simmer for 1 hour. Strain and measure. Reduce the stock over high heat to 1 cup. Set aside.

Pour the fat from the roasting pan into a small container and keep for later use. Pour the wine into the pan and bring to a simmer over moderately high heat, scraping up all the brown bits. Pour in the reduced stock and simmer over low heat while the duckling is being carved. Pour in any juices from the duckling. Taste for seasoning and add salt if necessary. Stir in the green peppercorns, crushing them a little. Pour the sauce into a sauceboat and serve with the duckling.

Serve with baked potatoes and a green vegetable. Drink a Beaujolais or other light dry red wine.

LE CANETON FAÇON DENISE HENRY

(Duckling à la Denise Henry)

SERVES 4.

This duckling has a most exciting mixture of flavors. It comes from M. Gueret of the Mapotel de Dieppe in Rouen; one can detect in this dish some influence from the French Caribbean.

1 duckling, about 4½ pounds	4 tablespoons butter, cut into bits
Salt, freshly ground pepper	1 teaspoon cane juice or sugar syrup
6 tablespoons rum	1 tablespoon green peppercorns
2 cups dry cider	
½ cup heavy cream	

Season the duckling with salt and pepper and truss it. Prick the skin of the fatty parts with a fork at ½-inch intervals. Put the duckling breast up in a baking pan and roast in a preheated moderate oven (350°F.) for 1 hour and 20 minutes. Remove from the oven and let the duckling stand for 10 minutes. Carve the duckling and arrange the pieces on a warmed serving dish. Warm 4 tablespoons rum and flame the duckling. Cover and keep warm.

Chop up the carcass of the duckling. Spoon off the fat from the baking pan and pour in the cider. Over moderate heat scrape up all the brown bits with a wooden spoon. Add the chopped-up bones and simmer over low heat, stirring from time to time, for 5 minutes. Remove and discard the bones. Reduce the cider to 1 cup, if necessary, then stir in the cream. Beat in the butter, bit by bit, adding each new piece when the previous piece is incorporated into the

(recipe continues)

sauce. Add remaining 2 tablespoons rum and the teaspoon of cane juice or sugar syrup. Add the green peppercorns, season to taste with salt, heat for 1 minute, and pour the sauce over the duckling.

Serve with baked apple slices (recipe follows). Drink a robust red wine such as a Burgundy.

BAKED APPLE SLICES

Peel 4 tart green apples, core them, and slice. Arrange slices in an ovenproof dish. Sprinkle with 1 tablespoon sugar, or less to taste, or use 1 tablespoon cane juice; dot with 2 tablespoons butter. Bake in a preheated moderate oven (350°F.) for 20 to 30 minutes, or until the apples are tender.

CONFIT D'OIE OU DE CANARD

(Preserved Goose or Duck)

Preserved goose or duck is essential for a really authentic *cassoulet*. Either bird is delicious as well because of its pungent, salty flavor. Though goose is really not practical for a small household, a duckling is. Making a *confit* is time-consuming, but no single step is difficult, so it is well worth the extra trouble. The preserved poultry can also be eaten with sautéed potatoes or boiled lentils. Just lift it out of the fat, and heat it through.

1 goose or duckling, cut into serving pieces Coarse salt, 4 to 8 tablespoons	Lard, about 2 pounds

Pull all the loose fat out of the bird. Chop it coarsely and put it into a saucepan with water to cover. Bring to a simmer and skim off any scum that rises. Simmer until the

206

water has evaporated. Pour the fat into a container and refrigerate it until ready to use.

Rub the pieces of goose or duckling with salt on both sides, using about 8 tablespoons for the goose, 4 tablespoons for the duckling. Put the pieces into a terrine, cover loosely, and set in a cool place, or refrigerate. Turn the pieces daily. Leave for 1 to 3 days.

Lift out the pieces of goose or duck and rinse under cold running water. Pat dry with paper towels. Discard the liquid and rinse out and dry the terrine. If the terrine is flameproof, add the reserved goose or duck fat and melt it over low heat. Pack the duck or goose pieces into the terrine. There should be enough fat to cover them completely; if not add lard as needed. If the terrine is not flameproof, use any heavy saucepan that will hold the poultry comfortably. Cover and cook over low heat for 1 to 2½ hours, until poultry is tender. Remove the poultry and set it aside. Simmer the fat until all the moisture has evaporated. Strain the fat through a sieve lined with cheesecloth.

Rinse out and dry the terrine and pack the poultry pieces in it. Pour the strained fat over them, cool, cover, and store in a cool place or in the refrigerator. To use, warm the terrine sufficiently to melt the fat and take out as many pieces as are needed. Make sure the remaining pieces are well covered with fat, and store. Keeps indefinitely.

MEATS

I am impressed with the ingenuity of French chefs and home cooks in creating meat dishes that do not rely on the finer cuts of beef or lamb. Roast beef and grilled or broiled steak or lamb chops are much the same everywhere. I have given only 4 recipes for fillet steak and 2 for beef stew, all of them different enough to be interesting. I found some splendid veal recipes with deliciously new flavors, some good robust lamb dishes and some delightful traditional recipes for ham in aspic, as well as luxurious sweetbread recipes. But for originality it was the rabbit recipes that impressed me most. Rabbit meat is lean and flavorful; it is an easy animal to handle. Excellent quality frozen rabbit, usually already cut up for cooking, is available in many supermarkets. Rabbit has not had the place in our kitchens that it deserves; I hope my small selection of rabbit recipes will go some way to altering this. I also found splendid tripe recipes, a variety meat we have neglected for too long.

LA PIÈCE DE BOEUF AUX SAUTERNES ET AU ROQUEFORT

(Fillet of Beef with Sauternes and Blue Cheese)

SERVES 2.

Many of us are eating less beef than we used to. This recipe from the greatly gifted Gascon chef André Daguin, proprietor of the Mapotel Hôtel de France at Auch, gives a new dimension to steak, turning a simple piece of beef into a magnificently original dish.

1 tablespoon butter	1 cup Sauternes wine
½ tablespoon vegetable oil	1 cup Veal Stock (see
2 fillet steaks, each ½	Index)
pound	2 teaspoons Roquefort
Salt and freshly ground	cheese mashed with 2
pepper	teaspoons butter
1 tablespoon finely	1 tablespoon slivered
chopped shallots	blanched almonds
1 tablespoon snipped chives	

Heat the butter and oil in a heavy skillet and sauté the steaks for 3 minutes a side. They should be rare but can be cooked longer if preferred. Lift out, season with salt and pepper, and keep warm. Pour out and discard the fat in the skillet and wipe it with paper towels. Add shallots and chives, pour in the Sauternes, and reduce over high heat until the wine has almost completely evaporated. Add the veal stock and reduce it over moderately high heat to ½ cup. Beat in the Roquefort-butter mixture. Arrange the steaks on a serving dish, pour the sauce over them and sprinkle them with the almonds.

Serve with broccoli. Drink a good Bordeaux red, a Saint-Émilion or Médoc; a fillet steak is worth it. I also like Cahors, a sturdy red wine from the Lot department of France, but this is a personal preference.

TOURNEDOS AU RAIFORT

(Fillet Steak with Horseradish)

SERVES 6.

This superb recipe was the creation of Claude Praz when he was the chef at the restaurant L'Alsace of the Frantel at Mulhouse. He has twice won awards for creating new dishes—in 1974 and 75. I find his recipes a delight. This one should be served with his Gratin de Poireaux (see Index), which I find a versatile dish.

6 tournedos (tenderloin steaks), each between 6 and 7 ounces Salt, freshly ground pepper 4 tablespoons very finely grated fresh horseradish	6 tablespoons butter 1 tablespoon vegetable oil 1 cup dry white wine, preferably Sylvaner 1 cup Veal or Beef Stock (see Index)

Season the steaks on both sides with salt and pepper, then lightly rub in the horseradish. Let them stand for 15 minutes or longer. When ready to cook, heat 2 tablespoons of the butter and the tablespoon of oil in a heavy skillet large enough to hold all the steaks comfortably, or use 2 skillets and divide the butter and oil between them. Lightly scrape off and reserve the horseradish. Sauté the steaks for 3 to 4 minutes on each side for medium rare. Lift steaks out of the skillet and keep warm. Pour in the wine and stir the pan with a wooden spoon to loosen any brown bits. Let the wine reduce to about half its volume, then add the veal stock and simmer for 1 or 2 minutes. Cut remaining 4 tablespoons butter into bits and whisk them into the wine and stock mixture, one at a time, adding a new piece as the previous piece is incorporated into the sauce. Stir in the reserved horseradish. Taste for seasoning and add salt and pepper if necessary. Nap the steaks with a little of the sauce and serve the rest separately in a sauceboat.

DAUBE À L'ALBIGEOISE

(Beef Stew Albi Style)

SERVES 6 TO 8.

M. Rieux of the Mapotel Hostellerie Saint-Antoine gave me this recipe for beef stew. Nothing is more satisfying than a good beef stew. This one is especially rewarding, enriched as it is by the calf's foot and the pig's foot. In a pinch, I've used 2 pig's feet when no calf's feet were to be had. There is the same gelatinous enrichment to the gravy. It is a gravy that cries out for bread to be dipped into it.

4 tablespoons lard or vegetable oil
2 pounds rump steak, cut into 2-inch cubes
4 medium-size carrots, peeled and sliced
2 medium-size onions, coarsely chopped
Bouquet garni: 2 or 3 parsley sprigs, 1 bay leaf, 1 thyme sprig

1 calf's foot, halved
1 pig's foot, halved
1 cup chopped fresh pork rinds
5 garlic cloves, peeled
4 cups dry red wine
Salt, freshly ground pepper

In a large, heavy flameproof casserole heat the lard or oil and sauté the steak, carrots and onions until the meat is lightly browned. Add the *bouquet garni,* the calf's foot, pig's foot, pork rinds, garlic and wine. Season with salt and pepper. Cover, and simmer over the lowest possible heat for 3 to 4 hours. Lift out the calf's and pig's feet; allow them to cool, then bone and cut into pieces. Return the pieces to the casserole and heat through before serving.

Serve with noodles or with whole boiled potatoes.

DAUBE DE BOEUF PROVENÇAL

(Provençal Beef Stew with Olives)

SERVES 8 GENEROUSLY

If I wanted to celebrate beef stew with homage to a single recipe, this is the one I would choose. I thank friends from Provence for helping me work it out. It is a great family dish, and a great party dish, and it is better if it is made ahead of time and reheated on the day you serve it.

3 tablespoons olive or vegetable oil
4 slices of bacon, chopped
4 pounds beef chuck or round, cut into 2-inch cubes
2 medium-size onions, finely chopped
2 garlic cloves, minced
2 medium-size carrots, scraped and chopped
¼ pound mushrooms, sliced
2 medium-size tomatoes, peeled and chopped

1 cup each of pitted black and green olives
Bouquet garni: ½ teaspoon thyme, ½ teaspoon rosemary, 1 bay leaf, 1½-inch strip of orange peel, 3 parsley sprigs, tied in a square of cheesecloth
3 cups dry red wine
Salt, freshly ground pepper
1 tablespoon butter
1 tablespoon flour

Heat the oil in a large skillet and sauté the bacon over moderately high heat until the pieces are crisp. Lift them out with a slotted spoon and transfer to a flameproof casserole. In the fat remaining in the pan sauté the beef, patted dry with paper towels, until it is lightly browned all over. Add it to the bacon. In the fat remaining in the pan, adding a little more oil if necessary, sauté the onions, garlic, carrots and mushrooms until the vegetables are soft. Add to the casserole with the tomatoes. If the olives are very salty, soak them in cold water for 10 minutes before adding them to

(recipe continues)

the casserole. Otherwise just rinse them thoroughly. Add the *bouquet garni.* Pour the wine into the skillet and bring it to a simmer over moderate heat. Scrape up all the brown bits and pour the wine deglazing into the casserole. Season beef and liquid with salt and pepper. Let the mixture marinate, covered, in a cool place or in the refrigerator overnight, turning it occasionally.

Let the casserole stand for at least 2 hours before cooking to come to room temperature. Bring to a simmer on top of the stove, cover with aluminum foil, then with the lid, and cook in a preheated slow oven (300°F.) for 2½ hours, or until the beef is tender.

Take the *daube* out of the oven. Remove and discard the cheesecloth bag with the *bouquet garni.* Skim the fat from the sauce. Mix the flour and butter together to make *beurre manié* and stir it, bit by bit, into the stew. Simmer gently until the sauce is thickened. Serve from the casserole or transfer to a warmed tureen or serving dish.

Serve with buttered noodles, or potatoes sprinkled with parsley, or rice.

The dish can be cooked ahead of time for 2 hours the previous day, to be finished on the day you serve it.

COEUR DE FILET AU POIVRE VERT

(Fillet Steak with Green Peppercorns)

SERVES 2.

We are all of us familiar with black peppercorns, the green sun-dried berries of *Piper nigrum,* and white peppercorns, the sun-dried ripe berries, but it was only about 10 years ago that the green peppercorns in their soft undried state were exported from Madagascar all over the world. French cooks took to the new spice as this recipe from chef Daniel Léron of the restaurant Daniel et Denise in Lyon shows. It is a lovely way to honor a fine piece of fillet of beef.

3 tablespoons butter
½ tablespoon vegetable oil
2 fillet steaks, 1 inch thick, each about ½ pound
Salt, freshly ground pepper
2 tablespoons dried currants

1 tablespoon green peppercorns
2 tablespoons Cognac
½ cup Beef Stock (see Index)

Heat 1 tablespoon butter and the oil in a heavy skillet and sauté the steaks over moderately high heat for 3 to 4 minutes a side for medium rare, or less or more time according to taste. Lift out, season with salt and pepper, and keep warm.

Drop the currants into a small saucepan of boiling water and blanch for 1 minute. Drain. In the fat remaining in the skillet sauté the currants and green peppercorns over very low heat for 1 minute. Remove from the heat. Warm the Cognac and flame the currants and peppercorns. Add the beef stock, bring to a simmer over moderate heat, and whisk in remaining butter in bits, adding a new piece as soon as the previous piece has been absorbed into the sauce. Taste for seasoning and add salt and pepper if necessary. Pour sauce over the steaks and serve immediately.

A puréed vegetable, potatoes, glazed carrots, mushrooms or broiled tomatoes are all suitable accompaniments to the steaks. Drink a good red wine such as a Médoc, a Côtes-du-Rhône, or Beaujolais-Villages.

PIÈCE DE CHAROLAIS À LA BEAUJOLAISE

(Fillet Steak with Beaujolais Sauce)

SERVES 4.

Daniel Robin of Chénas in the Beaujolais honors a fine piece of beef by cooking it in the simplest possible way and serving it with a small quantity of fine sauce.

2 cups Veal or Beef Stock (see Index)	1 tablespoon chopped shallot or scallion
2 medium-size onions, finely chopped	4 tablespoons butter
1 carrot, scraped and chopped	1½ pounds fillet steak, in 1 piece
1 cup Beaujolais or other dry red wine	Salt, freshly ground pepper

In a saucepan combine the veal or beef stock with the onions and carrot and simmer, partially covered, for 1 hour, or until vegetables are very soft and stock has reduced. Strain the stock, discarding the vegetables, and measure it. If necessary reduce it to 1 cup over high heat. Set it aside.

In a small saucepan combine the wine with the shallot and simmer until the wine is reduced to half. Add to the strained veal or beef stock.

Heat the butter in a roasting pan and quickly brown the fillet of beef all over. Roast the beef in a preheated hot oven (475°F) for 12 minutes for rare, 20 minutes for medium. Lift out the beef and place on a heated serving platter. Pour the stock and wine mixture into the roasting pan and reduce over high heat to 1 cup, stirring with a wooden spoon to scrape up all the brown bits. Season to taste with salt and pepper and nap the steak with the sauce.

Serve with French fried or matchstick potatoes, grilled whole small tomatoes, whole sautéed mushrooms and plain boiled green beans tossed with a little butter. Drink a Beaujolais or other young, full-bodied red wine.

PÂTÉ DE QUEUE DE BOEUF

(Oxtail Pâté)

SERVES 4 TO 6.

Oxtail is rich, flavorful and inexpensive, but it does require long slow cooking. A most gifted young French chef, Christian Delteil, now working at the Chewton Glen Hotel in Hampshire, England, has created this pâté which I like as the main course of a spring or summer luncheon, though properly speaking it is meant to be a first course. It is not only appetizing, but most attractive to look at.

3 pounds oxtail
  Salt, freshly ground
    pepper
1 medium-size carrot,
    scraped and sliced
1 medium-size onion,
    coarsely chopped
1 cup dry red wine
3 cups Beef Stock (see
    Index)
6 baby carrots, scraped
    and trimmed
1 bunch of scallions,
    trimmed, using some
    of the green part

½ pound whole green
    beans
10 small white onions
½ pound young white
    turnips, peeled and
    diced
4 tablespoons mixed
    chopped fresh herbs
    (chives, parsley,
    tarragon, chervil,
    basil, or whatever is
    available)
  Lettuce or watercress
    for garnish

In a flameproof casserole combine the oxtail, salt and pepper to taste, the sliced carrot and chopped onion with the wine and stock. Bring to a boil on top of the stove and cook, covered, in a preheated slow oven (300°F.) for 3 hours, or until oxtail is very tender. Remove from the oven. When oxtail pieces are cool enough to handle, shred meat from the bones and put meat into a bowl. Strain and reserve the stock.

(recipe continues)

217

Meanwhile cook the other vegetables in salted water until they are tender but still crisp. In an 8-cup mold, rinsed out in cold water, make a layer of the oxtail and sprinkle it with the herbs. Cover with a layer of carrots, scallions, green beans, onion and turnip, then make another layer of oxtail. If liked, make more than 1 layer of the vegetables, dividing up the meat and vegetables. Measure out 2 cups of the stock. Check if the stock will jell by putting a little on a saucer in the freezer. Oxtail is very gelatinous but the stock may need the addition of a little gelatin. If it does, soften 1 envelope unflavored gelatin (7 grams) in a little water and stir it into 1 cup of the stock, heated in a small saucepan. Dissolve the gelatin and mix it with the rest of the stock. Pour the stock over the oxtail in the mold, letting the liquid seep through to the bottom. Chill in the refrigerator until aspic is set.

Unmold on a platter garnished with lettuce or watercress.

Serve with Sauce Gribiche (recipe follows). Drink a Beaujolais or any fresh young red wine, or in summer weather a chilled *vin rosé*.

If serving the pâté as a main course, add a potato salad and a salad of sliced tomatoes, or whatever is liked.

SAUCE GRIBICHE

3 hard-cooked eggs, separated
Salt, freshly ground pepper
2 tablespoons white-wine or cider vinegar
¾ cup vegetable oil

1 tablespoon mixed chopped parsley, chervil and tarragon
1 teaspoon chopped capers
2 tablespoons chopped gherkins

Put the egg yolks into a bowl and mash them with salt and pepper to taste and the vinegar. Add the oil, drop by drop as if making mayonnaise. Add the herbs, capers, gherkins and the finely chopped egg whites.

ESCALOPES DE VEAU AUX AVOCATS ET COURGETTES

(Veal Scallops with Avocado and Zucchini)

SERVES 6.

Bernard Revire is a greatly talented Provençal chef. This delicious and unusual dish is one of his creations.

6 veal scallops, each 6 to 8 ounces
Salt, freshly ground pepper
Flour
¼ pound (1 stick) butter, approximately
1 tablespoon vegetable oil
3 medium-size avocados, peeled and sliced
3 medium-size tomatoes, peeled and sliced

½ pound Gruyère cheese, grated, about 2 cups
2 cups Veal or Chicken Stock (see Index)
¼ cup Tawny Port
2 pounds zucchini, chopped
2 garlic cloves, crushed
1 cup chopped parsley

Have the butcher flatten the scallops to ¼-inch thickness. Season the scallops with salt and pepper and dust lightly with flour. In a skillet heat 2 tablespoons of the butter and the oil and sauté the scallops until lightly browned on both sides, about 4 minutes a side. Do this in batches so as not to overcrowd the skillet. Add more butter and oil if necessary. Transfer the scallops to a buttered baking dish.

Arrange the avocado slices on top of the scallops and top with the tomato slices. Season with salt and pepper, sprinkle with the cheese, and dot with about 2 tablespoons butter. Bake in a preheated hot oven (400°F.) for about 10 minutes, or until the cheese is lightly browned.

(recipe continues)

Meanwhile combine the stock and Port in a saucepan and reduce over high heat to 1 cup. Taste for seasoning; add salt and pepper if necessary. Beat in 2 tablespoons butter, cut into bits, adding each new piece as the previous one is incorporated into the sauce. Nap the veal with the sauce when it has finished baking.

Add the chopped zucchini to a saucepan of briskly boiling salted water and boil for 5 minutes. Drain. Heat remaining 2 tablespoons butter in a large skillet and sauté zucchini for about 2 minutes. Stir in the garlic and parsley. Arrange the zucchini round the veal and serve.

Drink a chilled white wine, or a rosé, or a very lightly chilled red wine, according to preference and the weather. A rosé is perfect for a summer luncheon.

EMINCÉ DE FILET DE VEAU AU FENOUIL FRAIS

(Veal Fillet with Fresh Fennel)

SERVES 4.

This is an unusual and elegant way to serve veal. I have cooked it successfully with a less expensive cut than fillet. The recipe was given to me by Chef Gérard Truchetet of the Château d'Isenbourg in Rouffach, one of the Relais et Châteaux. He is a most enthusiastic cook, with his arms wide open to embrace all the kitchens of the world. It upsets him when nations fail to appreciate their own good food. We had a lovely time together, or perhaps I should say with proper modesty that I had a lovely time.

2 tablespoons vegetable
  oil
1 pound fillet of veal, or
  boneless veal, cut into
  strips 1½ inches by ½
  inch
  Salt, freshly ground
  pepper
¼ cup finely chopped
  shallots
¼ cup Pastis (Pernod,
  Ricard)

½ cup heavy cream
2 tablespoons Veal or
  Chicken Stock (see
  Index)
2 fennel bulbs
2 tablespoons lemon juice
2 tablespoons butter
1 tablespoon snipped
  chives

Heat the oil in a heavy flameproof casserole, add the veal strips, and cook until they are lightly colored and tender. Do not overcook veal. Season to taste with salt and pepper. Lift veal out of the casserole with a slotted spoon, and set aside. Add the shallots to the casserole and sauté until they are soft. Pour in the Pastis and stir. Add cream and stock and reduce over moderate heat, stirring from time to time, until the sauce has thickened lightly. Add salt and pepper to taste. Nap the veal with the sauce. Keep warm.

While the veal is cooking, cut off and discard the tops of the fennel. Halve the bulbs, then cut into thin lengthwise slices, about ⅛ inch wide. Drop the fennel slices into briskly boiling water with the lemon juice added, bring the water back to a boil over high heat, and cook for 2 or 3 minutes. Drain, rinse with cold water, drain thoroughly. At the last minute, heat the butter in a flameproof casserole, add the fennel, and cook for a few minutes. It should be tender but still crisp. Season with salt and pepper. Arrange the fennel round the veal. Sprinkle the fennel with the snipped chives.

Riesling is a pleasant wine with this.

MIGNON DE VEAU FRANC-COMTOIS

(Veal Scallops Franc-Comtois style)

SERVES 6.

Léopold Gohel, chef of the Besançon Frantel's restaurant, Le Vesontio, is widely traveled. He appreciates the principles of the *nouvelle cuisine* with its emphasis on natural tastes, and he likes to use the products of the region where he is working. The cheese in this dish is Comté, sometimes called Gruyère de Comté. It has been made in the Franche-Comté since Roman times. Regular Gruyère is fine to use instead.

12 veal scallops, each about 3 ounces (2¼ pounds altogether)
Salt, freshly ground pepper
6 to 8 tablespoons butter
3 cups finely chopped onions
1 cup dry bread crumbs, approximately
1 cup grated Gruyère cheese, approximately
¾ cup Veal or Chicken Stock (see Index)
¾ cup dry white wine
½ cup heavy cream

Have the butcher flatten the scallops to ¼-inch thickness. Season with salt and pepper. In a skillet heat 4 tablespoons butter and sauté the scallops until lightly browned on both sides, about 2 minutes a side. Lift out the scallops and arrange in a buttered ovenproof dish. Keep them warm.

In the skillet, adding more butter as necessary, sauté the onions until very soft. Season with salt and pepper. Divide the onions among the veal scallops, placing a spoonful on each scallop. Top the onions with a tablespoon of bread crumbs, pressing the crumbs down lightly. Top the crumbs with a tablespoon of the cheese. Flatten the cheese lightly. Heat the stock and wine and pour into the baking dish.

Bake in a preheated slow oven (250°F.) for 20 to 30 minutes, or until the liquid has almost evaporated. Pour the cream over the scallops, turn up the heat to hot (400°F.), and bake for about 5 minutes longer. Serve immediately.

Drink a chilled white wine such as a white Burgundy.

CÔTE DE VEAU AU GRATIN D'AVOCAT

(Veal Chops with Avocado)

SERVES 2.

This recipe is the invention of chef Jean Sarres of the restaurant Les Terrasses du Ponant at the Grande-Motte Frantel. I am particularly fond of it for a family supper for two, though the recipe can be doubled or trebled as needed.

2 large veal chops, about 1 inch thick
Salt, freshly ground pepper
2 tablespoons butter
1 medium-size avocado
½ teaspoon chopped chervil
1 teaspoon chopped shallot
4 ounces Gruyère cheese, cut into ⅛-inch slices

Season the chops with salt and pepper. Heat the butter in a skillet and sauté the chops for 4 minutes on each side. Lift out the chops and arrange them in a buttered ovenproof dish. Peel and pit the avocado and mash it with salt and pepper to taste, the chervil and the shallot. Top the chops with the avocado purée. Cover the purée with the slices of Gruyère cheese. Bake in a preheated hot oven (425°F.) for 15 minutes, or until the chops are tender and the cheese browned.

Serve with a green vegetable such as green beans and drink a chilled white wine or rosé.

VEAU À L'OSEILLE

(Veal Stew with Sorrel)

SERVES 6.

2 tablespoons vegetable
    oil
6 tablespoons butter
2 pounds boneless veal,
    cut into 1½-inch cubes
2 medium-size onions,
    finely chopped
1 carrot, scraped and
    finely chopped
½ pound sliced
    mushrooms
1 cup dry white wine
1 cup Chicken Stock (see
    Index) or water,
    approximately

1 sprig each of thyme and
    parsley
1 bay leaf
    Salt, freshly ground
    pepper
1 pound sorrel, about 4
    cups
¼ cup heavy cream
    (optional)

Heat the oil and 1 tablespoon of the butter in a skillet and
sauté the veal cubes until golden on both sides. If the skillet
is not large enough to hold all the veal at one time, do it in
batches. Lift out the meat and set it aside. Add 3 tablespoons of the butter to the skillet and sauté the onions and
carrot until the vegetables are tender. Add the mushrooms
and sauté for 5 minutes longer. In a flameproof casserole
combine the veal with the vegetables, pour in the wine and
enough stock or water barely to cover. Add thyme, parsley
and bay leaf. Season with salt and pepper. Cover and simmer over low heat until the veal is tender, about 1½ hours.

    While the veal is cooking, make a chiffonade of the sor-
rel (see Index), using the remaining 2 tablespoons of butter.
Set aside. Lift the veal out onto a serving dish and keep
warm. Over high heat reduce the cooking liquid to half. Stir

in the sorrel chiffonade and, if liked, the cream. Heat through and pour over the veal.

Serve with plain rice, noodles or potatoes, or with a mixture of young spring vegetables such as baby carrots and white turnips, snow peas or tiny green peas, or zucchini cooked in salted water, drained and tossed in a little butter.

AILLADE DE VEAU

(Veal in Garlic Sauce)

SERVES 6.

This is another of the beautifully simple recipes given me by Rémy André. The *aillades* are dishes from both Provence and Languedoc in which garlic plays an important role. It is not, however, an aggressive role. Cooking gentles the garlic, making it acceptable even from the point of view of nongarlic-eating neighbors.

2 tablespoons olive or vegetable oil	2 cups dry white wine Salt, freshly ground pepper
2 pounds veal, cut into 1-inch cubes	1 thyme sprig
10 large garlic cloves, peeled	1 bay leaf
⅔ cup freshly made bread crumbs	2 tablespoons lemon juice 2 tablespoon snipped chives

Heat the oil in a flameproof casserole. Add the veal and sauté until golden all over. Add garlic, bread crumbs, wine, salt and pepper to taste, thyme and bay leaf. Bring to a simmer, cover, and cook over low heat for 1 hour, or until veal is tender. Stir in the lemon juice. Sprinkle with chives just before serving.

Serve with rice pilaf. A dry white wine is a pleasant accompaniment.

POITRINE DE VEAU FARCIE

(Stuffed Breast of Veal)

SERVES 6.

This is a family recipe given me by the Vicomtesse du Breil de Pontbriand. It is simple and economical with a delicate flavor, and it can be served either hot or cold, making it a versatile dish.

1 breast of veal, about 3
    pounds
1 cup bread crumbs
¼ cup milk
1 cup finely chopped
    parsley
1 medium-size onion,
    minced
1 garlic clove, minced
⅛ teaspoon grated nutmeg
    Salt, freshly ground
    pepper

½ pound sausage meat
1 egg
2 tablespoons butter
1 tablespoon oil
4 cups Beef Stock (see
    Index)
½ cup dry red wine
1 tablespoon cornstarch
    (optional)

Have the butcher cut a pocket in the breast of veal and remove as many rib bones as possible. Soak the bread crumbs in the milk and squeeze them out. In a bowl combine the bread crumbs with the parsley, onion, garlic, nutmeg, salt and pepper to taste, and the sausage meat. Stir in the egg, mixing thoroughly. Season the veal pocket with salt and pepper and fill with the stuffing. Close the opening by sewing it up with string, or secure it with skewers and string. Heat the butter and oil in a large skillet and sauté the veal until it is lightly browned on both sides. Transfer it to a flameproof casserole just large enough to hold it comforta-

bly. Pour in the stock, bring to a simmer, cover with aluminum foil and the lid, and simmer over low heat for 2 hours, or until the veal is tender. Lift out the veal to a serving dish and remove the skewers and string. Cut meat into crosswise slices about ½ inch thick; cover and keep warm.

Pour 2½ cups of the stock into a saucepan with the red wine and reduce over high heat to 2 cups. If a thicker sauce is preferred, mix the cornstarch with a little water, stir it into the stock and simmer, stirring, until thickened. Taste for seasoning and add salt and pepper if necessary. Pour a little of the sauce over the veal and serve the rest in a sauceboat.

Serve with baby carrots, turnips and new potatoes, surrounding the veal in decorative heaps. To serve cold, accompany the veal with sliced tomatoes, potato salad and a green salad, or with any preferred salads. Strain the stock and reserve it for another use. Drink a young, full-bodied red wine such as a Beaujolais or a red Sancerre with the hot veal, and a chilled rosé or dry white wine with the veal served cold.

JAMBON PERSILLÉ À LA BOURGUIGNONNE

(Parsleyed Ham in Aspic, Burgundy Style)

SERVES 6 TO 8.

The Gauls of France first invented the salting and smoking of pork to produce ham, so it is no surprise that French ham dishes are so good. This is a very pretty one. Though popular at any time, this is the holiday dish served at Easter in Burgundy. The pink of the ham and the green of the

(recipe continues)

parsley are very springlike. I find this an ideal dish for a summer buffet. There are two versions which I like equally well. This one was given me by Marc Chevillot who began his career as an apprentice of Point's at Vienne; he is now owner and chef de cuisine of the Hôtel de la Poste at Beaune. The other recipe was given me by neighbors when I stayed at a friend's century-old stone farmhouse in the little Beaujolais village of Pruzilly. M. Chevillot uses a *jam-bonneau,* the nearest equivalent to which is a picnic shoulder, but any mild-cured smoked ham can be used.

1 mild-cured picnic shoulder, 5 to 6 pounds, scrubbed
1 onion, peeled, halved, and stuck with 2 cloves
2 garlic cloves, peeled
1 small celery rib
1 medium-size carrot, scraped and sliced
1 bay leaf
2 or 3 parsley sprigs
1 thyme sprig
6 peppercorns
1 calf's foot, washed and split, or 2 pig's feet, washed and split

2 cups dry white wine
8 cups Chicken Stock (see Index) or water, approximately
1 tablespoon unflavored gelatin, if necessary
Salt
2 cups finely chopped parsley
2 garlic cloves, minced
1 tablespoon heavy cream
1 tablespoon white-wine vinegar, or other fine white vinegar

If the ham is salty, soak it overnight in cold water to cover. Drain and discard the water. Put the ham into a large kettle or saucepan with the next 11 ingredients, ending with the chicken stock or water. Use enough stock or water to cover. Bring to a boil, reduce the heat, and simmer gently for 2 hours, or until the ham is tender. The water should barely move. Let the ham cool in the liquid. When it is cool

enough to handle, lift out and peel away the rind. Chop the ham coarsely, using both fat and lean. Transfer to a serving bowl and set aside.

Strain the stock through a double layer of dampened cheesecloth. Let it stand and skim off any fat. Discard the bones and vegetables. Measure the stock, pour it into a saucepan, and reduce it over brisk heat to 3 cups. If a calf's foot was not available and there is a doubt about the stock jelling, soften the gelatin in ¼ cup cold water and stir it into the hot stock until dissolved. Let the stock cool, taste for seasoning, and add a little salt if necessary. Stir in the chopped parsley, minced garlic, cream and vinegar, and pour the mixture slowly over the ham. Cover and refrigerate overnight.

Unmold on a serving plate and cut into ¾-inch slices. Serve with potato salad, green salad or sliced tomatoes and crusty bread and butter. The dish will keep, refrigerated, for about a week.

Variation: **JAMBON PERSILLÉ DE BOURGOGNE** (*BURGUNDY PARSLEYED HAM IN ASPIC*): Cook the ham in the same way, preferably using a mild-cured half ham instead of a picnic ham. Chop the ham and the fat and set them aside. Pour enough of the liquid aspic into a deep oblong dish, about 9 by 5 and 3 inches deep, to make a ½-inch layer. Chill until the aspic has set. Have ready 4 cups finely chopped parsley and the chopped ham and fat, mixed. Sprinkle a layer of parsley over the aspic, cover with a layer of ham, then one of parsley, and continue until the ham and parsley are used, ending with parsley. Slowly pour in more liquid aspic so that it seeps through, saving ½ cup for a garnish. Cover the dish and chill for 24 hours. Pour remaining aspic into a shallow bowl, cover, and chill. To unmold the ham, run a knife round the inside of the dish, invert a platter or flat serving dish over it, then invert the ham sharply on to the platter. Chop the reserved aspic and arrange around the ham.

LE CASSOULET DE CASTELNAUDARY

(Pork and Bean Casserole)

SERVES 10 TO 12.

I cannot resist a good cassoulet, especially one from Castelnaudary, which is claimed as the birthplace of the dish, of which there are a great many versions. Pierre Poggioli of the Mapotel Palmes et Industrie in Castelnaudary, whose cassoulet is justly famous, gave me his own recipe. It does involve quite a lot of work, but as it makes a hearty one-dish meal for 10 to 12, and is best made ahead of time, I find it splendid for entertaining. *Confit d'oie* (preserved goose) is an essential element of an authentic cassoulet, but I find a goose rather daunting in a small kitchen and make a *confit de canard* (preserved duck) instead. If pressed for time I substitute a roast duckling.

2 pounds Confit de Canard (see Index)

2 pounds Great Northern or Navy beans, about 4 cups

1 pork hock
  Pork rind from 4-pound pork shoulder, cut into strips and tied together with string
  Salt, freshly ground pepper

¼ teaspoon dried thyme

1 bay leaf

1 onion, halved and stuck with 2 cloves
  Fat from the Confit de Canard

4 pounds shoulder of pork, skin removed, boned, and cut into 2-inch pieces

½ pound piece of bacon, cut into ¼-inch cubes

4 garlic cloves, peeled and chopped

2 pounds garlic sausage, cut into 2-inch pieces

Make the *confit de canard* and set aside until ready to cook the cassoulet.

In a large saucepan cover the beans with cold water, enough to cover by about 2 inches. Bring to a boil over moderate heat, covered, and simmer for 5 minutes. Drain.

Discard the cooking water and return the beans to the saucepan. Add the pork hock, pork rind, salt and pepper to taste, thyme, bay leaf and the onion stuck with cloves. Pour in enough water to cover, bring to a simmer and cook, covered, until the beans are just tender, 1 to 1½ hours. Drain the beans, reserving the liquid. Remove the pork rind, discard the string, and cut the rind into squares. Set aside.

In a large skillet heat about 4 tablespoons of the fat from the *confit* and sauté the pork shoulder pieces until they are lightly browned all over. Transfer to a heavy flame-proof casserole. Add chopped bacon, garlic and water barely to cover. Bring to a simmer and cook, covered, until pork is tender, about 1½ hours. Strain and reserve the liquid. Set the meat aside.

To assemble the dish have a large earthenware casserole, or use any large heavy casserole. Make a layer of beans in the bottom of the pot. Add a layer of pork rind, pork, bacon and sausage. Make another layer of beans. Make a layer of the *confit de canard,* removed from its fat and cut into pieces. Make another layer of beans. Mix together the liquid from cooking the beans and the pork. Pour in just enough of the liquid to cover the beans. Put the casserole, uncovered, into a preheated slow oven (325°F.) and cook for 15 to 20 minutes, or until a crust has formed. Stir the crust into the casserole and repeat once more. Each time add ½ cup of the reserved mixed bean and pork liquids. Let a crust form once more, then serve.

Serve with a very light first course. Drink a Languedoc wine or any young full-bodied dry red wine. A green salad is the best other accompaniment.

Variations: If you like, 2 cups dry bread crumbs mixed with ½ cup finely chopped parsley may be sprinkled on the cassoulet and moistened with 4 tablespoons of the fat from the *confit* before the final baking.

Instead of the *confit,* roast a 4½-pound duckling and cut it into serving pieces. Add to the cassoulet.

Instead of the *confit* or the roast duckling, sauté 2½ pounds

(recipe continues)

lean boneless lamb, cut into 2-inch cubes, in pork fat. Season with salt and pepper and simmer with stock or water barely to cover, covered, until tender, 1 to 1½ hours. Drain and use in place of the duck.

The cassoulet may be refrigerated after it has been assembled and the cooking finished the following day. Bring the cassoulet to room temperature before the final baking.

PORC AU CIDRE
(Pork in Cider)

SERVES 6.

2 tablespoons butter	2 cups dry cider
2½ pounds pork—	Salt, freshly ground
shoulder, leg or	pepper
loin—boned and tied	¼ cup Moutarde de
2 garlic cloves, chopped	Meaux or Dijon
¼ cup Calvados or	mustard
Applejack	⅓ cup heavy cream

Heat the butter in a heavy flameproof casserole and brown the pork all over. Add the garlic and sauté for 1 or 2 minutes longer. Add the Calvados or Applejack, warmed, and ignite it. When the flame dies out, pour in the cider. Season pork with salt and pepper and bring the liquid in the casserole to a simmer. Cover the casserole with foil and the lid and cook in a preheated moderate oven (375°F.) for 2 hours, or until the meat is tender. Turn the meat halfway through the cooking.

When the meat is cooked, lift it out onto a serving platter and keep warm. Skim the excess fat from the liquid in the casserole and reduce it over high heat to half its volume. Stir in mustard and cream. Taste for seasoning and add salt and pepper if necessary. Slice the pork and pour a little sauce over it. Serve the rest of the sauce separately.

Serve with noodles or rice or a green vegetable such as broccoli, braised lettuce or green beans.

ROGNON DE VEAU ENTIER À L'ANCIENNE

(Whole Veal Kidney, Old Style)

SERVES 2.

This is a delicious way of serving veal kidneys and makes an out-of-the-ordinary yet inexpensive and easy-to-cook main dish. It is a favorite of chef Daniel Léron and his wife who run the charming small restaurant Daniel et Denise in Lyon.

1 veal kidney
5 tablespoons butter, approximately
Salt, freshly ground pepper
1 tablespoon finely chopped shallot

1 tablespoon *Lardons* (see Index)
8 small button mushrooms
1 cup dry white wine

Rinse the kidney quickly in cold water and pat it dry with paper towels. Trim away all the fat. Lightly butter a small baking dish just large enough to hold the kidney comfortably. Add the kidney and bake in a preheated hot oven (425°F.) for 10 minutes. Season the kidney with salt and pepper. It is important not to overcook kidney as it toughens easily. It should remain pink inside. Transfer the kidney to a serving dish, cover, and keep warm in the turned-off oven with the door open.

In a small skillet heat 1 tablespoon butter and sauté the shallot over moderate heat for 2 or 3 minutes. Add the *lardons* and mushrooms and sauté until mushrooms are lightly colored. Add the wine and any juices in the baking pan. Reduce the wine over high heat to ½ cup, stirring once or twice. Cut 3 tablespoons of butter into bits and beat it, bit by bit, into the sauce, adding each new piece as the previous

(recipe continues)

one is absorbed. Taste for seasoning and add salt and pepper if necessary. Pour any juices that have collected in the dish with the kidney into the sauce and heat it through. Quickly cut the kidney into ½-inch slices and pour the sauce over. Serve immediately.

Serve with rice or buttered noodles. Drink a red Burgundy or any full-bodied red wine.

FOIE DE VEAU AUX CÂPRES

(Calf's Liver with Capers)

SERVES 4.

Calf's liver is a delicacy as much appreciated in France as it is in the United States. The important thing is to sauté it quickly in very hot fat so that it is brown outside and pink inside. Overcooked liver loses its delicate texture and is tasteless and unappetizing.

1 pound calf's liver, cut
    into ¼-inch slices
    Salt, freshly ground
      pepper
    Flour
2 tablespoons olive oil
2 tablespoons butter
2 medium-size onions,
    finely chopped

1 garlic clove, minced
6 medium-size tomatoes,
    peeled and chopped
2 tablespoons capers,
    rinsed and drained
    Chopped parsley

Season the slices of liver with salt and pepper. Dredge with flour, shaking to remove the excess. In a heavy skillet large enough to hold the liver slices in 1 layer (or use 2 skillets), heat the oil and butter and sauté the liver over moderately high heat for 2 minutes on each side. Transfer to a serving

platter and keep warm. In the fat remaining in the skillet sauté the onions and garlic over moderate heat until onions are soft. Add the tomatoes and cook until the mixture is thick and well blended, about 5 minutes. Season to taste with salt and pepper. Stir in the capers. Pour in any juices that have collected on the platter with the liver and heat the sauce through. Pour the sauce over the liver and serve immediately. Sprinkle with chopped parsley.

Serve with rice or buttered noodles and a green vegetable. Drink a Beaujolais or any young red wine.

Variations: **FOIE DE VEAU AU POIVRE VERT** (*CALF'S LIVER WITH GREEN PEPPERCORNS*): Omit the capers and add 1 tablespoon green peppercorns to the sauce.

FOIE DE VEAU À LA MOUTARDE (*CALF'S LIVER IN MUSTARD SAUCE*): Sauté the calf's liver in 4 tablespoons clarified butter, transfer to a serving dish, cover and keep warm. In the fat remaining in the skillet sauté 1 medium-size onion, finely chopped, until soft. Stir in 1 cup dry white wine and reduce over high heat to ½ cup. Stir in ½ cup heavy cream and simmer until the sauce is lightly thickened. Stir in 2 tablespoons Dijon mustard. Pour the sauce over the liver.

FOIE DE VEAU AUX PRUNEAUX (CALF'S LIVER WITH PRUNES): Heat 4 tablespoons clarified butter in a skillet and sauté 1 medium-size onion, finely chopped, and 1 medium-size carrot, scraped and thinly sliced, until both the vegetables are soft. Season with salt and pepper and pour in 1½ cups beer and 2 tablespoons tomato paste. Stir to mix, cover, and simmer for 15 minutes. Add 1 cup pitted prunes and simmer uncovered for 15 minutes longer. Season the slices of liver with salt and pepper, dredge with flour, and sauté as in the master recipe. Transfer the slices of liver to a warmed serving dish. Surround with the prunes and cover with the sauce. If liked, fresh plums can be used instead of prunes. In that case, pit 1 cup of plums and partially cook them in plain water before adding them, drained, to the sauce to simmer for 15 minutes. Use red plums preferably, but any plums can be used.

LA PISTACHE

(Lamb and Bean Casserole)

SERVES 6.

This *pistache*, which comes from the Mapotel Poste et Golf in Luchon, is very different from the Pistache de Mouton made by Rémy André in Carcassonne, though both are fundamentally lamb stews. It is the sort of robust, satisfying dish that takes the chill out of a winter evening.

2½ cups dried white beans, preferably Great Northern

3 tablespoons vegetable oil

2 pounds boneless shoulder of lamb, cut into 1-inch cubes

3 cups chopped onions

2 medium-size carrots, scraped and sliced

¾ pound fresh or salt pork rind, cut into ½-inch pieces

4 garlic cloves

Bouquet garni: 1 bay leaf, 1 celery rib, 2 parsley sprigs, parsley, 1 thyme sprig, tied with a piece of cotton

Salt, freshly ground pepper

1 tablespoon chopped bacon

Soak the beans overnight, or if preferred bring the beans to a boil in a large saucepan with water to cover and boil for 2 minutes. Let the beans stand, not over heat, for 1 hour. Whichever soaking method has been used, the beans are now ready to cook.

In a large flameproof casserole heat the oil and sauté the lamb until the pieces are lightly browned. Add the onions and carrots and sauté for a few minutes longer. Add the pork rind, 2 chopped garlic cloves, the *bouquet garni* and the beans, with enough of the soaking water to cover the contents of the casserole by 1 inch. Season with salt and pepper. Cover, and cook for about 1½ hours, or until both beans and lamb are tender. Taste for seasoning and add

salt and pepper if necessary. Remove and discard the *bou-quet garni*. Stir in the chopped bacon with remaining 2 garlic cloves, and simmer for a few minutes longer.

MELON D'AGNEAU AUX FÈVES FRAÎCHES

(Stuffed Lamb with Fresh Broad Beans)

SERVES 6.

This is an unusual recipe, superb for a small dinner party. Serge Coulon of the restaurant Chez Serge in La Rochelle, its inventor, gave it to me. It has the added merit of being very easy to prepare.

2 tablespoons vegetable oil	1 small leg or shoulder of lamb, about 3½ pounds
2 lamb kidneys, skinned and chopped	4 or 5 slices of fat bacon
¼ pound lamb liver, chopped	3 tablespoons butter
¼ pound boiled ham, chopped	1 medium-size onion, finely chopped
1 tablespoon chopped fresh basil leaves	2 pounds broad beans, shelled, or use 2 cups baby lima beans
Salt, freshly ground pepper	½ cup heavy cream

In a heavy skillet heat the vegetable oil. Add the kidneys, liver and ham and sauté over moderately high heat for 1 minute. Add the chopped basil, season to taste with salt and pepper, and transfer to a bowl.

Have the butcher bone the lamb, or do it yourself. Season the lamb with salt and pepper and stuff it with the liver-kidney mixture. Skewer the lamb and tie it up roughly into the shape of a melon. Simmer the bacon slices in water to cover for 5 minutes, drain, pat dry, and lay over the lamb.

(recipe continues)

Put the lamb in a baking dish and put into a cold oven set at slow (325°F.). Bake for 1½ hours, or until a meat thermometer registers 140°F. for pink, juicy lamb. Let the meat stand in a warm place for 10 or 15 minutes before cutting into slices or wedges. Discard the bacon.

While the lamb is cooking, heat the butter in a saucepan and sauté the onion until soft but not browned. Add the broad beans, season with salt and pepper, and sauté for 1 or 2 minutes. Pour in the cream, bring to a simmer, cover, and cook until the beans are tender, about 35 minutes. Serve beans with the lamb.

GIGOT BRAISÉ À LA BEAUJOLAISE

(Braised Leg of Lamb, Beaujolais Style)

SERVES 6 TO 8.

4 pounds leg of lamb
2 garlic cloves, cut into slivers
Salt, freshly ground pepper
3 tablespoons vegetable oil
4 medium-size onions, chopped
2 medium-size carrots, scraped and thinly sliced

1 cup Beaujolais wine
2 cups Chicken Stock (see Index)
3 pounds potatoes, peeled and thinly sliced
½ cup finely chopped parsley
¼ cup snipped chives
1 tablespoon finely chopped chervil

With a small sharp knife make slits in the lamb and insert the slivers of garlic. Season the lamb with salt and pepper. In a large flameproof oval casserole heat the oil and brown the lamb all over. Lift out the lamb. Add the onions and carrots and sauté for 5 minutes, stirring from time to time. Lift out the vegetables with a slotted spoon. Pour off and

discard the oil. Pour the wine into the casserole and reduce it over high heat to half its volume, scraping to loosen all the brown bits. Lower the heat. Return the lamb to the casserole with the vegetables and pour in the chicken stock. Bring to a simmer on top of the stove. Cover the casserole with aluminum foil, then the lid, and bake in a preheated moderate oven (350°F.) for 3½ hours, turning the lamb halfway through the cooking.

When the lamb is within 45 minutes of being done, add the potatoes and the herbs. Check during the final cooking to see that there is enough liquid to keep the potatoes moist. Add a little stock if necessary. Lift out the lamb to a serving platter. Place the vegetables round the meat. Degrease any cooking stock that is left. Taste for seasoning, adding salt and pepper if necessary, and pour sauce into a sauceboat.

PISTACHE DE MOUTON

(Lamb with White Wine and Tomatoes)

SERVES 6 TO 8.

Rémy André and his wife are the proprietors of a small restaurant, Au Bon Pasteur, in Carcassonne, devoted to the cooking of Languedoc to which they have added something special of their own. Each says the other is the better cook. I refuse to judge, finding them equally good, with an instinctive feeling for the new attitudes to food. They generously gave me favorite recipes which could be described as simultaneously modern and traditonal. They are also wonderfully appetizing. Do not be put off by the amount of garlic, but do choose garlic with large cloves as peeling small ones is a tedious job. I find it a good idea to drop the unpeeled garlic cloves into boiling water for 1 minute, then peel them. It makes things easier and I have not been able to notice any difference in flavor if the cloves are first peeled, then blanched.

(recipe continues)

2 tablespoons olive or vegetable oil
4 pounds leg or shoulder of lamb, boned and tied
1 large onion, finely chopped
4 medium-size tomatoes, peeled and chopped
2 cups dry white wine
½ cup water
Salt, freshly ground pepper
1 thyme sprig
2 or 3 whole heads of garlic
1 cup freshly made bread crumbs (optional)

Heat the oil in a flameproof casserole large enough to hold the meat comfortably, and brown the lamb all over. Lift lamb out and set aside. In the fat remaining in the casserole, adding a little more if necessary, sauté the onion until very soft. Add the tomatoes, wine, water, salt and pepper to taste, and thyme, and cook for a few minutes. Return the lamb to the casserole, cover, and simmer over low heat for 1½ hours.

While the meat is cooking, separate the garlic cloves and drop them into briskly boiling water. Lift out after 1 minute and peel as soon as they are cool enough to handle. Add to the casserole when the meat has cooked for 1½ hours, and simmer for 30 minutes longer. If liked, stir in the bread crumbs to thicken the sauce, and simmer for 5 minutes longer.

Serve with cooked dried white beans (pea beans or Great Northern). Please yourself about the wine and drink either white, rosé or red. I prefer a fruity young red wine, but a dry rosé can be delightful in blazing summer weather which suits this robust dish surprisingly well.

RIS DE VEAU À L'OSEILLE

(Veal Sweetbreads with Sorrel Chiffonade)

SERVES 2 OR 3.

Italian greengroceries are the best place to look for sorrel. Its refreshing acidity is perfect with sweetbreads.

1 pound veal sweetbreads
2 tablespoons butter
4 slices of unsmoked
  bacon, chopped
2 medium-size carrots,
  scraped and thinly
  sliced
8 small white onions,
  peeled
4 small tomatoes, skinned
½ cup dry white wine
½ cup Beef Stock (see Index)

Bouquet garni: 2
  parsley sprigs, 1 thyme
  sprig, 1 bay leaf, tied
  together with cotton,
  or in a square of
  cheesecloth
Salt, freshly ground
  pepper
Sorrel Chiffonade
  (recipe follows)

Prepare the sweetbreads in the usual way (see Index), and cut into ½-inch slices. Heat the butter in a heavy casserole, add the bacon, and sauté over moderate heat for a few minutes. Add the sweetbreads, carrots and onions, and sauté until sweetbreads are golden on both sides, about 5 minutes. Add the tomatoes. Pour in wine and stock, add the *bouquet garni,* and season to taste with salt and pepper. Simmer, covered, over low heat for 30 minutes. Using a slotted spoon lift out the sweetbreads, bacon, carrots, onions and tomatoes to a heated serving dish. Remove and discard the *bouquet garni.* Reduce the sauce over high heat until it is lightly thickened. Taste for seasoning and add salt and pepper if necessary. Nap the sweetbreads with the sauce, and serve with sorrel chiffonade.

Sorrel Chiffonade

3 recipes Chiffonade
  d'Oseille (see Index)

2 tablespoons heavy cream

Make the chiffonade of sorrel. Stir the heavy cream into the chiffonade and heat through. Serve with the sweetbreads.

Variation: Lamb sweetbreads can be used successfully in this dish. As they are smaller than veal sweetbreads it will not be necessary to slice them. Just cut them into halves or leave them whole according to size.

241

RIS DE VEAU AUX PRUNEAUX

(Sweetbreads with Prunes)

SERVES 6.

This elegant dish is the creation of Christian Clément of the Bordeaux Frantel's restaurant Le Mériadeck. Sweetbreads are often available in supermarkets and from specialty butchers, and are worth looking for when cooking for a special occasion. The sweetbreads, spinach and prunes— rich, tart and acidy-sweet—make an exciting mix of flavors.

2½ pounds veal sweetbreads
Salt, freshly ground pepper
4 tablespoons butter
36 pitted prunes, about 12 ounces

¼ cup Port wine
1 cup rich Veal or Beef Stock (see Index)
1 cup heavy cream
2 pounds fresh spinach

Prepare the sweetbreads according to basic instructions (see Index). Cut sweetbreads into diagonal slices about ½ inch thick. Season with salt and pepper. In a large heavy skillet heat the butter and sauté the sweetbread slices until tender and golden on both sides. Add the prunes, cover the skillet, and cook for a few minutes longer. Remove sweetbreads and prunes to a dish, cover, and keep warm. Pour the Port wine into the skillet and simmer, uncovered, until the liquid has reduced to half. Add the stock and cook for about 5 minutes longer. Add the heavy cream and let it reduce until the sauce has thickened lightly.

While making the sauce, thoroughly wash the spinach, remove any wilted leaves, and trim any coarse stems. Have ready a large saucepan of briskly boiling salted water. Add the spinach, bring back to a boil, and simmer for 5 minutes. Drain thoroughly and squeeze out the water. An easy way to do this is to lay the drained spinach on a bamboo mat and roll the mat up while squeezing the bamboo cylinder

242

gently, or roll the spinach in a kitchen towel and squeeze out the moisture. Chop the spinach coarsely. Return it to the saucepan and heat it through briefly. Arrange the spinach on a serving dish. Top it with the sweetbreads. Arrange the prunes round the dish and nap with the sauce.

RIS DE VEAU AUX POMMES

(Sweetbreads with Apples)

SERVES 4 TO 6.

The acidity of the apples in contrast with the richness of the sweetbreads is very pleasing, a tribute to the talent and originality of Paul Pauvert, the young chef at the Nantes Frantel restaurant Le Tillac.

2½ pounds veal
    sweetbreads
    Salt, freshly ground
    pepper
4 tablespoons butter
2 tablespoons Calvados
1 pound apples, peeled,
    cored and chopped

1 cup dry cider
½ cup heavy cream
1 teaspoon Glace de
    Viande (see Index)
    Sautéed Apple Slices
    (see Index)

Prepare the sweetbreads according to basic instructions (see Index). Cut the sweetbreads into slices about ½ inch thick. Season with salt and pepper. In a large heavy skillet heat the butter and sauté the sweetbreads until slices are tender and golden on both sides. Warm the Calvados, pour over the sweetbreads, and ignite it. Transfer the contents of the skillet to a serving dish, cover, and keep warm.

Add the chopped apples to the skillet, pour in the cider and simmer, uncovered, until apples are tender, about 5 minutes. Add the cream and salt and pepper to taste, and simmer until the mixture is slightly reduced. Stir in the *glace de viande* and pour the sauce over the sweetbreads. Serve surrounded by the sautéed apple slices.

Drink cider, or dry white wine.

RIS DE VEAU À L'ORANGE

(Veal Sweetbreads in Orange Sauce)

SERVES 4.

This unusual recipe for sweetbreads comes from Les Antiquaires, the restaurant of M. Soalhat's Mapotel Pont Royal
in Paris. I find the contrast in flavors delightful.

2 pounds sweetbreads
Salt, freshly ground
  pepper
8 medium-size oranges,
  preferably thin-
  skinned

¾ cup sugar
½ cup white-wine vinegar

Prepare the sweetbreads according to the basic instructions
(see Index). Cut the sweetbreads into ½-inch slices, season
with salt and pepper, and set aside.

Peel the oranges and cut the rind (zest) into thin julienne strips about ¹/₁₆ by ¾ inch. Drop strips into a saucepan of briskly boiling water and simmer for 5 minutes.
Drain, pat dry, and set aside. Squeeze the juice from 6 oranges, and set it aside. Pull all the white pith from remaining 2 oranges and separate them into segments. Peel the
segments, or if preferred leave them unpeeled. Set them
aside.

Combine the sugar and vinegar in a small heavy saucepan and cook over moderate heat, stirring with a wooden
spoon, until the mixture forms a deep golden caramel. Off
the heat stir in the orange juice. Transfer the mixture to a
large saucepan or flameproof casserole. Add the zest of the
oranges and the sweetbreads. Taste for seasoning and add
a little salt if necessary. Cover and simmer gently for 20
minutes. Arrange on a warmed serving platter and surround with the orange segments.

Serve with rice.

RÂBLE DE LAPIN AUX OIGNONS CONFITS

(Saddle of Rabbit with Glazed Onions)

SERVES 3 OR 4.

I am indebted to my friend Richard Olney, author of the excellent book *Simple French Food,* for making sure I met Jean-Pierre Billoux of the Relais Gourmand Restaurant Bonnevay-Billoux in Digoin, Burgundy, a greatly gifted young chef who cooked for me, and gave me recipes. This was one I enjoyed very much. A ready-to-cook cut-up frozen rabbit can be used for this.

OIGNONS CONFITS

12 small white onions, peeled	4 tablespoons butter
	2 tablespoons sugar

Put the onions in a small heavy saucepan with the butter and let them brown very lightly. Add the sugar and enough water barely to cover. Cover, and cook over very low heat for 1 hour, shaking the saucepan from time to time. Set aside and keep warm until ready to use as a garnish.

RABBIT

1 rabbit, 2½ to 3 pounds, whole or cut into serving pieces	1 parsley sprig
	Salt, freshly ground pepper
1 medium-size onion, chopped	5 tablespoons butter
1 garlic clove, minced	2 tablespoons vegetable oil
1 medium-size carrot, scraped and chopped	2 tablespoons finely chopped shallots
1 bay leaf	¼ cup dry white wine

If using a whole rabbit, cut it up and bone it (see Index). Set aside the hind legs and the meaty saddle with the kid-

(recipe continues)

neys. Make a stock with the rib cage, forelegs and backbone, and the head if you have it: Put these parts into a saucepan with the onion, garlic, carrot, bay leaf, parsley, a little salt, and freshly ground pepper to taste. Pour in water to cover by about 1 inch. Cover the saucepan and simmer for 2 hours or longer. Strain, discard the solids, and reduce the stock over high heat to ½ cup. Taste for seasoning and add more salt and pepper if necessary.

In a flameproof casserole heat 2 tablespoons of the butter and the vegetable oil and sauté the legs and saddle pieces of the rabbit over moderate heat until lightly colored on both sides. Cover and cook over very low heat, turning once or twice, until rabbit is tender, about 1 hour. A lot will depend on the age of the rabbit. A really young one will cook in that time. An older one may need 30 minutes longer. Lift out the rabbit pieces and arrange them on a warmed serving dish. Surround with the glazed onions, cover, and keep warm.

Heat 1 tablespoon of the butter in a small heavy saucepan, add the shallots and the wine, and cook over low heat until the liquid has almost evaporated and the shallots are a moist purée. Add the reduced rabbit stock and simmer for 1 or 2 minutes. Whisk in remaining 2 tablespoons of butter, cut into bits, adding a new piece as soon as the previous one has melted. Nap the rabbit with the sauce.

Serve with a green vegetable such as broccoli, zucchini, or green beans. Drink a full-bodied young red wine, Burgundy or Beaujolais.

LE LAPIN AUX PRUNEAUX

(Rabbit Stuffed with Prunes)

SERVES 4.

This delicious recipe was given me by Mme Denise Olivereau-Capron of Le Domaine de la Tortinière at Montbazon after I had enjoyed it in the enchanting dining room of the château.

1 pound pitted prunes	½ cup chopped shallots
2½ cups dry red wine,	or scallions
preferably the soft	1 tablespoon finely
flowery Chinon of the	chopped parsley
Loire	Salt, freshly ground
4 slices of unsmoked	pepper
bacon, chopped	4 whole eggs
6 ounces lean pork,	1 rabbit, 2½ to 3 pounds
chopped	2 tablespoons oil
Heart, liver and	1 tablespoon butter
kidneys of the rabbit,	1 thyme sprig
chopped	1 bay leaf
2 medium-size onions,	1 carrot, scraped and
finely chopped	chopped

Put the prunes into a saucepan with 1½ cups of the wine, cover, and simmer for 15 minutes. Set aside. Combine the bacon, pork, heart, liver and kidneys of the rabbit with 1 chopped onion, the shallots, parsley, salt and pepper to taste and the eggs, mixing well. Drain the prunes and reserve the wine in which they were simmered. Stuff the rabbit with the meat mixture and the prunes, making a layer of stuffing, then one of prunes. Reserve the leftover prunes. Sew up the rabbit or fasten securely with skewers and string.

Heat the oil and butter in a large flameproof oval casserole, and brown the rabbit on both sides. Add the thyme, bay leaf, carrot, remaining onion, remaining cup of wine and the reserved wine from the prunes. Season with salt and pepper, cover, and simmer until the rabbit is tender, 1½ to 2 hours. Lift out the rabbit and remove the sewing thread or skewers and string. Keep warm on a serving dish. Strain the sauce and reduce it, if necessary, over high heat to 1½ cups. Add the reserved prunes and heat them through. Spoon the sauce over the rabbit, and garnish with the prunes.

Serve with rice.

For easier serving, the rabbit may be boned (see Index), using only the saddle and the hind legs. Use the rib cage and forelegs to enrich the sauce.

LAPIN AUX RAISINS FRAIS

(Rabbit with Grapes)

SERVES 3 OR 4.

The combination of black grapes and red wine turns this simple dish into a glamorous one, worthy of a special occasion. I was given it by grape-growing, wine-producing friends in the Beaujolais.

1 rabbit, 2½ to 3 pounds, cut into serving pieces	1 sprig each of thyme and parsley
Salt, freshly ground pepper	1 bay leaf
	2 cups dry red wine
1 carrot, scraped and chopped	1 tablespoon vegetable oil
	4 tablespoons butter
1 medium-size onion, chopped	2 tablespoons Cognac
	2 cups black grapes, seeded

Season the rabbit pieces with salt and pepper and put into a large bowl. Add the carrot, onion, thyme, parsley, bay leaf, 1½ cups of the wine and the vegetable oil; mix well. Marinate in the refrigerator overnight, turning once or twice.

When ready to cook, lift the rabbit pieces out of the marinade and pat them dry with paper towels. In a flameproof casserole heat the butter and sauté the rabbit pieces on both sides. Warm the Cognac, pour it over the rabbit, and ignite. Pour in the marinade with the solids, and cover the casserole. Simmer for about 50 minutes, or until rabbit is tender. Put the grapes in a bowl with remaining ½ cup wine. Lift rabbit pieces out of the casserole and keep them warm. Strain the liquid in the casserole and discard the solids. Return the liquid to the casserole and reduce over high heat to 1 cup. Add the grapes and the wine to the casserole with the rabbit pieces and simmer gently for 5 minutes.

Serve with boiled potatoes or plain white rice and a green vegetable.

LE LAPIN ET SA FEUILLE DE CHOU

(Rabbit and Stuffed Cabbage Leaves)

SERVES 4.

Since I love rabbit and love cabbage I enjoyed this dish very much. I was pleased when Yves Ternant, chef de cuisine of Les Ombrages, the restaurant of the Hôtel Frantel in Reims, told me how to make the dish.

RABBIT
- 1 rabbit, 2½ to 3 pounds
  Salt, freshly ground
    pepper
- 2 tablespoons butter
- 1 tablespoon vegetable oil
- 1 onion, finely chopped
- 1 garlic clove, chopped
- 1 medium-size carrot,
    scraped and chopped
- 1 thyme sprig
- 2 or 3 parsley sprigs
- 1 bay leaf
- 1 cup Chicken Stock (see
    Index.)
- 1 cup dry red wine

CABBAGE ROLLS
- ¼ pound sweetbreads,
    chopped
- 4 slices of bacon,
    blanched and chopped
- ¼ cup chopped shallots
- ¼ cup chopped
    mushrooms
  Salt, freshly ground
    pepper
- ¼ cup heavy cream
- 8 large leaves of Savoy
    cabbage
- 4 tablespoons butter, cut
    into bits

Cut up the rabbit (see Index). Scrape all the meat from the rib cage and forelegs, chop it, and set it aside. Cut the saddle into 2 equal pieces, crosswise, and separate the hind legs. Pat the pieces dry with paper towels and season with salt and pepper. Heat the butter and oil in a skillet and sauté the rabbit pieces until browned all over. Lift rabbit out into a flameproof casserole. In the fat remaining in the skillet sauté the onion, garlic and carrot and add to the casserole with the thyme, parsley, bay leaf and chicken stock. Pour the wine into the skillet over moderate heat and

(recipe continues)

scrape up any brown bits. Add to the casserole and set aside.

Mix the reserved chopped rabbit meat with the sweetbreads, bacon, shallots and mushrooms. Season with salt and pepper and mix in the cream. Drop the cabbage leaves into a large saucepan of boiling salted water. Cook only to soften the leaves, about 1 minute. Lift out and allow to cool. Stuff the leaves with the rabbit and sweetbread mixture and roll them up. Add them to the casserole with the rabbit pieces. Cover and simmer over low heat until rabbit is tender, 1½ to 2 hours.

Lift the rabbit pieces and cabbage rolls onto a serving dish and keep warm. Strain the liquid in the casserole, pour it back, and reduce it over high heat to about 1½ cups. Beat in the butter, bit by bit, with a whisk. Nap the rabbit pieces and the cabbage rolls with the sauce.

Serve with plain boiled baby carrots and small white tur- nips.

LAPIN BRAISÉ AUX COURGETTES

(Braised Rabbit with Zucchini)

SERVES 4.

A ready-to-cook cut-up frozen rabbit is fine for this appetiz- ingly light main course.

1 rabbit, 2½ to 3 pounds
1 onion, chopped
1 carrot, scraped and
   chopped
2 garlic cloves, chopped
1 bay leaf
1 sprig each of thyme and
   parsley
   Salt, freshly ground
   pepper

5 tablespoons butter
1 cup dry white wine
2 tablespoons tomato
   purée
2 tablespoons heavy cream
1 pound zucchini
2 tablespoons finely
   chopped fresh basil
   leaves

Cut up the rabbit (see Index). Reserve the saddle, left whole, and the hind legs, separated. Reserve the liver. Put the ribs, forelegs, and head if the butcher has included it, into a heavy saucepan with the onion, carrot, garlic, bay leaf, thyme, parsley, salt and pepper to taste and enough water to cover by about 1 inch. Bring to a boil, skim off any scum that rises, reduce the heat to low, cover, and simmer for about 2 hours. Cool and strain the liquid and return it to the saucepan. Reduce it to 2 cups. Remove the meat from the bones and keep warm.

Heat 4 tablespoons of the butter in a skillet and sauté the rabbit legs and saddle until golden brown on both sides. Put the rabbit pieces into a flameproof casserole with the 2 cups rabbit stock and the white wine. Cover and simmer over low heat until rabbit is tender, about 1½ hours. Lift rabbit out of the stock, cut the meat into 1-inch pieces, and keep it warm. Over high heat reduce the cooking liquid to 1½ cups. Reduce the heat and stir in the tomato purée and the cream. Taste for seasoning and add salt and pepper if necessary. Keep warm. Heat remaining tablespoon of butter in a small skillet and sauté the rabbit liver until it is browned on both sides but slightly pink inside, a matter of minutes. Cut the liver into chunks.

Slice the zucchini and cook it according to the instructions for Courgettes (see Index). To assemble the dish, put the rabbit liver in the center of the dish surrounded by the rabbit meat and, if liked, any meat from the forelegs and ribs. Surround the meat with the zucchini slices and nap with the sauce. Sprinkle with the chopped basil.

For easier assembly the zucchini can be served separately in a vegetable dish and any extra sauce can be served in a sauceboat.

SAUCISSONS AUX POMMES

(Sausages with Apples)

SERVES 2 TO 4.

This is a favorite of mine for a little supper or lunch.

2 tablespoons butter
4 large fresh pork
   sausages, such as fresh
   Bratwurst,
   approximately 1 pound

3 pounds tart apples,
   peeled, cored and
   thickly sliced

Heat the butter in a heavy skillet and brown the sausages all over. Lift them out and set aside. Add the apple slices to the skillet and sauté them in the fat for a few minutes, stirring to mix. Arrange the sausages on top of the apples, cover the skillet and cook, covered, over low heat for about 25 minutes, or until apples are tender. Arrange the apples in a warmed serving dish and place the sausages on top.

TRIPES BASQUAISES

(Tripe, Basque Style)

SERVES 4.

I find tripe dishes rich, simple and savory. Tripe once presented problems as it needed to be cleaned and cooked, but it is now sold cleaned and partially cooked. I often find that the tripe I buy needs no precooking but can simply be cooked briefly in a sauce. The best way to tell how much cooking is needed is to cut off a tiny bit of tripe, nibble it, and judge by how chewy it is.

4 tablespoons olive oil	4 medium-size tomatoes,
3 medium-size onions,	peeled and chopped
finely chopped	½ cup dry white wine
3 medium-size carrots,	1 garlic clove, chopped
scraped and thinly	1 thyme sprig
sliced	¼ pound cooked ham,
2 pounds tripe, cut into	cubed
squares or strips	
Salt, freshly ground	
pepper	

In a heavy flameproof casserole heat the olive oil and sauté the onions and carrots over moderate heat until onions are soft but not brown. Add the tripe and sauté for about 5 minutes longer. Season with salt and pepper. Add the tomatoes, wine, garlic, thyme and ham. Bring to a simmer, cover, and simmer for about 2 hours, or until tripe is tender. If the sauce is very abundant, cook with the casserole partially covered for the second hour of cooking time. Transfer the tripe to a serving dish and surround it with slices of bread rubbed with a cut garlic clove, sprinkled with olive oil and baked in a preheated hot oven (375°F) until browned, 10 to 15 minutes.

Serve with boiled potatoes and a green vegetable.

Variation: Add 1 large sweet red pepper, seeded and chopped, to the onion and carrot mixture.

For **TRIPES MAISON LA CHAUMETTE:** Use butter instead of oil to cook the onions and carrots. When the tripe is almost cooked stir in ¼ cup heavy cream and cook uncovered for the last 30 minutes. Serve with grated Parmesan cheese, boiled potatoes tossed in butter and sprinkled with parsley, and a green salad.

GRAS-DOUBLE AU CIDRE

(Tripe in Cider)

SERVES 4 OR 5.

This tripe recipe from Normandy could not be more different from the famous Tripes à la Mode de Caen, a marvelous dish but one that is very time-consuming to prepare.
Tripe in Cider is deceptively simple in spite of its rich, unc-
tuous sauce.

4 tablespoons butter
2 medium-size onions,
    finely chopped
3 pounds tripe,
    preferably honeycomb,
    cut into strips or 1-
    inch squares
Salt, freshly ground
    pepper

1 cup dry cider
1 sprig each of thyme and
    parsley
1 bay leaf
½ cup light cream
2 tablespoons lemon juice
1 large egg, lightly beaten

Heat the butter in a heavy flameproof casserole and sauté
the onions until very soft but not browned. Add the tripe
and salt and pepper to taste, stir to mix, and cook for 5
minutes longer. Pour in the cider, add the thyme, parsley
and bay leaf, and simmer until tripe is tender, about 1½
hours. If tripe is very watery, cook partially covered. Using
a slotted spoon, transfer the tripe to a heated serving dish
and keep warm.

Strain any liquid back into the casserole. Measure the
liquid in the casserole and reduce it over brisk heat to 1½
cups. In a bowl beat the cream and lemon juice into the
beaten egg until well blended. Pour the egg mixture into
the casserole and cook over low heat, stirring, until the
sauce is lightly thickened. Pour the sauce over the tripe.

Serve with boiled potatoes or noodles. Drink cider or a
light dry white wine.

EMINCÉ DE GRAS-DOUBLE AU VINAIGRE DE VIN

(Minced Tripe with Wine Vinegar)

SERVES 4.

Tripe is often overcooked before my butcher gets it, which makes it hard to give accurate cooking times. This is a traditional Beaujolais way of cooking tripe. My recipe comes from Gérard Cortembert, who runs the Auberge du Cep in Fleurie-en-Beaujolais. I acquired it during a recent summer when I was staying at a friend's house in the nearby small village of Pruzilly.

1½ pounds tripe, finely
    chopped
4 tablespoons olive oil
4 tablespoons butter
2 tablespoons red-wine
    vinegar
    Salt, freshly ground
    pepper

1½ pounds onions, finely
    chopped
2 medium-size tomatoes,
    peeled, seeded and
    chopped

Nibble a piece of tripe; if it seems to be about half-cooked, go ahead with the recipe. Otherwise cook it in salted water for a little longer, until it seems on the way to being tender. Heat half of the oil and half of the butter in a large heavy skillet and sauté the tripe, stirring from time to time, until it is lightly colored, 15 to 20 minutes. Stir in the vinegar and continue cooking until the vinegar has evaporated. Season with salt and pepper and set aside.

While the tripe is cooking heat remaining oil and butter in another skillet and sauté the onions until lightly browned. Mix together the tripe, onions and tomatoes. Put the mixture in a shallow ovenproof serving dish (a gratin dish) and finish the cooking in a preheated moderately hot oven (400°F.) for 30 minutes. Serve very hot from the dish.

Serve with potatoes and a green vegetable. Drink a Beaujolais, preferably a Fleurie, a lovely fruity wine.

GRAS-DOUBLE À LA LYONNAISE

(Tripe, Lyon Style)

SERVES 6.

4 tablespoons olive oil
2 pounds onions, finely
   chopped
3 pounds honeycomb
   tripe, cut into strips 1
   inch by ½ inch
1 cup dry white wine,
   approximately
   Salt, freshly ground
   pepper

⅛ teaspoon grated nutmeg
1 teaspoon red- or white-
   wine vinegar
1 tablespoon finely
   chopped garlic or
   shallots
2 tablespoons finely
   chopped parsley

Heat the oil in a heavy flameproof casserole and sauté the onions until golden. Add the tripe, pour in the wine, and season with salt, pepper and nutmeg. Cover and cook over very low heat until tripe is tender, about 2 hours, but test often for doneness as the cooking time for tripe varies greatly. Add more liquid if necessary; if tripe is very watery, cook uncovered.

When tripe is tender and the liquid reduced to a fairly thick sauce, stir in the vinegar and cook for a few minutes longer. Stir in the garlic and parsley mixed together. If preferred, use shallots instead of garlic.

CERVELLES FLAMBÉ AU WHISKY

(Brains in Whisky Sauce)

SERVES 2.

1 pound calf's brains
Salt
2 tablespoons butter
2 tablespoons Scotch
   whisky

½ cup heavy cream
Freshly ground pepper

Soak the brains in several changes of cold water for about 2 hours. Carefully remove the membrane covering the brains. Lift the brains gently into a saucepan filled with cold salted water. Bring to a simmer over moderate heat and simmer, covered, for 30 minutes. Let the brains cool in the cooking liquid, then lift them out, drain, and slice.

Heat the butter in a skillet and sauté the brains until they are lightly colored on both sides, 3 or 4 minutes. Warm the whisky, pour it over the brains, and ignite it. Lift the brains out to a serving dish and keep warm. Pour the cream into the skillet and reduce over high heat to half its volume. Season to taste with salt and pepper. Nap the brains with the sauce.

Garnish with Champignons Sautés au Beurre (see Index), and serve with rice.

VEGETABLES

The end of overcooking is the most important thing that has happened to vegetables in our time. I think this is at least in part an influence from Japan, Vietnam, Thailand and China. In none of these cuisines are green vegetables cooked until soggy. They are always crisp and full of flavor.

The new French cooking, *nouvelle cuisine,* early adopted this attitude to green vegetables. By now the idea has spread and almost everyone accepts *haricots verts* that are *croquant,* that is, cooked but still crisp, still crunchy, never limp.

The food processor has also changed the attitude to vegetables, particularly to root vegetables. It is so easy to purée vegetables in the food processor fitted with the steel blade. Two may be mixed together to modify a flavor and enhance texture. Separately puréed vegetables, carrots, turnips, spinach, may be served in heaps on the same plate, an interplay of flavor and color—orange, white and green— pretty for the eye, rewarding for the palate.

Vegetable gratins make good first courses as well as good accompaniments to a main course; they are also useful for vegetarians or those wishing to cut down on meat in the diet. A cauliflower or leek gratin makes a satisfying main course for lunch or supper. Vegetables are also being used more imaginatively as garnishes and accompaniments. Mousse de Navets (turnip mousse) (see Index) is light and delicate. Tiny spring vegetables, the *primeurs*—baby carrots and turnips, new potatoes, tiny white onions, little mushroom caps and skinny little *haricots verts* (green beans)—arranged in small decorative heaps on a plate to accompany a main course, are very appetizing as well as being good for one.

There are no hard and fast rules for serving vegetables. The cook is invited to use imagination, to make new combinations of flavor and color, and to make the fullest use of the bounty of nature at its freshest and best.

VEGETABLE PURÉES

Any of the following vegetables are suitable for puréeing: Root vegetables are very attractive if two are arranged in a vegetable dish—puréed carrots and potatotes, or puréed carrots and turnips, puréed beets and celeriac. Winter squash looks attractive with vegetables like parsnips and potatoes mixed, or celery root. Three-color combinations can use spinach, lima beans, green beans, peas or broccoli for a green section, with carrot, winter squash or yams for a golden-orange contrast, and potatoes, celery root, white sweet potatoes, parsnips or cauliflower for the third color. Think first of flavor and avoid two strongly flavored vegetables. Choose bland vegetables, for example, to go with parsnips or gentle the flavor of the parsnips by mixing them with potatoes. Choose colors that enliven the appearance of the dish.

I prefer to cook green vegetables rapidly in a large amount of boiling salted water, uncovered. The vegetables cook evenly, the color is preserved, and the speed of cooking minimizes vitamin loss. The following table gives approximate cooking times for vegetables suitable for this

cooking method, or for puréeing. If puréed vegetables seem at all watery (small white turnips do, for example), let them drain in a wire sieve and use the liquid in soups, sauces or stocks. After puréeing, and draining if necessary, return the purée to the saucepan, season with salt and pepper, and reheat with about 1 tablespoon of butter to 1 pound of vegetable. Add a little heavy cream to vegetables like cauliflower, Brussels sprouts, potatoes, parsnips and celery root (celeriac).

BEANS, wax or green: 8 minutes

BEETS, whole, unpeeled with 1 inch of beet top left on: 30 minutes to 1 hour according to age and size

BROCCOLI, stalks peeled: 8 to 10 minutes

BRUSSELS SPROUTS: 8 minutes

CABBAGE, shredded: 5 to 8 minutes; quartered: 10 to 15 minutes.

CARROTS, whole, young, scraped: 8 to 10 minutes; mature carrots: 15 to 30 minutes

CAULIFLOWER FLOWERETS: 5 to 8 minutes; whole cauliflower: 15 to 20 minutes

CELERIAC, CELERY ROOT, whole peeled: 20 to 30 minutes

CELERY HEARTS: about 10 minutes

CHARD, SWISS, leaves only: 2 to 3 minutes; stems: 10 to 15 minutes

CHESTNUTS, to prepare and cook, see Index

CHICORY: 2 minutes

CUCUMBER, peeled, quartered: 3 to 4 minutes

FENNEL, bulbs trimmed and peeled: may be blanched in boiling salted water for about 8 minutes before braising, otherwise follow recipe instructions

JERUSALEM ARTICHOKES, scraped and boiled whole: 10 to 15 minutes. Take care not to overcook, as the vegetable loses its crisp texture and turns mushy.

KALE: 5 to 8 minutes

KOHLRABI, peeled and cooked whole: 30 to 40 minutes; sliced or quartered: 20 minutes

LEEKS, sliced: 2 to 3 minutes; left whole: 8 to 10 minutes

PARSNIPS, peeled: 15 to 20 minutes

PEAS: 3 to 8 minutes, according to size. *Mange-tout* (snow peas) should be cooked only until the water returns to a boil, about 1 minute

POTATOES: 15 to 20 minutes, or until done

SPINACH: about 2 minutes

SWEET POTATOES, using the white sweet potato (boniato), peeled: 15 to 20 minutes

TURNIPS, peeled: 5 to 10 minutes

WINTER SQUASH (Hubbard, etc.), peeled and cut into large chunks or slices: 10 to 15 minutes

ZUCCHINI, young, sliced: 4 to 5 minutes

Note: Always bring the water back to a boil over high heat before starting to count the minutes.

Purées may also be used as the basis of a quickly made soup. Mix the purée with a well-flavored chicken or beef stock to the desired consistency. Heat the soup through, adding a little milk or cream if liked.

PURÉE DE FENOUIL ET BROCOLI

(Fennel and Broccoli Purée)

SERVES 6.

Broccoli is not a favorite vegetable in France. Combined with fennel, the flavor of both vegetables is remarkably enhanced.

1 pound fennel bulbs	4 tablespoons butter
Salt	Freshly ground pepper
1 pound broccoli	

Trim the fennel bulbs, discarding the tops. Halve the bulbs and cut them into ½-inch lengthwise slices. Add them to a

saucepan of boiling salted water, bring back to a boil, and simmer for 20 minutes. While the fennel is cooking trim the broccoli stalks; add these to the fennel when it has been simmering 20 minutes. Bring back to a boil and simmer for 10 minutes longer, or until both fennel and broccoli are tender. Drain thoroughly and purée in a food processor or blender in batches. Return the purée to the saucepan. Beat in the butter, season to taste with salt and pepper if necessary, and heat through.

PURÉE DE CAROTTES ET RUTABAGA

(Carrot and Rutabaga Purée)

SERVES 6.

Rutabaga is not used a great deal in French cooking, probably because of its pronounced flavor. The sweetness of the carrots gentles the rutabaga, giving a most pleasant result.

1 pound medium-size carrots, scraped and cut into 2-inch pieces	Salt
	4 tablespoons butter
	Freshly ground pepper
1 pound rutabaga (Swede turnip), peeled and cut into 2-inch chunks	2 tablespoons heavy cream (optional)

Drop the carrots and rutabaga into a saucepan of boiling salted water, bring back to a boil, and simmer until vegetables are tender, about 15 minutes. Drain thoroughly. Reduce to a purée in a food processor or in a blender in batches. Return the purée to the saucepan and beat in the butter over low heat. Taste for seasoning and add salt and pepper if necessary. If liked, add the cream and heat through.

PURÉE DE CHAMPIGNONS

(Mushroom Purée)

SERVES 6.

Of all vegetable purées this is the one I find most elegant, most luxurious. It enhances almost any main course and has a natural affinity for roast poultry. Cultivated mushrooms are fine but sometimes field mushrooms are available and these are even better.

4 tablespoons butter	Salt, freshly ground
¼ cup finely chopped	pepper
shallots, scallions, or	Pinch of grated nutmeg
small white onion	¼ cup heavy cream
1 pound mushrooms	

In a heavy skillet heat the butter and sauté the shallots until soft but not brown. Wipe the mushrooms and chop them coarsely, using caps and stems. Add mushrooms to the skillet and sauté over moderate heat until they have released all their liquid. Season with salt, pepper and the pinch of nutmeg. Purée in a food processor or in a blender in batches. Be careful not to overprocess as the purée should have some texture. Return the mixture to the skillet, stir in the cream, and cook for 3 or 4 minutes longer to heat through and reduce the liquid. If the purée is at all watery, cook for a few minutes longer.

PURÉE DE MARRONS

(Chestnut Purée)

SERVES 4 TO 6.

Chestnut purée makes a splendid accompaniment to roast poultry—pheasant, duck, goose, turkey—and to venison, pork and sausages.

2 pounds chestnuts,
  peeled (see Index),
  about 5 cups
2 cups Chicken or Beef
  Stock (see Index)

Salt, freshly ground
  pepper
4 tablespoons butter

Put the peeled chestnuts into a large saucepan with the stock, adding a little more stock or water if necessary to cover them by about 1 inch. Bring to a boil, lower the heat and simmer, covered, until the chestnuts are tender, about 30 minutes. Drain and reserve the stock. Purée the chestnuts in a food processor or in a blender in batches, using a little of the reserved stock if necessary. Return them to the saucepan and season with salt and pepper. Over low heat beat in the butter. Turn into a warmed vegetable dish.

BETTERAVES EN PURÉE

(Puréed Beets)

SERVES 6.

1 pound small fresh beets
  Salt, freshly ground
  pepper
4 tablespoons butter, cut
  into bits

¼ cup heavy cream
  (optional)
1 teaspoon lemon juice

Cook the beets until tender (see Vegetable Purées). Cool beets quickly under cold running water, cut off the tops and bottoms, and slip off the skins. Chop coarsely. Process in a food processor or a blender with salt and pepper to taste and the butter to a smooth purée. If liked, add the heavy cream. Add the lemon juice and process for a few seconds longer. Transfer to a saucepan and reheat for a few minutes. Serve as a vegetable accompaniment to fish or with other purées to accompany poultry, rabbit or sautéed sweetbreads.

GRATIN DE POIREAUX

(Leek Gratin)

SERVES 6 TO 8 AS A FIRST COURSE, 4 TO 6 AS MAIN COURSE.

I find leeks an indispensable vegetable and this gratin a versatile dish which I like as a first course, as a vegetable dish with plainly cooked meat or poultry, or as a main course for a light meal. Leeks need thorough washing; see Index for a simple, effective method.

12 medium-size leeks, about 2 pounds	2 cups milk
Salt	White pepper
	Pinch of grated nutmeg
5 tablespoons butter	1 cup grated Gruyère
4 tablespoons flour	cheese

Thoroughly wash the leeks, trim, and cut off all but about 2 inches of the green part. Cut the leeks into 2-inch slices and put into a saucepan with a little salt and water to cover. Bring to a boil, cover, and simmer for 10 minutes, or until barely tender. Drain and set aside.

Make Sauce Béchamel: In a heavy saucepan melt 3 tablespoons of the butter, stir in the flour using a wooden spoon and cook, stirring, over very low heat for 2 minutes without letting the flour brown. Still stirring, gradually pour in the milk and cook, stirring constantly, until the mixture comes to a boil; simmer for a few minutes. Remove sauce from the heat and season with salt, white pepper and nutmeg. Butter a shallow ovenproof baking dish and pour in a thin layer of the sauce. Arrange the leeks on top and cover with the rest of the sauce. Sprinkle with the grated cheese and dot with remaining butter. Bake in a preheated mod-

erate oven (375°F.) for 30 minutes, or until the top is browned and bubbling.

GRATIN DE CHOUFLEUR

(Cauliflower Gratin)

SERVES 4.

This makes a delicious first course, or a fine accompaniment to plainly cooked meat, poultry or fish. It is also good as the main course of a light meal.

1 large cauliflower,
    broken into flowerets
    Salt
2 cups Sauce Béchamel
    (see Index)
3 tablespoons butter,
    approximately

¼ cup grated Gruyère
    cheese
¼ cup grated Parmesan
    cheese

Drop the cauliflower flowerets into briskly boiling salted water and simmer for 5 minutes. Drain thoroughly. Purée in a food processor or blender, being careful not to over-process. The purée should retain some texture and not be too smooth. Fold in the Sauce Béchamel and pour the mixture into a buttered baking dish. Top with the cheeses and dot with 2 tablespoons butter. Bake in a preheated moderate oven (375°F.) for about 30 minutes, or until the top is golden brown.

Variation: Substitute 2 pounds cooked and puréed broccoli, or 2 pounds cooked and puréed Brussels sprouts, for the cauliflower.

GRATIN DE COURGE

(Winter Squash Gratin)

SERVES 4.

2 pounds winter squash, peeled and cut into ½-inch cubes
Salt, freshly ground pepper
2 tablespoons butter, approximately

2 cups Sauce Béchamel (see Index), seasoned with ⅛ teaspoon grated nutmeg
¼ cup grated Swiss cheese
¼ cup grated Parmesan cheese

Put the squash into a saucepan with boiling salted water to cover and simmer until barely tender, about 10 minutes. Drain thoroughly. Season with salt and pepper and put into a buttered baking dish. Pour in the Sauce Béchamel, sprinkle with the cheeses, and dot with 1 tablespoon butter cut into bits. Bake in a preheated moderate oven (375°F.) for 30 to 40 minutes, or until the top is golden brown.

Serve as a first course, or to accompany plainly cooked meat or poultry.

Variation: Use white sweet potatoes (*boniatos*) or tropical yams (not Louisiana yams or orange sweet potatoes).

GRATIN DAUPHINOIS

(Scalloped Potatoes)

SERVES 4.

It is a disappointment to be served a *gratin dauphinois* so liquid that it runs into the rest of the food on the plate. I was pleased and grateful when Lucien Ogier of the L'Aubergade at Pontchartrain gave me his recipe. He claims the secret lies in not rinsing or drying the potatoes after slicing so that the natural starch makes a fine liaison.

1 cup milk
1 pound potatoes, peeled and cut into ¼-inch slices
Salt, freshly ground pepper
2 tablespoons butter
3 tablespoons heavy cream
1 garlic clove
½ cup grated Gruyère cheese

Bring the milk to a boil in a saucepan and add the potatoes, salt and pepper to taste and butter. Bring back to a boil and add the cream. Simmer over very low heat, covered, for 30 minutes. Crush the garlic clove and rub the purée into an earthenware gratin dish. Turn the potato mixture into the gratin dish and sprinkle with the cheese. Bake in a preheated slow oven (325°F.) for 1 hour.

GÂTEAU DE POMMES DE TERRE AU MÜNSTER FERMIER

(Farm-Style Potatoes with Cheese)

SERVES 4.

1 tablespoon vegetable oil
2 tablespoons butter
1 pound potatoes, peeled and cut lengthwise into ⅛-inch slices
⅓ cup thin strips of Münster cheese
⅓ cup grated Gruyère cheese
Salt

Heat the oil and butter in a heavy flameproof casserole. Add one third of the potatoes, Münster and Gruyère. Repeat until all the potatoes and cheeses are used. Salt lightly. Cover and cook over very low heat for 30 to 40 minutes, or until potatoes are done. Turn the potato cake upside down on a warmed serving platter. If the cheese sticks to the bottom, use a spatula to scrape it out of the casserole and put it on top of the potatoes.

CHOU ROUGE À LA FLAMANDE

(Red Cabbage Flemish Style)

SERVES 6 TO 8.

This is a very good, uncomplicated way of cooking red cabbage. It can be cooked equally successfully in the oven or on top of the stove. Though thoroughly traditional, this recipe has the kind of simplicity that recommends itself to cooks today.

1 medium-size red
  cabbage
Salt, freshly ground
  pepper
1 tablespoon red-wine
  vinegar
3 tablespoons butter

1 cup dry red wine or
  Beef Stock (see Index)
3 tart apples, peeled,
  cored and quartered
1 tablespoon sugar, or less
  to taste

Wash the cabbage and remove any wilted leaves. Cut it into quarters and remove the white core. Shred the cabbage and season it with salt and pepper; add the vinegar, mixing well. Melt the butter in a casserole. Earthenware is best, but any heavy flameproof casserole will do. Add the cabbage mixture and the wine or stock. Cover and cook on top of the stove over very low heat, or in a preheated slow oven (300°F.), for about 1 hour, or until the cabbage is tender. Add the apples to the casserole, sprinkle with the sugar, and cook for 30 minutes longer. The cabbage can be cooked ahead of time as it reheats well.

This is very good with kielbasa or any garlic sausage such as cervelas, or with roast pork.

Variation: For a more robust version of the dish, **CHOUX ROUGES AUX POMMES ET AUX MARRONS** (*RED CABBAGE WITH APPLES AND CHESTNUTS*), wash, core, and finely shred the cabbage. Marinate it in 1 cup red-wine vinegar for 30 minutes. Heat 8 tablespoons goose or duck fat or vegetable oil in a flame-

proof casserole and sauté 1 finely chopped medium-size onion until soft. Add the cabbage with salt and pepper to taste, ¼ teaspoon sugar, all the marinating liquid, and ½ cup beef stock. Add 2 cloves and a bay leaf. Cook, covered, over very low heat on top of the stove, or in a preheated slow oven (300°F.), for 1 hour. Add 3 tart apples, peeled, cored and cut into quarters, and 20 chestnuts. Cook for 30 minutes longer. Serves 6 to 8.

FAR AU CHOU DU QUERCY
(Cabbage Pudding)

SERVES 4 TO 6.

Most of the *fars*, light puddings with vegetables or fruits, are usually thought of as Breton dishes. This one, given me by a friend, is from Quercy, once a county, now divided between the departments of Lot, Tarn and Garonne with Cahors as its principal town. I think an inventive cook could create many interesting variations of this, using combinations of vegetables.

1 pound cabbage, cooked, drained and chopped Salt, freshly ground pepper, pinch of sugar Butter	BATTER 1 cup all-purpose flour 1 teaspoon salt 3 whole eggs 1¼ cups milk

Mix the cabbage with salt, pepper and sugar to taste and pack into a well-buttered 6-cup soufflé dish or mold.

Make the batter: Sift the flour and salt into a bowl. Beat in the eggs, one by one, then beat in the milk until the mixture is smooth. Pour the batter over the cabbage. Bake in a preheated moderate oven (350°F.) for about 40 minutes, or until a cake tester comes out clean. Serve as a first course with tomato sauce, or as a vegetable dish with any meat or poultry.

CHOU FARCI AUX MARRONS

(Cabbage Stuffed with Chestnuts)

SERVES 6 TO 8.

At one of the first dinner parties I ever gave, in my green youth, I cooked a Sou-Fassum Provençale (stuffed cabbage Provence style) from a recipe in Escoffier's *Guide to Modern Cookery*. It was the main course of the dinner and I was very proud of it. One of my guests, then a young Navy lieutenant, but now a distinguished admiral, remarked at the end of the meal that he would have preferred a steak. I still enjoy the *sou-fassum* but I like equally well other stuffings, my fondness for cabbage having survived.

1 large Savoy cabbage, 2 to 2½ pounds
Salt
¾ cup diced unsmoked bacon
Oil
½ pound cooked ham, coarsely chopped
1 pound cooked chestnuts (see Index), coarsely chopped, about 2½ cups

¼ teaspoon grated nutmeg
½ teaspoon freshly ground pepper
4 tablespoons butter, melted
8 cups Beef or Chicken Stock (see Index), approximately
1 cup heavy cream

Trim the stalk of the cabbage and remove and discard any wilted leaves. Slide the cabbage into a large saucepan of briskly boiling salted water, bring back to a boil over high heat and simmer, uncovered, for 10 minutes. Drain in a colander and cool. On a work surface place a square of double cheesecloth large enough to envelop the cabbage. Place the cabbage in the center of the cheesecloth and very gently open out the leaves, taking care not to tear or detach them. Carefully cut out the heart of the cabbage, squeeze to re-

move excess moisture, and chop it finely. Set it aside in a bowl.

Sauté the bacon in a skillet, filmed with just enough oil to stop the bacon sticking, until bacon is lightly colored. Let it cool and add to the chopped cabbage heart. Add the ham, chestnuts, a little salt, the nutmeg and pepper. Mix thoroughly. The best and easiest way is to use the hands. Press the stuffing into a ball. The simplest way to stuff the cabbage is to gather up the cheesecloth and lift the whole cabbage into a large bowl, which will stop the leaves flopping about. Place the ball of stuffing in the cabbage where the heart was. Re-form the cabbage by folding the leaves, one by one, back over the stuffing, pressing gently in place. Pour the melted butter over the cabbage. Gather up the cheesecloth and tie it firmly with a piece of string. Lift the cabbage into a heavy saucepan just large enough to hold it comfortably, and pour in enough beef or chicken stock to cover it. (If no stock is available, use water with the addition of 2 medium-size carrots, scraped and chopped, 1 onion, halved and stuck with 2 cloves, and a few herbs—parsley, bay leaf, thyme.) Cover the saucepan and simmer over low heat for 2½ to 3 hours, adding more stock during the cooking, if necessary.

Lift out the cabbage into a bowl, and untie the cheesecloth. Cover the bowl with a deep serving dish and invert the cabbage into it. Pour off all but 1 cup of the stock, reserving the rest for another use. Transfer the cup of stock to a small saucepan, pour in the cream, and season to taste with salt and pepper. Bring to a boil and simmer for 1 or 2 minutes. Pour the sauce over the cabbage, or serve sauce separately in a sauceboat.

Variations: Cook the cabbage in the same way but use a different stuffing: Heat 2 tablespoons butter in a skillet and sauté 1 cup diced bacon until lightly colored. Add 2 finely chopped medium-size onions and 2 chopped garlic cloves and sauté until onions are tender. Add 1 pound ground pork and cook for 3 or 4 minutes

(*recipe continues*)

longer, stirring to mix. Transfer to a bowl. When the mixture is cool season with salt, a generous amount of freshly ground pepper, ½ cup finely chopped parsley, ½ cup chopped scallions using some of the green part, ¼ cup chopped fresh basil leaves, and the chopped cabbage heart. Mix thoroughly, form into a ball, and stuff the cabbage. Leftover cooked pork may be used instead of fresh pork. Omit the cream from the sauce. Serve a sauceboat of the stock.

SOU-FASSUM PROVENÇAL (*STUFFED CABBAGE PROVENCE STYLE*): Cook the cabbage in the same way, but use the following stuffing: Heat 1 tablespoon oil in a skillet and sauté ½ pound chopped lean bacon until lightly colored. Lift out the bacon with a slotted spoon to a bowl. Add the chopped cabbage heart. Add 1 tablespoon butter to the fat remaining in the skillet and sauté 2 finely chopped medium-size onions until soft. Add to the bowl with 1 pound ground fresh lean pork, 2 medium-size tomatoes, peeled, seeded and chopped, 1 crushed garlic clove, salt and freshly ground pepper to taste, ½ cup fresh young green peas, and ⅓ cup rice cooked in boiling salted water for 10 minutes, then drained. Mix thoroughly together, form into a ball, and stuff the cabbage.

OIGNONS GLACÉS À BLANC

(White Glazed Onions)

SERVES 6.

1½ pounds small white onions, about 24, peeled
3 tablespoons butter
1½ tablespoons sugar

½ cup Chicken or Veal Stock (see Index), or water
Salt

Put the onions into a saucepan or skillet that will hold them comfortably in a single layer. Add the butter, sugar, stock or water, and salt to taste. Bring to a boil, lower the heat, cover, and simmer until onions are tender. If necessary add

a little more liquid during the cooking. The onions will not brown, but be just faintly golden.

OIGNONS GLACÉS À BRUN

(Brown Glazed Onions)

(See preceding recipe for ingredients.)

Put the onions into the saucepan or skillet with the butter and stock or water to cover. Bring to a boil, lower the heat, cover, and simmer until onions are tender, about 20 minutes. Shake the pan from time to time to prevent sticking. Sprinkle onions with 1½ tablespoons sugar and cook, uncovered, until the sugar and butter form a rich brown glaze. Shake the pan during this part of the cooking to coat the onions evenly with the glaze. If they seem to be sticking, add a little stock or water. Put into a warm vegetable dish.

PETITS OIGNONS

(Little Onions)

SERVES 4 TO 6.

Pierre Hiély of the Relais Gourmand restaurant Hiély-Lucullus in Avignon gave me this recipe for tiny onions. It makes an attractive vegetable course with any plainly cooked meat or poultry dish.

2 pounds small white onions	1 thyme sprig
Butter	1 bay leaf
¼ cup raisins	⅛ teaspoon ground coriander
1 tablespoon fresh tomato purée	Salt, freshly ground pepper
1 cup dry white wine	¼ cup heavy cream
2 tablespoons olive oil	

(*recipe continues*)

Drop the onions into boiling water. Leave for 5 seconds, just long enough for the skins to loosen; drain, and rinse in cold water. Slip off the skins. Butter an ovenproof baking dish large enough to hold the onions in a single layer. Arrange the onions in the dish and sprinkle with the raisins. Mix together the tomato purée, wine, oil, thyme, bay leaf, coriander, salt and pepper to taste, and pour the mixture over the onions. Cover and bake in a preheated moderate oven (350°F.) for 30 minutes. Pour in the cream and cook, uncovered, for 15 minutes longer.

CAROTTES GLACÉES

(Glazed Carrots)

SERVES 6.

1½ pounds small young carrots, about 24, left whole, or larger carrots cut into 2- to 3-inch pieces	4 tablespoons butter 1½ tablespoons sugar Salt 2 tablespoons finely chopped parsley

Put the carrots, butter, sugar and salt to taste into a saucepan with water barely to cover. Bring to a boil, cover, and simmer until carrots are tender and the liquid has reduced to a syrupy glaze, 30 to 40 minutes. If the liquid has not all evaporated, cook uncovered for the last 15 minutes of cooking, shaking the pan from time to time so the carrots are evenly coated. Transfer to a heated vegetable dish and sprinkle with the parsley.

Variation: Small white turnips and celery root, peeled and cut into 2-inch pieces or into olive shapes, can be cooked in the same way as the carrots.

GNOCCHI DE POTIRON

(Winter Squash Gnocchi)

SERVES 4 AS AN ACCOMPANIMENT, 2 AS MAIN COURSE.

I like to serve these *gnocchi* instead of noodles, rice or potatoes with any meat or poultry dish that has a sauce, especially one based on tomato. They also make a good first course or a light luncheon dish if gratinéed.

1 pound winter squash
   such as Hubbard,
   peeled and cubed,
   about 2 cups
1 cup flour
2 tablespoons heavy
   cream
   Salt, freshly ground
   pepper

GRATIN
⅓ cup heavy cream
½ cup grated Gruyère
   cheese
2 tablespoons butter, cut
   into bits

Grate the squash as fine as possible in a food processor fitted with the steel blade. Add the flour, cream and salt and pepper to taste, and process until the flour is thoroughly mixed into the vegetable. The squash can also be puréed in a blender. Lacking these utensils, don't cube it, but grate it on the fine side of a grater.

Have ready a large saucepan of boiling salted water. Form the squash mixture into dumplings, about 1 tablespoon each, and slide them gently into the water. Do not have the water at a rolling boil; it should just move. When they are done, the *gnocchi* will rise to the surface. They take about 10 minutes. Lift out with a slotted spoon and keep warm if serving as an accompaniment to a main course.

If serving gratinéed, arrange *gnocchi* in a buttered ovenproof dish, drizzle with the cream, sprinkle with the cheese, dot with the butter, and brown under a moderately hot broiler.

MARRONS BRAISÉS

(Braised Chestnuts)

SERVES 4 TO 6.

3 tablespoons butter
1 pound chestnuts, peeled
   (see Index)
2 cups Chicken, Veal or
   Beef Stock (see Index)

2 tablespoons Port or
   Madeira wine
Salt, freshly ground
   pepper

Butter a flameproof casserole large enough to hold the chestnuts without heaping them up. Put in the chestnuts and pour in the stock and the Port or Madeira. Season to taste, and add remaining butter. Bring to a simmer, cover, and cook over very low heat until chestnuts are tender and most of the liquid has cooked away. Uncover and cook, shaking the casserole from time to time, until the stock has reduced to a glaze, coating the chestnuts. Serve with poultry.

Variations: Combine the braised chestnuts with 1 cup raw long-grain rice cooked in 2 cups chicken stock. The rice should be quite dry when the chestnuts are added. If liked, stir in 1 or 2 tablespoons butter.

   Combine the cooked chestnuts with 1 pound cooked Brussels sprouts.

CHAMPIGNONS SAUTÉS AU BEURRE

(Sautéed Mushrooms)

SERVES 2.

½ pound mushrooms
   Salt, freshly ground
   pepper

2 tablespoons butter
½ tablespoon vegetable oil

If possible choose mushrooms of a uniform size. Wipe the mushroom caps and remove the stems. (Use stems in stocks or sauces.) If mushrooms are small, leave whole; if large, quarter them. Season the mushrooms with salt and pepper. In a heavy skillet heat the butter and oil. Add the mushrooms and sauté over moderately high heat until they have released all their moisture and are lightly browned, about 5 minutes. Use as directed in recipes, or serve as a vegetable.

CHAMPIGNONS À LA DIJONNAISE

(Mushrooms, Dijon Style)

SERVES 4 TO 6.

1 pound mushrooms, if small left whole, if large, quartered
Salt, freshly ground pepper
3 tablespoons lemon juice
2 tablespoons butter
¼ cup finely chopped shallots

½ cup heavy cream
½ cup dry white wine
2 tablespoons Dijon mustard
2 tablespoons finely chopped parsley

Trim the mushrooms and wipe the tops with a damp paper towel. Put them into a flameproof casserole and season with salt and pepper; add the lemon juice and 1 tablespoon of the butter. Cover and simmer over very low heat for 5 minutes. Heat remaining tablespoon of butter in a small skillet and sauté the shallots until soft, but do not let them brown. Add them to the casserole and continue to cook, covered, over low heat for a few minutes longer. Mix together the cream, wine and mustard and stir into the casserole. Stir and cook until the sauce is heated through and the mushrooms are tender. Serve sprinkled with the parsley.

MOUSSE DE NAVETS AUX FINES HERBES

(Mousse of White Turnips with Herbs)

SERVES 4 GENEROUSLY.

I think all of us get tired of vegetables cooked in a routine way so I was delighted when Georges Paineau, who runs the Relais Gourmand Le Bretagne at Questembert, served a delicious *mousse de navets* as a vegetable accompaniment. Nothing that Georges Paineau cooks is ordinary or dull, and just eating his food stretches one's own culinary imagination.

2 pounds small white turnips, peeled and halved	Freshly ground pepper
Salt	Cayenne pepper
4 egg whites	Butter
6 tablespoons and 1 cup heavy cream	½ cup finely snipped chives

Put the turnips in a saucepan with salted water to cover, bring to a boil, and simmer until the turnips are tender, about 15 minutes. Drain thoroughly. Purée in a blender or food processor fitted with the steel blade. Drain the purée in a sieve, letting it stand for about 10 minutes. (The drained-off liquid can be added to stock.) Turn the purée into a bowl and set it in a larger bowl filled with ice cubes or crushed ice. Gradually beat in the egg whites, then the 6 tablespoons of cream. Season to taste with salt, pepper and a little cayenne. Butter 8 small cylindrical (ramekin) molds, or a 1-quart soufflé dish. Fill the molds with the mousse batter. Set the molds in a pan with water to come about halfway up. Cook in a preheated moderate oven (350°F.) for 20 minutes, or until set.

In a small saucepan reduce the cup of cream to ½ cup. Keep it warm and at the last minute stir in the chives. Un-

mold the small pots onto plates, two to a serving, and surround with a ribbon of the cream and chives mixture. If you used the soufflé dish, serve the mousse directly out of the dish and spoon a little of the cream at the side of each serving.

LAITUES BRAISÉES AUX RAISINS

(Lettuce Braised with Grapes)

SERVES 6.

6 Boston lettuces
  Salt, freshly ground
    pepper
½ cup Chicken Stock (see
  Index)

½ cup dry white wine
2 cups small white
    seedless grapes
4 tablespoons butter, cut
    into bits

Trim the lettuces and remove any wilted leaves. Have ready a large saucepan of briskly boiling salted water, add the lettuces, and bring the water back to a boil over high heat. Boil for 1 minute, then plunge the lettuces into cold water, drain, and pat dry, gently squeezing out the excess moisture. Halve the lettuces lengthwise and arrange them, pushed closely together, in a heavy skillet or flameproof casserole. Season with salt and pepper, pour in the stock and wine, and sprinkle with the grapes. Bring to a simmer, cover, and cook over low heat for 10 minutes, or until lettuces are tender. Lift out with a slotted spoon to a vegetable dish, lifting out the grapes at the same time. Over high heat reduce the liquid in the pan until it is syrupy. Beat in the butter, bit by bit, adding each new piece as soon as the previous bit is incorporated into the sauce. Taste for seasoning, adding salt and pepper if necessary. Pour the sauce over the lettuces. This is particularly good with roast or sautéed chicken, duckling or other poultry.

CHOUFLEUR AU BEURRE NANTAIS

(Cauliflower in White Butter Sauce)

SERVES 4 TO 6.

1 medium-size cauliflower
Salt
1 recipe Beurre Nantais
   (see Index)

1 large egg, lightly beaten
⅓ cup heavy cream

Slide the whole cauliflower into a large saucepan of briskly boiling salted water, bring back to a boil over high heat and simmer, uncovered, for 15 to 20 minutes, or until cauliflower is tender. Drain and put into a warmed vegetable dish. Keep warm. While the cauliflower is cooking make the Beurre Nantais. Over low heat whisk the egg into the sauce; when sauce has thickened lightly, whisk in the cream. Nap the cauliflower with the sauce.

COURGETTES

(Zucchini)

SERVES 6.

2 pounds zucchini, 3 to 6
   inches long, with
   smooth shiny skins

Salt

Wash the vegetables and trim the stem and blossom ends but do not scrape or peel except to remove a blemished spot. Cut into ⅛-inch slices. Have ready a saucepan of briskly boiling salted water. Add the zucchini, bring back to a boil over high heat and simmer, uncovered, over moderate heat for 4 to 5 minutes. Small young vegetables will need only 4 minutes. Drain in a colander. Put into a

warmed vegetable dish with a tablespoon or 2 of butter, if liked.

Variation: Purée the cooked zucchini in a blender or food processor, drain through a wire sieve, and return to the saucepan with 2 tablespoons butter. Toss over heat to melt the butter and heat the vegetable through. Transfer to a heated vegetable dish and grind a little pepper on top, or sprinkle with a little ground coriander.

ÉPINARDS EN BRANCHES AU BEURRE NOISETTE

(Spinach with Brown Butter)

SERVES 4.

2 pounds fresh spinach   Salt

Thoroughly wash the spinach. Remove any coarse stems and wilted leaves. Drain. Drop the spinach into a large saucepan of briskly boiling salted water. Bring back to a boil over high heat and boil for 2 minutes. Drain. To remove the water, lay the spinach on a bamboo mat, roll up the mat and squeeze out the water, or roll the spinach in a kitchen towel and press out the moisture. Return the spinach to the saucepan and shake, over moderate heat, until the vegetable is dry and heated through. Transfer the spinach to a warmed vegetable dish and pour the beurre noisette (brown butter) over it.

BEURRE NOISETTE

(BROWN BUTTER)

In a small, heavy saucepan cook 4 tablespoons of clarified butter over low heat until it turns a golden brown.

CRÊPES VONNASSIENNES

(Potato Pancakes Vonnas Style)

SERVES 6.

This is a favorite recipe of Georges Blanc of the Relais La Mère Blanc in Vonnas, a lovely inn where, if you are lucky, you can hear nightingales sing as well as eat potato crêpes and other delights. The recipe is well known but Georges Blanc agreed with me when I said I could not bear to leave it out. I like the crêpes with main courses of meat or poultry, with a little sugar as a dessert, or just by themselves.

1 pound potatoes, peeled and quartered	4 tablespoons flour
Salt	6 large eggs
½ cup milk	¼ cup heavy cream
	Butter

Cook the potatoes in boiling salted water to cover until tender, 15 to 20 minutes. Drain potatoes thoroughly, then steam them dry over low heat for 1 or 2 minutes. Mash the potatoes or purée them in a food processor. Stir in the milk, then chill the potatoes thoroughly. In a food processor fitted with the steel blade, or in a blender, combine the potatoes with the flour. With the machine running, add the eggs one by one, then stir in the cream. Beat the batter until it is very smooth and has the consistency of heavy cream. Taste for seasoning and add a little salt if necessary.

In a heavy skillet heat a tablespoon of butter. When the foam subsides, pour in about 1 tablespoon of the batter, or enough to make a 3-inch crêpe. Cook over moderate heat

until browned. Turn and brown the other side. Make crêpes with remaining batter in the same way, adding butter to the skillet as needed. Transfer the crêpes as they are done to a dish lined with paper towels and keep them warm.

POMMES DE TERRE AUX OIGNONS ET AU LARD

(Potatoes with Onion and Bacon)

SERVES 6.

¼ pound bacon, about 4 slices, chopped
2 pounds potatoes, about 6 medium-size, peeled and thinly sliced
2 pounds onions, chopped

¼ pound butter (1 stick), chilled and cut into bits
Salt, freshly ground pepper

In a large heavy casserole make a layer of the bacon. Top the bacon with one third of the potato slices, half of the onions and one third of the butter. Season with salt and pepper. Repeat with another third of the potatoes, the rest of the onions, and another third of the butter. Season with salt and pepper. Make a final layer with remaining potatoes and butter. Season with salt and pepper. Cover the casserole and bake in a preheated hot oven (425°F.) for 1 hour. Stir to mix.

This is delicious with baked ham or roast pork.

RIZ CRÉOLE

(Creole Rice)

SERVES 6 TO 8.

This is a popular way of cooking rice in France. The technique was adopted from the Creoles. The rice emerges dry and fluffy.

2 cups raw long-grain rice   6 cups water
1 teaspoon salt

Thoroughly wash the rice in several changes of water. In a large heavy saucepan combine the salt and water and bring to a rolling boil. Pour in the rice and bring back to a boil over high heat. Simmer, uncovered, for 15 minutes. Drain, rinse quickly under cold running water, and return to the saucepan. Cover and cook over the lowest possible heat until rice is tender and quite dry, about 20 minutes. Use an asbestos mat, if necessary, to prevent the rice sticking.

DESSERTS AND BREADS

Elaborate or rich desserts are marvelous but do not belong, I feel, with everyday meals. I often prefer, as do guests, fresh fruit, sometimes served with cheese, or just cheese with a glass of red wine to finish a meal. But there are occasions when a dessert served with a glass of Sauternes will end a meal on a splendid note. I have made a modest collection of desserts I have enjoyed, and of some breads as well.

There are also the *sorbets* (sherbets) which have come into their own with the new attitudes to food. Once relegated to the role of palate refresher to be served in the middle of long, rich, elaborate meals, they are now served as light and delicate desserts at the end of meals where a rich sauce of an exquisitely concentrated flavor makes the palate crave the tart airiness of a fruit *sorbet*.

SORBETS

(SHERBETS)

A successful *sorbet* can be made by hand, the freezing process interrupted several times and the mixture beaten with a whisk, but this is tedious, and not always successful. A young Parisian friend of mine recently asked me if I had a *sorbetière* and urged me, if I didn't, to get one immediately. It is, he assured me, as essential a kitchen tool as the food processor. Excellent electric ice-cream and/or *sorbet* makers are available to take advantage of the new approach to this lightest of desserts.

A wide range of fruits and mixtures of fruits and juices can be used. A pretty notion is to have a palette of *sorbets,* small servings of a number of different flavors arranged on a large plate like an artist's palette, or several *sorbets* arranged on a plate with a small amounts of the appropriate fresh fruit arranged decoratively with them. There is no end to the charming arrangements an imaginative cook can make following the basic inspiration of the new ideas. Oranges can be hollowed out and filled with sherbet, and lemons can be hollowed out, frozen, and filled with *sorbet de citron,* the frozen shell making an amusing and attractive container. Fruit *sorbets* are made from sugar syrup and fruit purée or juice, using equal amounts of purée or juice to syrup. To make the syrup:

4 cups water
3 cups sugar

In a heavy saucepan combine the water and sugar and bring to a boil over a moderate heat. Simmer for about 3 minutes. If any sugar crystals cling to the sides of the pan, wash them back into the syrup with a pastry brush dipped into cold water. Let the syrup cool. Pour it into a jar or jug and refrigerate until ready to use.

Wine *sorbets* are made in the same way, using sugar syrup. If using wine such as Madeira, Port, Champagne, or

Sauternes, use 2 cups wine to 2 cups syrup, adding lemon juice to taste.

Sorbets made with liqueurs, Calvados for example, need only ½ cup liqueur to 3½ cups syrup.

SORBET AUX POIRES

(Fresh Pear Sherbet)

MAKES ABOUT 1 QUART.

3 large pears, peeled, cored, and quartered	1½ cups sugar syrup
⅓ cup water	1 to 2 tablespoons lemon juice

In a heavy saucepan combine the pear pieces with the water and simmer, covered, until pears are tender, about 5 minutes. Cool, drain, setting the liquid aside, and purée the pears in a blender or a food processor fitted with the steel blade. Use the reserved liquid when making the sugar syrup in place of the equivalent amount of water. Makes about 1½ cups purée.

Combine purée with 1½ cups sugar syrup and stir in 1 to 2 tablespoons lemon juice, according to taste. If liked, a tablespoon of *eau de vie de poire* (pear liqueur) may be used as well as, or instead of, the lemon juice to heighten the flavor. Freeze in an ice-cream freezer or *sorbetière*. Canned fruit can also be used.

Variations: Make *sorbet* with any of the following fruits: apple (cooked and puréed), pineapple, raspberry, strawberry, blueberry, cranberry, mango, blackberry, black currants, kiwi fruit, cherries. Bananas are too bland to be used alone and should be puréed with a mixture of orange and lemon juice, or with pineapple juice. Fruits full of tiny seeds like raspberries should be sieved. Orange or lemon sherbet should be made with orange or lemon juice and the grated or julienned rind of the fruit.

Herbs like mint are often used for *sorbets.*

SORBET DE MENTHE

(Mint Sherbet)

MAKES ABOUT 1½ QUARTS.

This unusual *sorbet* is the invention of chef Michel Gonod of the Relais et Châteaux Le Prieuré at Villeneuve-lès-Avignon. It has a most refreshing taste.

  3 cups water
2¼ cups sugar
  2 cups mint leaves

1 to 2 tablespoons lemon juice (optional)

In a saucepan combine the water and 2 cups sugar and cook over moderate heat, stirring with a wooden spoon, until the sugar is dissolved. Bring to a boil and simmer for 3 minutes. Wash down the sugar crystals clinging to the sides of the pan with a pastry brush dipped into cold water. Let the syrup cool.

In a bowl mash the mint leaves with remaining ¼ cup sugar, bruising the mint thoroughly. Add the mint mixture to the cooled syrup and let it infuse for at least 1 hour. Strain. Freeze the mixture in an ice-cream freezer or in an electric refrigerator ice-cream freezer or a *sorbetière*.

If a sharper flavor is preferred, stir 1 to 2 tablespoons of lemon juice into the mixture before freezing.

FROMAGE BLANC AVEC CRÈME FRAÎCHE

(Fresh Cheese with Cream)

SERVES 2.

Fresh white cheese masked with cream and sprinkled with sugar is a favorite dessert in France. With the aid of chefs I have been able to put together a reasonable facsimile of the original. In Bourg-en-Bresse I bought cup-size plastic tumblers with holes on the bottom and sides for making fresh cheese. The holes let the whey drain out. The cheese can then be inverted onto a serving plate in a neat pyramidal shape. These cups are nice to have, but a sieve lined with cheesecloth does the same job. A great aspect of this dessert is that it can be made from low-calorie yogurt or skim milk, and anyone wishing to can make his own yogurt, or junket (see recipes following), for cheese.

4 cups plain or low-fat yogurt	Crème Fraîche (see Index) or heavy cream
Pinch of salt	Sugar

Line a large sieve with a double layer of dampened cheesecloth. Pour in the yogurt and add the salt. Set over a bowl. Let the yogurt stand until the whey has drained out and the cheese is firm, about 6 hours. Makes about 2 cups.

Mound the cheese on 2 plates, mask with *crème fraîche* or heavy cream, and sprinkle with sugar.

If liked serve with fresh fruit such as strawberries or raspberries.

Variations: Omit sugar and sprinkle the cheese with 1 tablespoon finely chopped fresh herbs including chives, parsley, tarragon, basil and chervil, mixed according to taste and availability.

For a richer cheese, add 1 cup heavy cream to 3 cups yogurt, and drain through cheesecloth.

To Make Yogurt

4 cups milk, either whole or skim milk	2 tablespoons homemade or commercial yogurt

Heat the milk in a saucepan to lukewarm (110°F.). Remove from the heat. Beat the yogurt with a fork until it is liquid and stir it into the milk. Pour the mixture into a bowl, cover, and leave in a warm place, such as an oven with the pilot light on, until the mixture is thick, 6 to 8 hours. Use to make fresh cheese.

(recipe continues)

To Make Junket Cheese

4 cups milk, either whole or skim milk	Pinch of salt
	2 junket (rennet) tablets

In a large saucepan heat the milk with the salt to lukewarm (110°F.). Pour into a bowl. Crush the junket tablets to powder and mix with a little water. Add to the milk; stir once, quickly. Cover and let stand for about 15 minutes, or until set. Pour carefully into a sieve lined with a double thickness of dampened cheesecloth set over a bowl and leave until the cheese is lightly firm, about 30 minutes. Pour off and discard the whey. Serve masked with *crème fraîche* or heavy cream and sprinkled with sugar. Makes 1⅓ cups.

CHARLOTTE

SERVES 6.

This modestly named recipe is the luscious invention of chef Michel Gonod of the Relais et Châteaux Hostellerie Le Prieuré at Villeneuve-lès-Avignon.

24 single ladyfingers, 2 by 4 inches, approximately	CHOCOLATE MOUSSE
	6 ounces sweet dark chocolate
SYRUP	10 tablespoons strong black coffee
2 cups water	10 tablespoons butter
1 cup sugar	2 eggs, separated
½ cup dark rum, approximately	Whipped cream

Make the syrup: In a saucepan combine 2 cups water with the sugar and stir over moderate heat until sugar is dissolved. Cool and stir in the rum. Taste and add a little more rum if liked. Pour a little of the syrup into a rimmed soup plate or shallow bowl and set the rest aside.

Quickly dip the ladyfingers, one at a time, into the syrup

in the soup plate and put them, curved side down, into the bottom of a 6-cup charlotte mold, cutting them into wedges to fit. Put the rest of the ladyfingers upright round the sides of the mold, close together with their curved sides against the mold. Set the prepared mold aside.

Make the mousse: Melt the chocolate in the top part of a double boiler over hot water and over low heat, and pour in the coffee, stirring to mix. Remove from the heat and let the mixture cool for a minute or 2. Beat in the butter bit by bit, then beat in the egg yolks, one at a time. Cool. Beat the whites until they stand in firm peaks and fold them into the cooled chocolate mixture. Pour the mousse into the prepared charlotte mold. Cover the mold with the remaining ladyfingers. Refrigerate, covered with plastic wrap, for 12 hours. Just before serving pour the reserved rum syrup over the charlotte to saturate the ladyfingers. Serve with whipped cream.

LES FRAISES MARINÉES

(Strawberries in Wine)

SERVES 6.

It may seem like gilding the lily, but using wine is a good way of escaping from the temptation of adding cream to strawberries in the traditional fashion. This version is from Raymond Vuillet, the chef at the Mapotel Impérator in Nîmes; and it is the the Port wine that makes the difference.

1½ pounds strawberries	Confectioners' sugar
1 cup dry red wine	(optional)
½ cup Port wine	

Rinse and hull the strawberries and put them into a shallow glass bowl. Pour in the red wine and the Port and refrigerate for 1 hour. Just before serving, the strawberries may be sprinkled with a little confectioners' sugar to taste.

TARTE CHAUDE AUX POIRES

(Warm Pear Tart)

SERVES 1.

I remember with pleasure the pear tart I had at the restaurant Le Drouet of the Hôtel de la Paix in Reims. It was simplicity itself. Make it when pears are at their finest and most abundant. Recipe can be increased to any number.

¼ recipe Pâte Feuilletée
  (see Index)
1 egg yolk
1 teaspoon water
1 large ripe pear, peeled,
  cored and cut into
  lengthwise slices

1 tablespoon sugar
1 tablespoon butter plus
  butter for baking sheet
Heavy cream (optional)

Roll out the puff pastry ¼ inch thick and into a rectangle 3 by 5 inches. Prick the pastry with a fork and brush with egg wash made by beating the egg yolk with the water. Cut a ½-inch-wide strip of pastry and lay it round the edge of the rectangle on top of the egg wash. Press it gently into place. Brush with egg wash. Arrange the slices of pear on the pastry and sprinkle with sugar. Dot with butter and place on a buttered baking sheet. Bake in a preheated hot oven (425°F.) for 15 to 20 minutes, or until the pastry is delicately browned. Serve immediately accompanied by a bowl of cream, if liked.

FLAN AUX POIRES DU POITOU

(Warm Pear Tart)

SERVES 8.

Pears are one of my favorite fruits, and walnuts a favorite nut, both deliciously combined in this tart. M. Robert, of the Mapotel de France in Poitiers, was kind enough to share this recipe with me.

1 recipe Pâte Brisée
   Sucrée (see Index)
1 cup walnut pieces

2 large or 3 small pears,
   peeled, cored and
   sliced

CRÈME PÂTISSIÈRE (Pastry Cream)

3 egg yolks
⅓ cup sugar
⅓ cup all-purpose flour

1 cup milk
Butter

Make the pastry, and chill until ready to use.

    Make the pastry cream: In a bowl beat the egg yolks and sugar together until they form a ribbon. Gradually beat in the flour. In a small saucepan bring the milk to boiling point. Slowly pour the milk into the egg-yolk mixture while continuing to whisk it. Transfer the mixture to a saucepan; stirring constantly over moderate heat, bring the *crème* to a boil and cook, still stirring, for 2 minutes. Remove from heat. Dot with a little butter, and cool.

APRICOT GLAZE

1 cup apricot jam
3 tablespoons Kirsch or
   Cointreau

Make the glaze: Put the jam in a small saucepan with the liqueur and stir constantly over moderate heat until the mixture is well blended. Strain through a sieve. Makes about 1 cup.

TO ASSEMBLE THE TART

Roll out the pastry and line a 10-inch pie pan. Spread the pastry with half the pastry cream. Cover the cream with the walnut pieces, then arrange the sliced pears on top. Cover with remaining pastry cream. Bake in a preheated hot oven (425°F.) for 1 hour. Allow the tart to cool to warm. Serve with the apricot glaze, which may be put into a small bowl and spooned over the tart.

GARGOUILLAU CREUSOIS

(Pear Pudding)

SERVES 6 TO 8.

This delicious pear pudding is from the Limousin where I first enjoyed it and acquired this recipe. It could hardly be easier to make. Though it is served warm, any leftover pudding is equally delicious cold.

8 medium-size pears, peeled and cored	2 eggs, lightly beaten
½ cup flour	¾ cup milk
¾ cup sugar	½ cup heavy cream
	3 tablespoons butter

Cut the pears into ½-inch slices and set aside. In a large bowl mix together the flour and ½ cup of the sugar. Stir in the eggs. Add the milk and the cream little by little, stirring with a wooden spoon, or combine the ingredients in a blender or food processor and mix until smooth. The batter will be quite thin. Fold in the pears. Butter the sides and bottom of a 2-quart casserole and pour in the mixture. Sprinkle with remaining ¼ cup sugar and dot with remaining butter. Bake in a preheated hot oven (425°F.) for 40 to 50 minutes.

COURONNE DE SEMOULE AUX FRAISES

(Farina Pudding with Strawberries)

SERVES 6 TO 8.

This simple and delicious dessert was given me by Madame la Vicomtesse du Breil de Pontbriand who has turned her 15th-century home, Manoir du Vaumadeuc at Pléven on the Côtes-du-Nord, into an elegant 10-bedroom hotel. It has been described, I think most aptly, as a poem in stone. The recipe is a family one and I enjoyed it made by the family cook. I made it myself in summer when strawberries were at their best and again enjoyed it, as did my guests.

¾ cup sugar
1 vanilla bean
3 to 3½ cups milk
1 cup farina
5 egg yolks
3 tablespoons unsalted
  butter
1 teaspoon grated lemon
  rind

½ cup slivered almonds
2 egg whites
6 cups strawberries
1 cup dry red wine
¼ cup Ruby Port
2 tablespoons Cointreau

In a large saucepan combine ½ cup sugar, the vanilla bean and 3 cups of the milk. Heat, stirring with a wooden spoon, until the sugar has dissolved. Remove the vanilla bean and keep for another use. Pour the farina into the milk in a thin, slow, steady stream and, stirring constantly, bring to a boil over moderate heat. If the mixture seems very thick, stir in the remaining ½ cup milk. Off the heat stir in the egg yolks, one by one, then stir in the butter, grated lemon rind and almonds. Cool. Beat the egg whites until they stand in firm unwavering peaks, then fold them lightly into the cooled farina mixture. Butter a 1½-quart savarin (ring) mold and pour in the mixture. Set the mold in a baking tin with water to come halfway up the mold. Cover the mold with buttered wax paper. Bake in a preheated moderate oven (350°F.) for about 35 minutes, or until a cake tester comes out clean. When cool, run a knife round the edges of the cake and unmold onto a serving plate.

In a bowl combine 4 cups of the strawberries, choosing the best ones, and macerate them in the red wine and Port for 1 to 2 hours. Purée remaining 2 cups of strawberries with remaining ¼ cup sugar and the Cointreau. When ready to serve, drain the berries and put them in the center of the ring mold. Mask the pudding with some of the strawberry purée and serve the rest in a sauceboat.

TARTE FINE AUX POMMES

(Special Apple Tart)

SERVES 6.

This is my favorite apple tart, which I first enjoyed at Lameloise at Chagny. "Special" is not really the proper translation of *fine,* but fine or delicate does not quite convey the quality of the tart.

1 recipe Pâte Brisée (see Index), using all butter instead of the vegetable shortening-butter mixture	3 tablespoons butter, approximately 1 pound crisp apples ⅓ cup sugar

Make the pastry and refrigerate for at least 1 hour before using. Butter a baking sheet. On a lightly floured surface roll out the pastry to a circle about 12 inches across. Drape the pastry over the rolling pin and transfer it to the baking sheet. Roll up the edges to form a border all round and pinch with thumb and first finger.

Peel the apples, quarter and core them. Cut apple quarters into lengthwise slices ⅛ inch thick and arrange them in overlapping circles in the pastry. Sprinkle apples with the sugar and dot with 2 tablespoons butter cut into bits. Bake in a preheated moderate oven (375°F.) for about 30 minutes, or until apples are tender and lightly browned. Slide the tart onto a flat round platter, and serve hot. The tart may also be served at room temperature or cold. If you like, accompany with heavy cream or whipped cream.

Variations: Make a thick applesauce using 2 pounds apples, peeled, cored and chopped, then cooked, covered, in a heavy saucepan over low heat until tender, about 15 minutes. Stir in ½ cup sugar, or to taste, according to the tartness of the apples. Beat until smooth. Cool. Spread applesauce on the bottom of the pastry. Add the sliced apples and bake as in the master recipe.

Stir ½ cup apricot preserves over low heat in a small saucepan until melted. Stir in 2 tablespoons Cointreau or Kirsch, or any similar liqueur, then rub through a sieve. Paint the tart with the apricot glaze, using a pastry brush or spoon, as soon as the tart is taken from the oven.

Fruit tarts of all kinds are extremely popular in France. For *TARTE AUX ABRICOTS (APRICOT TART)* or *TARTE AUX PÊCHES (PEACH TART)*, drop 10 apricots or 4 medium-size peaches into boiling water and remove immediately. Slip off the skins, pit and slice the fruit. For *TARTE AUX POIRES (PEAR TART)*, peel, core and slice 1 pound pears. For *TARTE AUX QUETSCHES (PLUM TART)*, cut 1½ pounds plums into lengthwise quarters. Arrange the fruit in the pastry, sprinkle with ⅓ cup sugar, and dot with 2 tablespoons butter. Bake in a preheated moderate (375°F.) oven for 30 to 40 minutes, or until the fruit is lightly colored. Serve warm or cold.

TARTE AUX NOIX

(Walnut Tart)

SERVES 6.

Périgord is famous for its walnuts. The recipe for this delicious walnut tart was given me by M. Leyssalles of the Mapotel Cro-Magnon at Les Eyzies-de-Tayac, in Périgord.

1 recipe Pâte Brisée
   Sucrée (see Index)

FILLING
1 cup heavy cream
½ cup sugar
1 cup ground walnuts

1 teaspoon vanilla extract,
   or cinnamon
1 cup halved walnuts,
   approximately

Make the *pâte brisée sucrée* for an 8- to 9-inch pie shell, and bake it blind. Let it cool for about 1 hour.

In a bowl mix together the cream, sugar, ground walnuts, vanilla or cinnamon. Pour the mixture into the pastry shell. Bake in a preheated slow oven (285°F.) for about 15 minutes, or until set. Cool. Garnish with the walnut halves.

299

SOUFFLÉS SUCRÉS

(DESSERT SOUFFLÉS)

A large mythology has grown up around soufflés, and many beginning cooks are afraid to make them, whether for entrées or desserts. I was lucky, as no one told me of the hazards. Since I had no soufflé molds, I first made my soufflés in a large English pudding basin. When I learned that the dish I made so casually was as temperamental as a prima donna, it took me several weeks to recover my nerve and I never had the courage to use my pudding basin again. I went out and bought a proper set of soufflé dishes. I've never had a failure, and if certain simple rules are followed no one need fail. Soufflés make a most glamorous dessert. There is one problem: since the soufflé waits for no man or woman, timing must be right. However, that is not as difficult as it sounds. Let the guests linger over an extra glass of wine while the soufflé rises to airy, delectable heights.

BASIC DESSERT SOUFFLÉ

SERVES 4.

This is a dessert soufflé without flavoring. Flavoring, as indicated, can be added to give an almost infinite variety of dishes.

Butter	4 whole eggs
4 tablespoons flour	1 extra egg white
⅓ cup sugar	Pinch of salt
¾ cup milk	Confectioners' sugar

Butter a 6-cup soufflé mold and set it aside.

In a bowl combine the flour and sugar and gradually add the milk, stirring until the mixture is smooth. A wire whisk is good for this. Pour the mixture into a saucepan and stir constantly over moderate heat until it comes to a boil. Cook, stirring, for 1 minute. It will be very thick. Remove from the heat and cool slightly.

Separate the eggs. Beat the yolks, one by one, into the sauce and put the whites into a large bowl with the extra white and the pinch of salt. Beat the whites until they form firm unwavering peaks. Stir one quarter of the whites into the sauce, then fold in the rest with a spatula, very lightly but thoroughly. Pour the mixture into the prepared mold. Bake in a preheated moderate oven (375°F.) for 30 to 35 minutes, or until the soufflé is puffed and golden and a cake tester or thin skewer comes out clean; or cook at the higher temperature of 425°F. for 10 to 15 minutes. Sprinkle the soufflé with confectioners' sugar and serve immediately. Serve with a large spoon and fork, or with 2 large spoons, breaking lightly into the top of the soufflé.

The soufflé may be made 1 or 2 hours ahead of time and refrigerated before baking.

Flavorings: Add to the sauce 2 tablespoons vanilla extract for SOUFFLÉ AU VANILLE (*VANILLA SOUFFLÉ*), or any liqueur such as Cointreau or Grand Marnier for SOUFFLÉ AU COINTREAU, etc., or any *eau de vie* such as Eau de Vie de Poire (pear).

For a ginger soufflé add 3 tablespoons finely chopped candied ginger roots. For a soufflé with almonds or other nuts, add ½ cup pulverized nuts to the sauce mixture. Inventive cooks are invited to experiment with other fruits and flavors.

SOUFFLÉ AU CITRON

(Lemon Soufflé)

SERVES 4.

This soufflé, the creation of chef Michel Gonod of Jacques Mille's charming Relais et Châteaux Hostellerie Le Prieuré at Villeneuve-lès-Avignon, has a satisfying but not cloying sweetness, balanced by the fresh, sharp flavor of lemon. No flour is used.

(recipe continues)

5 egg yolks
½ cup plus 1 tablespoon
  sugar
4 tablespoons lemon juice

2 teaspoons grated lemon
  rind
5 egg whites
Butter

In a bowl beat the egg yolks with ½ cup sugar, using a wooden spatula, a whisk or an electric beater, until they form a ribbon. Add the lemon juice and grated rind. In a separate bowl beat the whites until they stand in firm unwavering peaks. Fold egg whites lightly into the egg-yolk and sugar mixture. Butter a 6-cup mold and sprinkle it with 1 tablespoon sugar. Spoon the soufflé mixture into the mold. Bake the soufflé in a preheated moderate oven (375°F.) for 18 to 20 minutes, or until it is puffed and golden.

SOUFFLÉ AU CHOCOLAT

(Chocolate Soufflé)

SERVES 4.

Because chocolate is heavy, no flour is used in this recipe.

Butter
Sugar
4 ounces semisweet baking
  chocolate, broken into
  bits
2 tablespoons strong
  coffee

1 cup heavy cream
1 tablespoon Cognac
3 egg yolks
5 egg whites
Pinch salt
Confectioners' sugar

Butter a 6-cup soufflé mold, sprinkle with sugar, and shake to remove the excess. In a saucepan combine the chocolate with the coffee and cream. Melt the chocolate over very low heat, stirring in the coffee and cream until the mixture is smooth. Remove from heat and beat in 1 tablespoon Cognac and 3 egg yolks. Let the mixture cool. In a large bowl beat 5 egg whites with a pinch of salt until they stand in firm unwavering peaks. Fold egg whites very lightly into the chocolate mixture. Pour the mixture into the prepared mold. Bake the soufflé in a preheated hot oven (425°F.) for 12 to 15 minutes, or until a cake tester or skewer comes out clean. Sprinkle with confectioners' sugar and serve immediately.

FAR AUX POMMES

(Apple Pudding)

SERVES 4 TO 6.

This is a dessert version of the Far au Chou du Quercy (Cabbage Pudding) in the vegetable chapter. This is a favorite in Brittany. I was given the recipe by a Breton friend who always serves it with *crème fraîche* or whipped cream.

Butter	½ cup sugar
1½ pounds crisp apples, peeled, cored, and cut into ¼-inch slices	1 recipe for batter for Far au Chou du Quercy (see Index)

Generously butter a 6-cup soufflé dish or mold and arrange the apples in layers, sprinkling the layers with ¼ cup of the sugar. Make the batter according to the recipe but reduce the salt to ⅛ teaspoon and add the remaining ¼ cup sugar. Pour the batter over the apples. Bake in a preheated moderate oven (350°F.) for about 40 minutes, or until a cake tester comes out clean. Serve warm with *crème fraîche* or with whipped cream flavored with 2 tablespoons Calvados or Applejack.

Variation: Use any fruits in season—plums, cherries etc., or used dried fruits such as apricots, raisins, previously soaked in water but not cooked.

CLAFOUTIS AUX RAISINS

(Grape Pudding)

SERVES 4 TO 6.

A perfect dessert for a cook in a hurry, this is another of the recipes given me by my vineyard-owning friends in the Beaujolais.

Butter	¼ cup sugar
4 cups seedless green or black grapes	⅓ cup all-purpose flour, sifted
2 large eggs, lightly beaten	1 tablespoon rum
	1 cup milk
⅛ teaspoon salt	Confectioners' sugar

Butter an 8-cup baking dish deep enough to hold the grapes and batter, about 1½ inches. Fill the dish with the grapes. In a large bowl, or in a blender or food processor, combine the the eggs, salt, sugar, flour, rum and milk; beat or blend until the batter is smooth. Pour the batter over the grapes. Bake the pudding in a preheated moderate oven (350°F.) until it is puffed and golden and a cake tester comes out clean, about 30 minutes. Cool slightly and sprinkle with confectioners' sugar. Serve warm.

Variations: In the Limousin, in the cherry season, a cherry *clafoutis* is a favorite dessert. Traditionally the fruits are unpitted as it is said that the pits add a special flavor to the dish—a wonderful excuse for anyone not wanting the task of pitting them, but the dish is better with pitted cherries regardless of the work. Use 4 cups pitted black cherries for a really traditional dish. Red cherries are good too. Substitute cherries for grapes in the master recipe.

Use apples, plums, peaches or apricots instead of grapes, or any soft fruit like blackberries, according to the cook's fancy. If ever I grew raspberries, and really had lots of them, I would love to make a raspberry *clafoutis*. I'm sure it would be exquisite.

CRÈME DE LA RESURRECTION

(Resurrection Cream)

SERVES 3 OR 4.

This oddly named dessert was given me by chef Bernard Passevent of the Relais Gourmand Hôtel de Paris at Moulins-sur-Allier. It is simple to make and delicious.

6 large egg yolks
½ cup dry white wine
¼ cup fine granulated
  sugar
1 teaspoon grated lemon
  rind

2 tablespoons lemon juice,
  strained
2 tablespoons Marc de
  Bourgogne or Cognac

In the top part of a double boiler set over hot water, over low heat, combine the egg yolks, wine and sugar and cook, stirring constantly with a wooden spoon, until the mixture has thickened. Add the grated rind, lemon juice and liqueur. Serve in small dessert bowls with rich cookies.

CRÈME DE RHUBARBE

(Rhubarb Cream)

SERVES 6.

I inherited a rhubarb plant from the previous owner of our house and garden and was happy to find this recipe to help me keep up with the plant's generous output. It is light and delicious, a mixture of tart and sweet.

1½ pounds tender young rhubarb, cut into 1-inch pieces	1 cup water
	1 tablespoon apricot jam
1 cup sugar	½ cup heavy cream

In a saucepan combine the rhubarb, sugar and water and simmer, covered, until rhubarb is tender, about 3 minutes. Strain, reserving the liquid. Set the rhubarb aside. Return the liquid to the saucepan and reduce it over moderate heat to the consistency of syrup. Stir in the apricot jam, mixing thoroughly. Chill the syrup lightly. Whip the cream until it stands in peaks and fold half of it into the rhubarb syrup. Add the reserved rhubarb pieces to the syrup and pour the mixture into a glass dessert bowl. Decorate with rosettes of the remaining whipped cream, or serve the cream separately.

CRÈME DE CHÂTAIGNES À LA BORDELAISE

(Chestnut Cream Bordeaux Style)

SERVES 6.

2 cups granulated sugar
2 tablespoons water
4 cups chestnut purée
   (about 2 pounds raw
   chestnuts)
1 teaspoon vanilla extract
½ cup semisweet white
   wine such as
   Sauternes

12 ladyfingers
1 cup heavy cream
3 tablespoons
   confectioners' sugar

Put the granulated sugar and the water in a heavy saucepan and melt the sugar over low heat, but do not let it caramelize. Stir in the chestnut purée and cook, still over low heat, for 5 minutes, stirring from time to time with a wooden spoon. Stir in the vanilla. Pour into a mold rinsed out in cold water and chill in the refrigerator for 12 hours.

Pour the wine over the ladyfingers and let them stand for 2 hours. Mash the ladyfingers. Beat the cream until it stands in firm peaks and fold it into the ladyfingers. Add the confectioners' sugar, mixing lightly. Unmold the chestnut cream on a glass dish and surround it with the cream mixture.

TUILES

(Almond Biscuits)

MAKES ABOUT 24.

These light crisp biscuits or cookies are perfect with *sorbets* and delicious at any time with any dessert or by themselves. They are called *tuiles* (tiles) from their shape, which is like the curved terracotta roof tiles of the houses of the Provençal villages where the biscuits originated. With very little practice it is easy to shape them; by the end of the first half dozen one is an expert.

½ cup sugar
4 tablespoons flour
Pinch of salt
½ cup egg whites, about
    3 large, lightly beaten
4 tablespoons butter,
    melted and cooled

1¼ cups slivered blanched
    almonds
Butter and flour for
    baking sheet

In a bowl combine the sugar, flour and salt. Stir in the egg whites and the melted butter, mixing thoroughly. Stir in 1 cup of the almonds. Lightly butter and flour a baking sheet, a heavy one if possible as it is easier to remove the biscuits. Drop the mixture by heaped teaspoons about 2 inches apart onto the baking sheet and flatten with a fork or spoon. The mixture should be runny; if necessary add a little more egg white. Sprinkle with the remaining ¼ cup almonds. Bake in a preheated hot oven (425°F.) for about 5 minutes, or until the edges are golden. Remove the biscuits with a spatula and wrap round a rolling pin or bottle or similar object to

shape them. While the biscuits are warm they are easy to shape. Put the baking sheet with the biscuits back in the oven for a few minutes if they become too cool to be pliable. Cool biscuits on a wire rack before storing in an airtight tin where they will keep fresh and crisp for some time.

For large *tuiles* drop by tablespoon onto the baking sheet, to make about 12. For LA GROSSE TUILE (*GIANT-SIZE ALMOND BISCUIT*) like those that the Frères Trois-gros, Jean and Pierre, serve at their restaurant in Roanne, divide the mixture into 4 parts and spread it as thinly as possible on the baking sheet, probably one at a time. These big ones are quite tricky to make but are so attractive it is worth the effort.

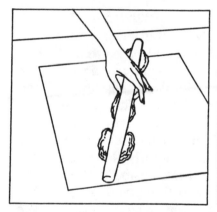

1. Lay a rolling pin on the *tuiles* when they are hot from the oven, and gently curve them around the pin, holding them for a minute until cooled and set.

2. The *tuiles* will hold their curved tile shape when cold.

PAIN DE NOIX

(Walnut Bread)

MAKES 2 LOAVES.

I have very much enjoyed walnut bread as it is served with cheese in many parts of France. It is easy to make and keeps well refrigerated. I warm it up in the oven to freshen it.

2 envelopes active dry yeast, 7 grams each	3 cups rye flour
1 teaspoon sugar	1 cup white flour
1½ cups lukewarm water (105° to 115°F.)	2 teaspoons salt
	1 cup walnut meats
	Butter

In a small bowl mix the yeast with the sugar and ½ cup lukewarm water. In a large bowl combine the rye and white flours. When the yeast mixture is bubbly, make a well in the center of the flour and pour in the yeast. Dissolve the salt in the remaining cup of water and mix it into the flour, using just enough water to make a fairly stiff dough. The amount will depend on the flour so use less or more as needed. Turn the dough out on a lightly floured surface and knead it until it is smooth and satiny, about 10 minutes. Return it to the bowl, sprinkle with flour, and cover with a cloth. Stand the bowl in a warm draft-free place and leave until the dough has doubled in bulk, about 2 hours.

Punch the dough down and turn it out on a lightly floured board. Cut it into halves and knead each piece separately until it is very smooth, about 3 minutes. Work ½ cup walnut meats into each of the pieces. Shape each piece into a loaf approximately 3 by 8 inches. With a sharp knife make 2 or 3 diagonal slashes on top. Put loaves on a buttered baking sheet, cover with a cloth, and set them again in a warm draft-free place to rise until doubled in bulk, about 1 hour or longer.

Bake on the middle shelf of a preheated hot oven (425°F.) for about 30 minutes. The loaves are done when they sound hollow if tapped on the bottom with the knuckles. Transfer the loaves to a wire rack to cool. Serve with butter and a platter of cheese.

FOUACE

(Walnut Hearth Cake)

MAKES 1 LOAF.

This is another version of the walnut bread that is made with a mixture of white and rye flours. Sugar can be added to the *fouace* if a sweeter bread is preferred.

1 envelope active dry yeast, 7 grams
½ cup lukewarm milk (105° to 115°F.)
1 tablespoon sugar
2 cups flour
½ teaspoon salt

4 tablespoons butter, cut into bits
1 egg, lightly beaten
1 cup walnut meats
Egg wash: 1 egg yolk beaten with 1 teaspoon water

In a small bowl mix together the yeast, milk and sugar and let it stand in a warm place until the yeast is bubbly. Sift the flour and salt into a large bowl. Blend in the butter until the mixture resembles coarse meal. Make a well in the center of the flour and pour in the egg and the yeast mixture. Mix to a soft but not sticky dough. If necessary, add a little water. Turn the dough out on a lightly floured board and knead until it is smooth and satiny, about 10 minutes.

Knead the walnuts into the bread. Form the bread into a ball and place it on a buttered baking sheet. With a sharp knife slash the bread in 4 equidistant places. Cover with a cloth and leave in a warm draft-free place until it has doubled in bulk, about 2 hours.

Brush the bread lightly with the egg wash. Bake the loaf

(recipe continues)

in a preheated moderate oven (350°F.) for about 30 minutes, or until it is browned and the bottom sounds hollow when tapped with the knuckles. Transfer the bread to a rack to cool. It may be served warm or at room temperature.

This bread is pleasant with cheese. It is also good buttered, or toasted and buttered, as a breakfast bread.

Variation: For those who prefer a sweeter bread, add ⅓ cup sugar to the flour when sifting it.

POMPE AUX GRATTONS

(Bread with Bacon Rinds)

MAKES 1 LARGE LOAF.

Grattons are the brown bits from pork, goose or duck fat. A restaurant can have a generous supply of these crispy bits, which are also called *frittons*. The domestic kitchen is unlikely to have the half pound needed for this recipe. I use the type of *grattons* from the Île de la Réunion (Île Bourbon) which are the same as Latin-American *chicharrones*. They can be bought in supermarkets packaged as bacon rinds or from Latin-American markets, and when crumbled do very well for the *pompe*. Chef Bernard Passevent of the Hôtel de Paris at Moulins-sur-Allier, a Relais Gourmand, showed me how to make this bread, which enlivens a simple meal.

1 envelope active dry yeast, 7 grams	1 teaspoon salt
¼ cup lukewarm water (105° to 115°F.)	4 eggs
½ teaspoon sugar	½ pound bacon rinds, or grattons
3 cups flour	5 tablespoons each of butter and lard

In a small bowl mix the yeast with the lukewarm water and the sugar. Sift the flour and salt into a large bowl. Mix in 3 eggs, lightly beaten, and the yeast to make a soft sticky dough. Turn the dough out on a lightly floured surface and knead until it is smooth and no longer sticky, adding a little flour as necessary. Using the fingers, or a wooden spatula, mix in the bacon rinds and the butter and lard, cut into small bits and softened at room temperature. When the dough has absorbed the fat, put it back in the bowl, cover with a kitchen towel, and let it rise in a warm draft-free place until it has doubled in bulk, about 2 hours.

Butter a 2-quart brioche or charlotte mold. Twist off one quarter of the dough and roll it into a ball. Smooth remaining dough into a ball and fit it into the mold. Put the small ball of dough on top. Cover and leave it to rise again for about 2 hours.

Separate the remaining egg; reserve the white for another use. Lightly beat the yolk and brush the dough with it. Bake the loaf in a preheated moderate oven (350°F.) for about 40 minutes, or until a cake tester comes out clean.

The dough may also be made in a food processor: In a bowl combine the yeast with the lukewarm water and the sugar. When the yeast mixture is bubbly, sift in 1 cup flour and stir to mix. Cover with a cloth and leave in a warm place to rise for about 1 hour, or longer if necessary. Transfer the sponge to a food processor fitted with the steel blade. Add the salt, eggs and remaining flour, and spin on and off until well mixed, about 30 seconds. Drop the butter through the feed tube bit by bit and spin until mixed; add the lard in the same way. When the fats are well incorporated, process 30 seconds longer. Add the bacon rinds and spin very briefly. Turn the dough out on a floured surface and knead it until smooth. Put the dough in a bowl, cover with a cloth, and leave to rise until doubled in bulk, about 2 hours.

Put the dough into a brioche or charlotte mold as in the handmade method, let it rise again, and bake.

PAIN DE CAMPAGNE

(Country Bread)

MAKES 1 LARGE LOAF OR 2 MEDIUM-SIZE LOAVES.

This firm crusty bread is the one the French eat with pâtés, soups and salads. It is the easiest of all breads to make; when it is baking, it fills the kitchen with an enticing aroma. It contains nothing but flour, salt, yeast and water, yet despite this simplicity has a tantalizing flavor. Unbleached hard-wheat bread flour gives the best results, but ordinary all-purpose flour gives a good loaf too.

2 packages active dry
    yeast, 7 grams each
1½ cups lukewarm water
    (105° to 115°F.)
4 cups unsifted
    unbleached bread
    flour or all-purpose
    flour

1 teaspoon salt,
    preferably sea salt

In a small bowl mix the yeast with ½ cup of the lukewarm water and set it aside to proof. If the yeast is fresh small bubbles will appear on the surface, usually in 10 to 15 minutes.

Put the flour and salt into a large bowl. Make a well in the center and add the yeast mixture and the rest of the water. Stir with a wooden spoon to mix, then work the mixture with the hands, kneading it in the bowl until the dough comes away smoothly from the sides. If it is very sticky, sprinkle a little more flour over it and work the flour into the dough. Form the dough into a ball, sprinkle a little flour over it, cover it with a towel, and set it in a warm draft-free place to rise until it is doubled in bulk. This will take about 1 hour, according to the temperature of the kitchen. A gas oven with the pilot light on is a good place for the rising.

When the dough has doubled in bulk, punch it down and turn it out on a lightly floured board. Knead dough thoroughly until it is smooth and elastic. Form it into a ball once more and replace it in the bowl. Sprinkle with flour, cover with a towel, and leave it to rise a second time, until doubled in bulk.

When dough has risen, turn it out of the bowl, punch it down, and knead it for 2 or 3 minutes. Form it into a slightly flattened ball and slash it, quite deeply, with a razor blade or sharp knife crosswise both ways. Sprinkle with flour and place on a floured baking sheet. Cover with a towel and leave to rise again until doubled in bulk, about 30 minutes.

Bake the loaf in a preheated moderate oven (350°F.) for 1 hour and 15 minutes, or until it is golden brown and the bottom sounds hollow when tapped with the knuckles. Check the loaf when it has been baking for 1 hour as ovens vary and it may be ready. Replace it for the extra 15 minutes if necessary.

If preferred, make 2 loaves, dividing the dough after the second rising, or make the dough into sausage shapes and slash diagonally at regular intervals down the length.

INDEX

Aillade de Veau, 225
Almond Biscuits, 308-309
Alsace, L', Mulhouse, 211
Anchoïade, L', 71
Anchovies, 54-55, 70, 81
Anchovy Sauce, 71
André, Rémy, 62, 180, 200, 225, 236, 239
Anglerfish, 152-153
Anglerfish and Mussels, 155-156
Anglerfish in Cider, 156-157
Anglerfish in Dry White Wine, 154-155
Anglerfish Stew, 158-159
Anglerfish with Mushrooms, 151-152
Anglerfish with White Beans, 149-150
Anguille des Abbayes, 170-171
Antiquaires, Les, Paris, 244

Apple Pudding, 303
Apple slices, baked, 206
Apple tart, 298-299
Apples, sautéed, 202
Apricot glaze, 295
Asparagus, 140
Aspic, 6
Assiette des Pêcheurs, 163-164
Au Bon Pasteur, Carcassonne, 62, 180, 200, 239
Au Bon Vieux Temps, Sedan, 129
Aubergade, L', Pontchartrain, 194, 268
Auberge Bressane, Bourg-en-Bresse, 67, 141, 192
Auberge de l'Ill, Illhaeusern, 107
Auberge du Cep, Fleurie, 168, 255

Aubriet, *M.*, 133, 160
Aux Armes de Champagne, L'Epine, 76
Avocado with Vinaigrette and Chervil, 40-41
Avocat au Vinaigrette et Cerfeuil, 40-41

Bacon, 24-25
Baked apple slices, 206
Baked Fish Provencal Style, 147
Barrier, Charles, 126
Basic Dessert Soufflé, 300-301
Basque-Style Squash Soup, 102-103
Baudroie à l'Aigo Sau, 158-159
Baudroie aux Champignons, 151-152
Beaujeu, Marc, 142, 181
Beef, 210-216
Beef stew, 213-214
Beef Stew Albi Style, 212
Beef stock, 3
Beets, 265
Belons, 46
Berthelotiere Salad, 76
Betteraves en Purée, 265
Beurre Blanc, 9
Beurre d' Escargots, 11
Beurre Fondu, 54
Beurre Manié, 10
Beurre Nantais, 9
Beurre Noisette, 283
Billoux, Jean-Pierre, 65, 172, 173, 245
Blanc, Georges, 166, 284
Blanc de Turbot au Miel et aux Oranges, 134-135
Blanquette de Lotte, 159
Bocuse, Paul, 107, 158
Boni, Roger, 70
Bossée, Jean-Paul, 50, 186

Brains in Whisky Sauce, 257
Braised Anglerfish *Tortinière,* 152-153
Braised Chestnuts, 278
Braised Chicken with Watercress Sauce, 196-197
Braised Leg of Lamb, Beaujolais Style, 238-239
Braised Pheasant with Port, 202-203
Braised Pike *Tourangelle,* 126-127
Braised Rabbit with Zucchini, 250-251
Bread cases, 14-15
Bread with Bacon Rinds, 312-313
Breil de Pontbriand, Vicomtesse du, 61, 226, 296
Bretagne, Le, Questembert, 48, 124, 280
Broad Bean Soup, 105
Broccoli, 262-263
Brochet aux Noix, 125-126
Brown Glazed Onions, 275
Brown sauce, 10
Brown stock, 3
Burgundy Parsleyed Ham in Aspic, 229
Butter, 11
   to clarify, 11
Butter sauce, 9, 54

Cabbage, 148-149, 172, 270-271
Cabbage Pudding, 271
Cabbage rolls, 249
Cabbage soup, 100-101
Cabbage Stuffed with Chestnuts, 272-274
Calamars, 173
Calf's Liver with Capers, 234-235

Calf's Liver with Green Pepper-corns, 235
Calf's Liver with Prunes, 235
Canard Duchambais, 201-202
Caneton au Poivre Vert, 204
Caneton Facon Denise Henry, Le, 205-206
Carottes Glacées, 276
Carrot and Rutabaga Purée, 263
Carrots, 14, 276
Casseroles (equipment), 29
Cassoulet de Castelnaudary, Le, 230-232
Cauliflower Gratin, 267
Cauliflower in White Butter Sauce, 282
Cazaudehore et La Forestìere, Saint-Germain-en-Laye, 49, 56-57
Celery Soup, 95
Cèpes, 78
Cervclat, 41
Cervelles Flambé au Whisky, 257
Chaîne, Roger, 113, 191
Champignons à la Dijonnaise, 279
Champignons à l'Anchoïade, 70-71
Champignons Sautés au Beurre, 278-279
Chapotin, Bertrand F., 58, 128
Charlotte, 292-293
Chateau d'Isenbourg, Rouffach, 37, 134, 193, 220
Cheese, 290-291
Cheese Puffs, 64-65
Chervil soup, 93-94
Chestnut Cream Bordeaux Style, 307
Chestnut Purée, 264-265
Chestnuts, 42, 198, 270-271, 272-273, 278
to prepare, 25
Chevillot, Marc, 73, 228

Chez Serge, La Rochelle, 148, 149, 198, 237
Chicken, 76, 196-197, 200-201
to bone, 27
Chicken, Arles Style, 188
Chicken Breasts St. Antoine, 191
Chicken Breasts with Scallions, 190-191
Chicken Curry, 178-179
Chicken Fricassee with Vinegar, 181
Chicken in Cream Sauce with Tarragon, 192-193
Chicken in Still Champagne, 176
Chicken in White Wine, 180, 182-183
Chicken Liver Mousse, 67-68
Chicken Liver Pâté and Ham Loaf, 66-67
Chicken livers, 38-39
Chicken, Nantes Style, 195-196
Chicken Sauté, Grenoble Style, 194-195
Chicken Sautéed with Garlic and White Alsatian, 193
Chicken stock, 2
Chicken Stuffed with Pâté de Foie, 177-178
Chicken with Cucumbers, 183
Chicken with Grapes, 185
Chicken with Green Pepper-corns, 189
Chicken with Hazelnuts, 184
Chicken with Leeks, 186-187
Chicken with Thyme, 187
Chiffonade d'Oseille, 13
Chocolate Mousse, 292-293
Chocolate Soufflé, 302-303
Chou Farci aux Marrons, 272-274
Chou Rouge à la Flamande, 270-271
Choufleur au Beurre Nantais, 282

INDEX

Choux Rouges aux Pommes et aux Marrons, 270-271

Clafoutis aux Raisins, 304-305

Clement, Christian, 242

Clos Saint-Vincent, Le, Ribeauville, 58, 128

Coconut, 44

Coeur de Filet au Poivre Vert, 214-215

Confit de canard, 82, 206-207, 230

Confit d'oie, 82, 206-207, 230

Conger Eel Soup, 89-90

Coquilles Saint-Jacques au Safran, 164-165

Coquilles Saint-Jacques Georges Blanc, 166

Cortembert, Gérard, 168, 255

Côte de Veau au Gratin d'Avocat, 223

Coulis de Tomates Fraîches, 12

Coulon, Serge, 148, 149, 198, 237

Country Bread, 314-315

Courgettes, 282-283

Courgnaud, Jacques, 52, 176

Couronne de Semoule aux Fraises, 296-297

Court Bouillon, 6-7

Couscoussière, 30, 187

Crab soup, 109

Crayfish Poached in Still Champagne, 52-53

Cream, 26

Cream of Chervil Soup, 93-94

Cream of Cucumber Soup, 96

Cream of Sorrel Soup, 92-93

Crème de Châtaignes à la Bordelaise, 307

Crème de Concombres, 96

Crème de la Resurrection, 305

Crème de Rhubarbe, 306

Crème Fraîche, 26

Crème Nignon, 106-107

Crème Patissière, 295

Creole Rice, 286

Crêpes Vonnassiennes, 284-285

Croustades, 14-15

Croûtes, 15

Croûtes à l'Ail, 15

Croûtons, 15

Crusts, 15

Cucumber soup, 96

Curried Mussels, 167

Curry de Volaille à l'Indienne, 178-179

Daguin, André, 116, 210

Daniel et Denise, Lyon, 56, 132, 215, 233

Daube à l'Albigeoise, 212

Daube de Boeuf Provençal, 213-214

Daube de Congre, 169

Daurade à la Provençale, 145-146

Délice de Sole à la Mousse de Tomate Fraîche, 124-125

Delteil, Christian, 217

Devauchelle, Michel, 119

Dinde Farcie aux Oeufs Brouillés et Marrons, 198-199

Dindonneau à la Basquaise, 199

Domaine de la Berthelotière, Le Nantes, 76, 118, 151, 163, 187

Domaine de la Tortinière, Le, Montbazon, 152, 246

Drouet, Le, Reims, 294

Duck, 206-207

Duck with Vinegar and Mustard, 201-202

Duckling, 82

Duckling à la Denise Henry, 205-206

Duckling with Green Pepper-corns, 204
Duvauchelle, Pierre, 104, 133
Duxelles, 14

Écrevisses à la Nage au Champagne, 52-53
Eel, Abbey Style, 170-171
Eel in Red Wine, 168-169
Eel soup, 89-90
Eel stew, 169
Eggs, Burgundy Style, 73-74
Embeurrée aux Poissons, 148-149
Emincé de Filet de Veau au Fenouil Frais, 220-221
Emincé de Gras-Double au Vinaigre de Vin, 255
Épinards en Branches au Beurre Noisette, 283
Escalopes de Saumon en Papillote, 118-119
Escalopes de Veau aux Avocats et Courgettes, 219-220

Faisan Braisé au Porto, 202-203
Far au Chou du Quercy, 271
Far aux Pommes, 303
Farina Pudding with Strawber-ries, 296-297
Farm-Style Potatoes with Cheese, 269
Fava, Bruno, 131, 178
Fava, Jean-Pierre, 164-165, 178
Fennel and Broccoli Pureé, 262-263
Feuilleté d'Escargots à la Crème d'Ail, 56
Feuilleté d'Oseille au Parfum d'Anchois, 54-55
Filet de Bar au Basilic, 141
Filet de Poisson à la Tahitienne, 44-45

Filet de Rascasse aux Concombres, 142-143
Filet de Sole à l'Oseille, 130-131
Filet de Sole en Court-Bouillon au Tomate, 122
Filet de Turbot à l'Oseille, 128-129
Filets de Barbue "Rosa Bonheur," 133-134
Filets de Flétan Interallie, 138-139
Filets de Saint-Pierre à l'Estragon, 137
Filets de Turbotin à la Moutarde, 132-133
Fillet of Beef with Sauternes and Blue Cheese, 210
Fillet of Sole Poached in Tomato Stock, 122
Fillet Steak with Beaujolais Sauce, 216
Fillet Steak with Green Pepper-corns, 214-215
Fillet Steak with Horseradish, 211
Fillets of John Dory with Tarra-gon, 137
Fillets of Sole with Fresh Tomato Mousse, 124-125
Fish
 to bone, 28
Fish Fillets, Rosa Bonheur, 133-134
Fish Fillets with Asparagus, 140
Fish Fillets with Honey and Oranges, 134-135
Fish Fillets with Mustard, 132-133
Fish Fillets with Sorrel, 128-129
Fish salad, 45
Fish sauce, 145
Fish soup, 86-88
Fish stew, 163-164
Fish Stew, Dieppe Style, 162-163

Fish stock, 6-7
Fish, tahitian style, 44-45
Fish with Orange, 136-137
Fish with Sorrel Sauce, 129-131
Fisherman's Soup, 86-87
Fisherman's Stew, 160-161
Flamiche aux Poireaux, 62
Flan aux Poires du Poitou, 294-295
Flétan aux Noix, 138
Foie de Veau au Poivre Vert, 235
Foie de Veau aux Câpres, 234-235
Foie de Veau aux Pruneaux, 235
Foie gras, 37, 82, 177
Foie Gras Salad with Turnips and Spinach, 36
Fouace, 311-312
Fraises Marinées, Les, 293
Frantel, Mulhouse, 70
French salad dressing, 8-9
Fresh Cheese with Cream, 290-292
Fresh Pear Sherbet, 289
Fricassée de Volaille au Vinaigre, 181
Fromage Blanc avec Crème Fraîche, 290-292
Fruit tarts, 299
Fumet, 6-7

Gargouillau Creusois, 296
Garlic flavored *Croûtes,* 15
Garlic-flavored toasted bread, 15
Garlic, Tomato and Chili Pepper Sauce, 88
Gâteau de Foies Blonds, 67-68
Gâteau de Foies de Volaille et Jambon, 66-67
Gâteau de Pommes de Terre au Münster Fermier, 269
George Blanc's Scallops, 166

Gigot Braisé à la Beaujolaise, 238-239
Gigot de Lotte au Mogettes, 149-150
Glace de Viande, 4
Glazed Carrots, 276
Gnocchi de Potiron, 277
Gohel, Léopold, 222
Gonod, Michel, 290, 296, 301
Goose, 206-207
Gougères, 65
Gourmand de Volaille, 177-178
Gourmet Salad, 40
Grape Pudding, 304-305
Gras-Double à la Lyonnaise, 256
Gras-Double au Cidre, 254
Gratin Dauphinois, 268-269
Gratin de Choufleur, 267
Gratin de Courge, 268
Gratin de Pireaux, 266-267
Green Bean Soup, 97-98
Green Pea Soup, 99
Green salad, 81
Grilled Striped Mullet with Fennel, 143
Guerárd, Michel, 1
Gueret, *M.,* 205
Guinea fowl, 200-201

Haeberlin, Paul, 107
Halibut, 50-51, 132-136, 138-139
Halibut with Walnut Sauce, 138
Ham, 66-67, 227-229
Hazelnuts, 184
Hiély, Pierre, 86, 140
Hiély-Lucullus, Avignon, 86, 140
Hostellerie Claire-Fontaine, Remiremont, 112, 177
Hostellerie Claire-Fontaine, Saint-Nabord, 60

Hostellerie La Chenaudière Colroy-la-Roche, 50, 186
Hostellerie Lenoir, Auvillers-les-Forges, 184, 189
Hostellerie Saint-Antoine, Albi, 113, 191, 212
Hot Potato Salad, 75
Hot Sausage, Poitiers Style, 74-75
Hôtel Bérard, Saint-André-de Corcy, 142, 181
Hôtel de France, Auch, 116-117, 210
Hôtel de France, Poitiers, 74, 170, 295
Hôtel de l'Aigle Noir, Fontaine-bleau, 104, 112, 160
Hôtel de la Paix, Reims, 137
Hôtel de la Poste, Beaune, 73, 228
Hôtel de Paris, Moulins-sur-Allier, 80, 100, 120, 125, 201, 305, 312
Hôtel des Berceaux, Épernay, 52, 176
Hôtel des Frères Troisgros, Roanne, 309
Hôtel Jules César, Arles, 158, 188
Hôtel-Restaurant Quincan-grogne, Dampmart, 106
Hôtellerie du Bas-Bréau, Barbizon, 131, 164-165, 178
Hugues, Houard, 76
Huîtres de Belons au Champagne, Les, 46
Huîtres en Paquets, Les, 48
Huîtres Fremies avec la Laitue de Mer, 47

Jambon Persillé à la Bourgui-gnonne, 227-229

Jambon Persillé de Bourgogne, 229
Jellied Rabbit, 56-58
Junket cheese, 292
Jus Lié, 10

Keller, Arthur, 106

Laitue de mer, 47
Laitues Braisées aux Raisins, 281
Lamb, 237-239
Lamb and Bean Casserole, 236-237
Lamb with White Wine and To-matoes, 239-240
Langoustines au Chou, 172-173
Lapin aux Pruneaux, Le, 246-247
Lapin aux Raisins Frais, 248
Lapin Braisé aux Courgettes, 250-251
Lapin en Compote, 56-58
Lapin et sa Feuille de Chou, Le, 249-250
Lardons, 24
Lardoons, 24
Lasserre, René, 138
Lasserre, Paris, 138
Laustriat, Francois, 80, 100, 201
Le Divellec, Jacques, 45, 47, 54-55, 136, 167
Leek Gratin, 266-267
Leek Quiche, 62
Leeks, 161-162
  to wash, 20
Lemon Souffle, 301-302
Lenoir, Jean, 184, 189
Leron, Daniel, 56, 132, 215, 233
Leterme, Jean-Claude, 129
Lettuce and Walnut Salad, 83
Lettuce Braised with Grapes, 281
Lettuce Salad, 80-81
Lettuce Soup, 96-97

INDEX

Leyssalles, *M.*, 43, 114, 299
Little Onions, 275-276
Lobster, 172-173
Lotte au Cidre, 156-157
Lotte au Muscadet, 154-155
Lotte aux Moules, 155-156
Lou Païrol, Montpellier, 78
Loustau, Michel, 78

Manoir, Le, Fontenay-Trésigny, 39, 64
Manoir de Vaumadeuc, Pléven, 61, 296
Mapotel Cro-Magnon, Les Eyzies-de-Tayac, 43, 114, 299
Mapotel de Dieppe, Rouen, 205
Mapotel Empérator, Nimes, 293
Mapotel Pont Royal, Paris, 44
Marrons Braisés, 278
Mayanelle, La, Gordes, 70, 71, 90
Mayard, *M.*, 70, 71, 90
Mayonnaise, 8
Meat glaze, 4
Melon d'Agneau aux Fèves Fraîches, 237-238
Mennetret, Lucien, 146
Mère Blanc, La, Vonnas, 166, 284
Mériadeck, Le, Bordeaux, 242
Meurette d'Anguille Vigneronne, 168-169
Mignon de Veau Franc-Comtois, 222-223
Mille, Jacques, 301
Minced Tripe with Wine Vinegar, 255
Mint Sherbet, 290
Mirepoix, 14
Mixed Fish Stew, 163-164
Mixed Fish with Leeks, 161-162

Mixed Green Salad with Anchovies, 81
Moitry, Monique, 112
Morel soup, 109
Mouclade, 167
Moules à la Marinière, 21
Mousse de Brochet, 53-54
Mousse de Navets aux Fines Herbes, 280-281
Mousse of White Turnips with Herbs, 280-281
Mulet Grillé au Fenouil, 143
Mushroom Purée, 264
Mushroom Soup, 94-95
Mushroom Tartlets, 62-63
Mushrooms, 14, 38, 182, 278-279
Mushrooms, Dijon Style, 279
Mushrooms with Anchovy Sauce, 70-71
Mussels, 167
    to clean, 21
    steamed, 21

Oeufs Bourguignons, 73-74
Ogier, Lucien, 194, 268
Oignons Confits, 245
Oignons Glacés à Blanc, 274-275
Oignons Glacés à Brun, 275
Oil and vinegar dressing, 8-9
Olive and Anchovy Spread, 70
Olivereau-Capron, Denise, 152, 246
Ombrages, Les, Reims, 249
Omelet Mountaineer Style, 72
Onion Tart, 60-62
Onions, 274-276
Onions, glazed, 245
Oxtail Pâté, 217-218
Oysters Cooked with Seaweed, 47
Oysters in Packets, 48

Oysters Poached in Still Champagne, 46

Pain de Campagne, 36, 314-315
Pain de Noix, 310-311
Paineau, Georges, 48, 124, 280
Palmes et Industrie, Castelnaudary, 230
Parsley Soup, 98-99
Parsleyed Ham in Aspic, Burgundy Style, 227-229
Passevent, Bernard, 120, 125, 201, 305, 312
Pastry cream, 295
Pastry shell, 17
Pastry-topped soups, 107-109
Pâte Brisée, 16
Pâte Brisée Sucrée, 17
Pâté de foie, 36, 37, 82, 177
Pâté de Queue de Boeuf, 217-218
Pâte de Saumon, 49
Pâté Feuilletée, 18-19
Paul, Jean Louis, 142, 181
Pauvert, Paul, 40, 58, 79, 80, 115, 243
Pear Pudding, 296
Pear Salad, 79
Pear Sherbet, 289
Pear Tart, 294-295
Petit Saumon Saint-Patrick, 116-117
Petite Marmite Dieppoise, 162-163
Petite Marmite du Pêcheur, 86-87, 160-161
Petits Oignons, 275-276
Petrini, Roland, 158, 188
Peyrafitte, *M.*, 69
Pheasant, 202-203
Pie shell, 17
Pecè de Boeuf aux Sauternes et au Rouquefort, La, 210

Piece de Charolais à la Beaujolaise, 216
Piecrust, 16
Pigonnet, Le, Aix-en-Provence, 146
Pike, 126-127
Pike Mousse, 53-54
Pike with Walnuts, 125-126
Pinard, Yves, 82, 116
Pistache, La, 236-237
Pistache de Mouton, 239-240
Pistou, 91
Poggioli, Pierre, 230
Poisson au Four Provençale, 147
Poisson Fumé en Salade, 45
Poissons aux Poireaux, 161-162
Poitrine de Veau Farcie, 226-227
Pommes de Terre aux Oignons et au Lard, 285
Pompe aux Grattons, 312-313
Porc au Cidre, 232
Pork and Beans Casserole, 230-232
Pork in Cider, 232
Potage au Potiron, 103
Potage Crème de Cerfeuil, 93-94
Potage de Céleris, 95
Potage de Laitues, 96-97
Potage de Petits Pois, 99
Potage de Printemps, 106
Potato Pancakes Vonnas Style, 284-285
Potato salad, 75
Potato Soup, 106-107
Potatoes, 268-269
Potatoes with Onion and Bacon, 285
Potted Minced Rabbit, 58-59
Poulet à l'Arlesienne, 188
Poulet au Blancs de Poireaux, 186-187
Poulet au Champagne, 176

Poulet au Poivre Vert, 189

Poulet au Reisling, 182-183

Poulet au Thym, 187

Poulet aux Concombres, 183

Poulet aux Noisettes, 184

Poulet aux Raisins, 185

Poulet Braisé au Sauce Cresson, 196-197

Poulet en Alicotte, 180

Poulet Nantaise, 195-196

Poulet Sauté à la Crème d'Ail et au Sylvaner, 193

Poulet Sauté Grenobloise, 194-195

Praz, Claude, 41, 211

Preserved Goose or Duck, 206-207

Prieuré, Le, Vileneuve-les-Avignon, 290, 292, 301

Provençal Beef Stew with Olives, 213-214

Provencal Fish Sauce, 145

Puff pastry, 18-19

Puff Pastry Stuffed with Sorrel and Anchovy Purée, 54-55

Puff Pastry with Snails in Garlic Sauce, 56

Purée de Carottes et Rutabaga, 263

Purée de Champignons, 264

Purée de Fenouil et Brocoli, 262-263

Purée de Marrons, 264-265

Puréed Beets, 265

Quiche Lorraine, 60

Rabbit, 56-59, 209, 245-246, 250-251

  to bone, 22-23

Rabbit and Stuffed Cabbage Leaves, 249-250

Rabbit Soup, 104-105

Rabbit Stuffed with Prunes, 246-247

Rabbit with Grapes, 248

Râble de Lapin aux Oignons Confits, 245-246

Ragout of Guinea Fowl, 200-201

Ramequins au Fromage, 64

Rascasse Fillets with Cucumber, 142-143

Red Cabbage Flemish Style, 270-271

Red Cabbage with Apples and Chestnuts, 270-271

Red Mullet Broiled with Fennel, 144

Red Porgy Provence Style, 145-146

Renardias, *M.,* 137

Restaurant Bonnevay-Billoux, Digoin, 65, 172, 173, 245

Resurection Cream, 305

Rétirade, La, Clermont-Ferrand, 119

Revire, Bernard, 219

Rhubarb Cream, 306

Rice, 286

Rice with Almonds and Raisins, 179

Rieux, *M.,* 113, 212

Rillettes de Lapin Clementine, 58-59

Ris de Veau à l'Oiseille, 240-241

Ris de Veau à l'Orange, 244

Ris de Veau aux Pommes, 243

Ris de Veau aux Pruneaux, 242-243

Riz Créole, 286

Robert, *M.,* 74, 170, 294

Robin, Daniel, 53, 216

Rochard, Jacques, 49, 56-57

Rock Lobster Tails with Cabbage, 172-173

Rognon de Veau Entier à l'Ancienne, 233-234

Rôti de Lotte Tortinière, Le, 152-153

Rotonde, La, Luchon, 69, 72, 236

Rouget Grillé au Fenouil, 144

Rouille, 87, 88

Roussel, *M.*, 112, 177

Royal Salad, 37

Rutabaga, 263

Ryngel, Gérard, 76, 118, 151, 163, 187

Saddle of Rabbit with Glazed Onions, 245-246

Salad dressing, 8-9

Salad Gourmet's Fancy, 78

Salad of Spring Vegetables with Smoked Salmon, 43

Salade Berthelotière, 76

Salade Bigouden, 80-81

Salade Caprice Gourmand, 78

Salade Chaubuisson, 39

Salade de Choucroute Crue et Cervelas, 41

Salade de Courgettes, Haricots Verts, Avocat et Foie de Volaille, 38-39

Salade de Crevettes au Pamplemousse, 80

Salade de Foie Gras aux Navets et Épinards, 36

Salade de Laitue aux Noix, 83

Salade de Petits Légumes au Saumon Fumé, 43

Salade de Poire, 79

Salade de Pommes de Terre Chaude, 75

Salade de Printemps, 76-77

Salade de Tomates, Haricots Verts et Champignons, 38

Salade des Gastronomes, 40

Salade Mixte aux Anchois, 81

Salade Royale, 37

Salade Veronique, 82

Salmis de Palombes, Le, 68-69

Salmis de Pintade, 200-201

Salmon, 43, 45, 76-77, 116-117

Salmon Baked in Cooking Parchment, 118-119

Salmon Pâté, 49

Salmon Pie, 120-121

Salmon (Sea) Trout with Sorrel Watercress, 119-120

Salmon Terrine with Watercress Sauce, 50-51

Sandre de la Loire Braisé à la Tourangelle, 126-127

Sarres, Jean, 223

Sauce Béchamel, 10

Sauce Gribiche, 218

Sauce Velouté, 10

Sauce Vert de Martigues, 145

Sauce Vinaigrette, 8-9

Saucisson Chaud Poitevin, 74-75

Saucissons aux Pommes, 252

Sauerkraut and Cervelat Sausage Salad, 41

Sausage, 74-75

Sausages with Apples, 252

Sautéed apple slices, 202

Sautéed Mushrooms, 278-279

Sax, Richard, 50

Scalloped Potatoes, 268-269

Scallops, 166

Scallops in Saffron Sauce, 164-165

Seaweed, 47

Sherbets, 288-290

Short paste, 16

Shrimp and Grapefruit Salad, 80

Shrimp, Artichoke Heart and Avocado Salad, 39

Shrimps, 37, 52, 76, 78, 172

Small Salmon St. Patrick, 116-117
Smoked Fish Salad, 45
Snail butter, 11
Soalhat, *M.*, 244
Sole, 50-51, 122, 124-125, 130-131
Sole au Vermouth, 123
Sole Fillets with Sorrel, 130-131
Sole with Vermouth, 123
Sorbet aux Poires, 289
Sorbet de Menthe, 290
Sorbetière, 288
Sorbets, 288-290
Sorrel, 112-113, 119-120, 128-129, 224-225, 240-241
Sorrel Chiffonade, 13
Sorrel soup, 92-93
Sou-Fassum Provençal, 274
Soufflé au Chocolat, 302-303
Soufflé au Citron, 301-302
Soufflés Sucrés, 300
Soup with Two Vegetables, 92
Soupe au Lapin de Garenne, 104-105
Soupe au Pistou, 90-91
Soupe aux Champignons, 94-95
Soupe aux Choux, La, 100-101
Soupe aux Deux Légumes, 92
Soupe aux Haricots Verts, 97-98
Soupe aux Truffes, 107, 108-109
Soupe de Congre, 89-90
Soupe de Crabe, 109
Soupe de Morilles, 109
Soupe de Persil, 98-99
Soupe de Poisson, 87-88
Soupe de Potiron Basquaise, 102-103
Sourisseau, Jacques, 39, 64
Special Apple Tart, 298-299
Spinach, 36, 48, 76, 112-113, 115

Spinach with Brown Butter, 283
Spring Salad, 76-77
Spring Soup, 106
Squab Salmis, 68-69
Squash, 268, 277
Squash Soup, 102-103
Squid, 173
Steak, 210-211, 214-216
Steamed Fish with Cabbage, 148-149
Stocks, 1-5
  to clarify, 4
Strained Fish Soup, 87-88
Strawberries, 296-297
Strawberries in Wine, 293
Striped Bass Fillets with Fresh Basil, 141
Striped Mullet, 143
Stuffed Breasts of Veal, 226-227
Stuffed Cabbage Provence Style, 274
Stuffed Halibut Fillets, 138-139
Stuffed Lamb with Fresh Broad Beans, 237-238
Suprême de Turbot à l'Oseille, 129-131
Suprême de Turbots aux Asperges, 140
Suprêmes de Poulet aux Oignons Nouveaux, 190-191
Suprêmes de Poulet Saint-Antoine, 191
Sweet short pastry, 17
Sweetbreads
  to prepare, 24
Sweetbreads with Apples, 243
Sweetbreads with Prunes, 242-243

Tapenade, 70
Tarte à l'Oignon, 60-62

Tarte aux Noix, 299
Tarte Chaude aux Poires, 294
Tarte Fine aux Pommes, 298-299
Tartelettes aux Champignons, 62-63
Ternant, Yves, 249
Terrasses du Ponant, Les, 223
Terrine de Saumon avec Sauce au Cresson, 50-51
Tillac, Le Frantel, Nantes, 40, 58, 79, 115
Toit de Bigorre, Le, 82, 116
Tomates Farcies aux Noix et Marrons, 42
Tomato, Green Bean and Mushroom Salad, 38
Tomato Purée, 12
Tomato Soup, 100
Tomato vinaigrette, 13
Tomatoes
  to peel, 12
Tomatoes Stuffed with Walnuts and Chestnuts, 42
Tortilla Montagnarde, 72
Tourin aux Tomates, 100
Tournedos au Raifort, 211
Tourte de Saumon, 120-121
Trimbach, Hubert, 128
Tripe, 255
Tripe, Basque Style, 252-253
Tripe in Cider, 254
Tripe, Lyon Style, 256
Tripes Basquaise, 252-253
Tripes Maison la Chaumette, 253
Troisgros, Jean and Pierre, 309
Trout Stuffed with Sorrel and Spinach, 112-113
Trout Stuffed with Spinach, 115-116
Trout with Herbs, 114
Trout with Mixed Herbs, 113-114

Truchetet, Gérard, 37, 134, 193, 220
Truffle Soup, 108-109
Truite aux Fines Herbes, 113-114
Truite aux Herbes, 114
Truite de Mer à l'Oseille et Cresson, 119-120
Truite Farcie aux Épinards, 115-116
Truite Nano, 112-113
Tuiles, 308-309
Turbot avec d'Orange, 136-137
Turkey, Basque Style, 199
Turkey Stuffed with Scrambled Eggs and Chestnuts, 198-199
Turnips, 14, 36, 280-281

Ulva lactuca, 47

Veal, 226-227
Veal Chops with Avocado, 223
Veal Fillet with Fresh Fennel, 220-221
Veal in Garlic Sauce, 225
Veal Kidney, 233-234
Veal Scallops Franc-Comtois Style, 222-223
Veal Scallops with Avocado and Zucchini, 219-220
Veal Stew with Sorrel, 224-225
Veal stock, 5
Veal sweetbreads, 242-243
Veal Sweetbreads in Orange Sauce, 244
Veal Sweetbreads with Sorrel Chiffonade, 240-241
Veau à l'Oiseille, 224-225
Vegetable purées, 260-262
Vegetable Soup with Basil and Garlic, 90-91
Velouté de Fèves, Le, 105

Velouté d'Oseille, 92-93
Veronica Salad, 82
Vesonitio, Le, Besançon, 222
Vignes, Christian, 82
Vinaigrette de Tomates Fraîches,
  13
Vinaigrette dressing, 75
Volaille à la Crème d'Estragon,
  192-193
Vuillet, Raymond, 293
Vullin, Jean-Pierre, 67, 141,
  192

Wakame, 47
Walnut Bread, 310-311
Walnut Hearth Cake, 311-312
Walnut Tart, 299
Warm Pear Tart, 294-295

Watercress sauce, 51, 196-197
White butter sauce, 9
White Glazed Onions, 274-275
White sauce, 10
White veal stock, 5
Whole Veal Kidney, Old Style,
  233-234
Winter Squash Gnocchi, 277
Winter Squash Gratin, 268

Yachtman, Le, La Rochelle, 45,
  47, 54, 136, 167
Yogurt, 291

Zucchini, 219-220, 282-283
Zucchini, Green Bean, Avocado
  and Chicken-Liver salad,
  38-39